WHEN THE SUN REACHES THE MOUNTAIN

Christine Cassano

Copyright © 2017 Christine Cassano

All rights reserved.

ISBN-13: 978-1545354278
ISBN-10: 1545354278

DEDICATION

To my children Robert, Christa, Desiree, and John,
they have heard many of the stories but not all.
May this book give them a glimpse of how the human spirit can
persevere.

CONTENTS

	Acknowledgments	viii
	Foreword	x
	Prologue	1
1	The Posts	7
2	Take a Deep Breath and Hold It	37
3	Cushman Indian Hospital	59
4	Taking the Cure	81
5	Spaghetti for Breakfast	113
6	The Wheelchair	139
7	13 Mile Cabin	159
8	Make Us Proud	195
9	The Candle	247
10	I Was There	269
	Epilogue	295

ACKNOWLEDGMENTS

It has been a long journey to this point of my life, yet when I think back, the years seem to have melted away. Few people write their life story. It is like unrolling a bolt of fabric that you made and had tucked away in the closet. You take it out and dust it off. What you see will surprise you. You see just who you are and what you are made up of. In it all, you see the important people that helped you, guided you, inspired you and cared about you in one way or the other. I am lucky to have had so many. There isn't room to write them all down. I will do my best.

First of all, I would like to thank my family: my son, Bob Cassano and Joan Cassano, my granddaughters Alexandra Cassano and Samantha Cassano, my daughter, Christa Cassano, Ernesto Gomez, my daughter Desiree Cassano, Curtis Rew, and Kay Courville.

I would like to give a special thanks to Desiree and Curtis for encouraging me in the beginning to write my story. When I look back, I'm sure my story would not have been told without them. They took training in my school and heard some of my life stories used to encourage the students with their problems. I remember Curtis saying, "Duke, your story has to be told."

I would also like to give a special thanks to Bob for spending many, many hours editing, explaining, encouraging and guiding me throughout the writing of the book. The one thing he said to me that really helped, "Ma, don't let anybody change the way you talk. It's your voice that makes it your book." Somehow, it made me stand up a little taller.

I would like to thank my granddaughter Alex for helping me with the meaning of words and how to use them. Somehow, she figured out I had a few things going for me. She said, "Grandma, if you went to college we would be rich." She made me feel like I could have been the

President of the United States. Yeah, I'm wiser than that.

Also, a special thanks to Kay. She played a very important part in helping me raise the children. I could always depend on her to be there while I worked. Times were tough and she knew how to stretch a dollar for the next meal.

I would like to thank my friends that gave me a place to rest my weary bones after the school was closed to help me save for my home: Bob and Joan, Desiree and Curtis, Johnny and Cindy Propp, Judy Ellis, Betty Henderson, the late Dotty Erickson, Mike and Vangie Duffy.

Also, my friends that read my transcript during the writing and gave me their advice and encouragement: Carol McGirk, Lequetta Kennedy, Linda Bunch, Jeanie Youngblood-Rainert, and Doree Anderson.

Without the guidance, leadership and friendship of Mrs. Olney, Mr. Abey, and Mrs. Cady, I would never have succeeded in school or life. Their steadfast belief in me gave me strength and courage to continue.

I would like to thank all the students that attended my school, Christine's Institute of Hair Design. It was a wonderful time in my life. Yes, they made me proud.

A special thanks to all the models who wore my hairstyles like a crown. Donna DeRose who wore the crown jewel that won the International American Cup.

My clients who supported me through the years raising my family and those at the end of the line as I saved to build my home. Without them I would have been on the soup line. They kept gas in my little pickup and my brown bag full.

Also, after my home was built I want to thank Curtis and Desiree, Bill Trudell and Daryle Marchand for helping me complete the major projects around my home. It's all beautiful and I'm happy.

The State of Washington and Indian Health Care for the care in the sanatoriums that gave me a second chance to live and realize all my dreams and goals.

The Washington State Rehabilitation Program for the training and support it gave me that started me on my life journey. It makes me wonder what I would have done without the help.

When I say my prayers, I can see His Great Hand in my life that has guided me throughout the years. Everything that has happened brought me to this point. After all, I dodged several bullets to get here!

FOREWORD
By Robert Cassano

In the pages of *When the Sun Reaches the Mountain*, my mom reveals the personal and intimate details of a young girl battling incredible adversity. With her deepest thoughts, emotions, and fears, she bares her soul. In so doing, she demonstrates not only how experience shapes the person, but how the person shapes the experience. Her story is inspiring and infuriating, touching and troubling.

Flashbacks of her childhood describe a way of life that is virtually unheard of in today's age. Growing up on the Colville Indian Reservation, she and her two brothers were blissfully unaware of the poverty in which they were raised. Rising to succeed in life despite the many disadvantages that she has faced is truly amazing. Her unique tale could have been similar to many others but for the absence of means and education many take for granted; typical if not for the presence of courage and determination uncommon to most.

I coach high school football and when I talk to my players about true toughness, that it is not about how much you can dish out but about how much you can take, I always tell them that the toughest person I know is my little, 5' 1" mother. I tell the story about when we were hunting on an unfamiliar mountain. We drove up a logging road early in the morning until the snow was too deep to drive any farther. We spent the rest of the day hunting up and down the ridges and bucking through knee-deep snow. We lost our sense of direction and ended up going the wrong way when we thought we were heading back to my truck. As night fell around us and we still had no idea where we were, I remember thinking that there was nobody else that I'd rather be with. I knew that she wouldn't give up. I knew that she would keep stepping forward, no matter how long it took, until we finished the job of getting out of those mountains. Sometime around 2:00 AM, we stepped out of the woods and onto the highway.

She approached that predicament like she approaches everything in her life. Don't worry about where your last step is coming from. Don't even worry where your next step is going. Just know what you want and step forward. The shortest, or the easiest, or even the best path has nothing to do with it. Just step. Keep going. Hang in there. If you worry about the obstacles or how long it will take, you'll stop. And it's not that she never has doubts. Many times, she has had to struggle with the thought that she was never going to make it. Yet those doubts, the moments of despair, have always ended up as just another obstacle left behind.

It's been said that adversity doesn't build character, it reveals it. When you read the story of my mother's early life, you can truly understand the character of a person who refuses to give up. It tells of a world that only a few people have experienced and most have not survived. Poverty, sickness, agony and abuse are met with love, courage, hope, and most of all… endurance.

Prologue

Mama, Daddy, if you can see me, if you can hear me, I've come home. Look at my home. The walls are made of wood, not of canvas. The roof doesn't leak. There is a mattress on the bed, not boughs from a tree. The food is kept cool by a refrigerator, not in a box down by the creek. The heat in the house is kept at 70 degrees at all times, it's not kept warm from a campfire.

I wish I could have come home sooner, years sooner. I could have made life easier for the both of you. But, I'm here now, where it all began. It shaped me into who I am. It gave me strength, it gave me purpose. Mama, you made me believe in myself. Daddy, I never forgot your words, "Respect yourself and others will respect you."

It's December 2004. The past has been haunting me and I just had to go back to the place I can first remember at the age of three. Our camp was 13 miles south of Republic, Washington. It sat off the highway beyond a creek and was well hidden from view.

There was about two feet of snow. I parked my pick-up on the side of the highway and started up the old road leading to the place where we camped, our home. The road had not been used for years. Fir trees and bushes had grown up, but were still visible where the road banked on the sides.

Making my way up the little hill, through the snow, the clearing where the camp was came into view. At the far end, to the left, there had been a big fir tree that leaned to one side leaving a bare spot in the snow. Our camp was set beneath it and shielded us from the weather. The tree no longer stood, someone had cut it down. The little log cabin that Mama and Daddy built that winter burned down some years back.

I wanted to come here at the same time of year to see what it was like back then. I walked to where the big tree stood and I looked up the mountain. It took me back in time. I could almost hear Mama and Daddy chopping and sawing the logs for the cabin.

Ernie was five years old, I was three, and Manny was a year and a half. Our playground was our bedding. Mama and Daddy cut fir boughs, interwove them, then covered them with a canvas to make the mattress. Blankets covered the canvas making it soft to lay on. Another canvas, larger than the bed, covered everything from the weather. During the night, we slept under this canvas. During the day, if the weather allowed, it was opened for us to play on. Our dog Trixie was our babysitter and kept us on the bedding. If any one of us kids wandered off the canvas, she would bark and keep barking until Mama or Daddy would come from the woods and see what the trouble was.

As I stood there reminiscing, a tear ran down my cheek. Blinking to clear it away, I looked around at the snow in the clearing. Two old deer tracks made dimples in the smooth surface of the snow. There were mounds of snow that were covering something underneath. I could imagine how it looked when we slept under the canvas after a snowstorm. We were like the wild birds, such as grouse, that burrow under the snow during a storm to keep warm. The snow was our added blanket and there, under the canvas, was Trixie who lent us her heat to keep us warm.

When Mama and Daddy went hunting, Trixie would bark if anything came close to camp. When we got cold or sleepy, we would pull the blankets and canvas over us and say the little prayer Mama taught us, "Please, God, let Mama and Daddy get a deer because we're hungry." Trixie would lie on top of the canvas and lean against us while we waited for their return.

Driving back home, my heart ached for the past. It was like a dream. I have made a full circle back to the Colville Indian Reservation, where it all began.

By the time I reached the road that led to my house, it was dark. I had to watch closely since there was no indication of a road, only an orange ribbon hanging from a tree marking the turnoff for the construction workers that built my house.

Driving on the bumpy road, I made the turn where trees hid my house from the highway. The headlights brought the house into view. The brightness from the light and the cedar color of the house with the white trim seemed to glow in the night making everything else disappear.

It has taken ten years of saving to buy the five acres of land that my house sits on. The house has two extra bedrooms, making sure I have a place for my family or friends to stay the night. The back of the house faces east overlooking Lake Roosevelt which is the backwater of the Grand Coulee Dam.

In the evenings, I stand on the patio and listen to the sounds of the night. I hear the owl hooting in the distance and the coyotes bark. I watch the birds flying around, looking for a tree to spend the night. Every now and then a deer comes out from the trees before realizing I'm standing there, then scampers off. Wild turkeys stroll by and stare at me as I stand still. This wildlife means I will never be alone.

My home is still so new and I've unpacked for the last time. It's hard for me to settle in and attach myself to the present. Only the mountains tell me I'm at home. The road back home taught me how to fight for what I wanted and not to settle for less. Now that the fight is over, there is only one thing that matters, having a home where there is peace and tranquility.

However, unpacking the many boxes that were kept in storage the past ten years had its moments. I sat out boxes marked "Garbage", "Goodwill", and "Keep". Dishes, pots, pans, etc., were washed and put in place. I went through it all, taking my time. Some items, such as a set of glasses, a mixing bowl, a set of salt and pepper shakers, would make me smile and I would say to myself, "Oh, I remember this." This went on for days. It was like old friends that you never forgot and were surprised to see.

After I completed the kitchen, it was time to go through the clothing and bedding, what a job. Goodwill, Goodwill, Goodwill! I gave away more than I kept. Looking at my clothes, "Man, I made this? I bought this? What was I thinking?" The 80's and early 90's are long gone and those clothes were so out-dated. I'm telling you, ten years really makes a difference, not only in style of the day but to your mind. Looking at the pile of clothes that was going to the Goodwill, I felt a little fear, maybe they won't take them, even the ones that still had price tags on them. Oh well, I'll put them in a box, tape it shut, write "Clothes" and smile when I hand it to the man.

Now it was time to go through the nitty-gritty of the bathroom stuff and the old papers. This was really time consuming. The bathroom stuff didn't take that long, it was the old papers. My whole life, my family, the ups, the downs, the heartbreaks, the happy times, all flashed before my eyes. The report cards of my children, the notes from their teachers, their drawings, notes from their friends... it was all there and it made me cry, day after day. Since my house and land are located near a cemetery, I'm sure my spirit friends looked in the big picture windows, bowed their heads and cried with me. I think I used up a whole roll of toilet paper drying my eyes. When it was done, I felt drained, empty and alone. But, that is life and I must accept it and go on. The best way to deal with it is to make plans for tomorrow, next month, next year and work at it.

Now, I look out the big windows of my home and think of the

times my two brothers and I roamed the mountains chasing squirrels and chipmunks, not knowing there was a world beyond the horizon.

It seems like I've been fighting my way home ever since they took me away those many years ago.

Mama, circa 1930

Chapter 1

THE POSTS
Age 15

It's the summer of 1951, I will turn 16 in August. It's daybreak and Daddy wakes Manny and me up. "Get up, you kids. It's daylight in the swamp and we have to beat the heat. Get up."

I opened my eyes and felt the ache in my muscles from the day before. I turned over and looked at Manny. "Oh my gawd, I don't think I can move."

He peeked out from under the blankets, with a twinkle in his eye, "Bet I can beat you to the creek!" He jumped up and made a dash for the end of the truck bed. Soon I could hear him splashing in the creek, taking his bath.

This morning, I didn't care who got to the creek first. Turning over in bed, I started coughing again. It seemed like I coughed all the time. I crawled to the end of the truck bed, hung my head over and coughed until I had dry heaves. The stuff I coughed up had blood in it. I figured it was from straining too hard when I coughed.

"Come on, you kids. Mush on the tab. Come and get it!" This was Daddy's last call.

Daddy had light brown eyes, sharp features and a fair complexion. His skin did not tan from the sun but took on a pink color. He stood 5'8" and had a slender build, almost on the skinny side. By the time he was twenty-five, his hair turned white. He was a happy person and found humor in most things. He had a quick wit, when he was asked a question, his answers were short and to the point. He had a hot temper, but when he got angry he had good reason. His advice, "Don't look for trouble, but when it comes your way, don't back down!"

Coming up from the creek with his hair wet, "Hey, Sis. You're not moving too fast these days. What's the matter, can't handle it?" Manny said, sprinting around flexing his muscles.

"Oh, shut up. I can out work you any day." He annoyed me. Manny was 15 months younger than me. He had a sparkle in his eye and an energy about him. Sleeping was a waste of time to him, he couldn't wait to start the next day. Both of my brothers and I were about 5'1" and weighed less than 100 pounds.

With a dish in my hand, I looked over the pancakes and tried to find the smallest one. I loved Daddy's cooking but just the smell of food made me sick. I knew I had to eat due to the long day ahead.

Daddy had got the order for 2500 cedar posts and it was time to make the move to Lynx Creek near Inchelium where we would set up camp. Inchelium is a little town that sprang up by the Columbia River in the 1800's located on the eastern side of the Colville Indian Reservation. When Grand Coulee Dam was being built, Inchelium had to be moved above the water line. It was not until around 1942 that the dam was finished. When the dam was closed off, the water backed up and swallowed what was Old Inchelium. About 25 miles up the river is Kettle Falls where the Indians came from all over to catch salmon. As the water backed up, the Indian campgrounds and the falls slowly disappeared. Only the name remains.

My brother Ernie and I were to ride Sherry and Cheyenne the 50 miles northeast to our new camp. Daddy said, "I want the both of you to saddle up and get moving. It's going to take you all day to get there. We will load up the truck. I'm sure we can take everything in one load. Now, grab a couple biscuits, you'll need it."

The ride on those two horses, I will never, never forget. It was terrible! When we left, we took a short cut down the mountain to the highway instead of going around on the road. It took off a few miles.

At first it wasn't so bad, but as the day wore on and the sun beat down on us, we felt like we were being fried alive. Sherry's body was so wide, I felt like I was being split in two, so we decided to change horses now and then.

As the horses lumbered along, we sat upright, we laid back with our heads on their rumps, we hung over the saddle, we all but stood up. We even led the horses to rest our bottoms. The countryside moved by at a snail's pace. It was torture of the worst kind! And, not knowing the country and the mileage, it seemed like we would never get to the end. The only indication we could go by was the sun. Daddy said it would take us all day and into the night.

Late in the night, seeing the light of the campfire was like seeing the "light at the end of the tunnel" we felt would never end. We could see Mama and Daddy sitting by the fire. When they heard us coming, they came to meet us. Daddy took the reins.

"Oh Mama, help me down. I don't think I can walk." I cried. "I never want to ride another horse for the rest of my life!"

With a smile, Daddy told us, "I'll feed and water the horses. You kids get something to eat. I know you had a hard day."

1940 – Age 5

The sun reached the mountain so we knew it was time to go home. We were hungry. We put on our clothes and headed back to camp. We dug around, trying to find something to eat. We found some leftover pancakes from breakfast and some deer meat from the day before. With our hunger satisfied, we talked about what a wonderful day we had. Soon, the remaining daylight faded into the night. Looking out at the meadow, the sky was clear and the moon was full. The trees at the edge of the meadow cast shadows. We knew animals would come out now that we were gone, so we waited.

Whispering, Ernie started to make up scary stories. Whenever we whispered, Trixie would perk up her ears. With each scary story, we would huddle closer together. I'm sure Ernie scared himself too.

Then we saw a bear come out of the trees. It made the hair stand up on the back of our necks! The bear lumbered along the creek stopping now and then, sniffing around. Then he followed our tracks that brought him to our camp. We watched as he came up to the house, smelled around and went around to the back. We knew if he tried to get into the house, Trixie would bark. As it was, she just growled. After several minutes, Trixie calmed down which told us the bear left.

We heard an owl hoot close by. Looking at each other, our eyes shining from the moon showing through the window, we made our way to Mama and Daddy's bed and crawled under the blankets. It made us feel safe. Huddled close together, we fell asleep with Trixie on the top of the covers, leaning against us.

Waking up early the next morning, we peeked down and saw Mama and Daddy asleep. Sometime in the night, they had come home and moved us kids to the top bunk without waking us. Slowly, we got down and tip-toed to the grocery box and started to dig through it. Mama always put some candy at the bottom of the box for us to find. There were times we found apples or oranges and sometimes, nothing. We didn't fuss about it because we knew there wasn't any in town.

Mama, Daddy and Manny had the camp all set up. A lean-to sat up against a large tree. An 8x8 foot frame was built out of poles Daddy cut from the brush along the creek to support a canvas that served as the roof. Another canvas wrapped around the poles that supported the roof. It served to block the wind. The side facing the fireplace was left open.

The old cupboard Mama built many years before which we used everywhere we camped was nailed to the tree. Our grub box and anything that had to be kept dry was put under the canopy. When it rained, we stood under it and ate. The cupboard lid opened and served as our table or work area when we cooked.

The whole area of the camp was swept clean of weeds, brush and rocks. Large rocks were brought from the creek to form the fireplace. Special rocks were placed so a pot or frying pan could be used for cooking. Blocks of wood were brought from home for seating around the fireplace.

Daddy had cut lodge poles to make a frame on the back of the truck where we would sleep. He placed a canvas over it and the sides of the truck to block the wind. Two full size mattresses were put in the bed of the truck, cross-ways. Daddy slept on the end, Mama next to him, me, then Manny. Ernie slept against the cab. It served him well, he was always the last one to get up in the morning.

Sitting by the campfire, after that long ride, I looked around the campsite. "Oh Mama, Daddy, it is so good to be home. Everything looks nice. I can't believe you got so much done." Looking over at the truck, "I can't wait to lay down. I may never get up!"

The wood on the fire was reduced to ashes that shone red-orange on our faces as the five of us sat staring into it. Coffee in our hands, each in our own thoughts and very, very tired. The bones in the cheeks of my butt throbbed. When I stood up, I felt bow-legged.

Daddy looked up at the sky, "Looks like we will have good weather for the next few days." Looking around at the four of us, "You people look pretty worn out. We better turn in. Manny, put out the fire." Taking a block of wood with him, he placed it so we could climb into the back of the truck.

It took all the strength I had to climb up. Taking my place by Mama, I eased myself down. Then, I began to cough and cough. Afraid I would throw up, Mama and Daddy had to lift up their feet so I could crawl and hang my head over the back end of the truck.

Returning to my place, I began to cry, "Mama, breathing is too much. I can't stop coughing. It just wears me out."

My coughing fit would last about five minutes. Many times, I coughed until I threw up. This took place every night. Soon as I would lay down, I would start coughing. Mama and Daddy automatically lifted their feet.

Up with the sun, Daddy's call and the smell of coffee and bacon. For as long as I could remember, breakfast meant sourdough pancakes from the starter Daddy had going for years, mush and, when we had extra money, bacon. Oh yes, slab bacon. None of that sliced bacon. He was so funny. Since having bacon was such a treat, he smiled as he sliced it and stood there with a fork in his hand and watched it cook.

"Get up you kids. You will lay down a long time after you're dead. Get up." From the tone in his voice we knew it was his last call.

Manny and I jumped up and raced for the creek, Manny got there first. I went back to the camp and stopped to see how Mama was feeling. She was sitting up in bed. Daddy had given her a cup of coffee and was rolling a cigarette for her.

"How do you feel this morning, Mama?" I asked

Holding her hand on top of her head and with pain in her eyes, "Sissie, when you take your bath, wet a wash rag so I can put it on my head. When it's cold, it dulls the pain."

Mama was heavy set and her hugs made me feel so secure and loved. Her brown hair hung down in two braids and framed her high cheekbones. When her head ached, she wore a headband. We all adored Mama, she was the foundation of our family.

"Go ahead and dish her up, Tissie. Eat a good breakfast, you will need it. You have a long day ahead of you," Daddy said.

After breakfast Daddy gave his orders. "Tissie, you and Manny come with me. I will show you what trees to cut down. Ernie, I want you to harness Sherry and have him ready to drag the logs in this afternoon."

1943 – Age 7
Before Mama and Daddy got out of sight with a load of wood, Ernie headed for the pigpen. Manny and I ran behind him and climbed on the logs to watch him. Ernie jumped into the pen and started to chase the biggest one. They went round and round. Ernie couldn't get a hold of the pig. All the pig done was squeal and dodge around. When Ernie would grab hold, the pig would back up and Ernie would fall in front of it.

At one point, he had the pig in the corner facing him. Ernie jumped on backwards and the pig squealed like it was being killed. With Ernie on its back, the pig went around the pen and jumped the trough. Ernie went over its head, making the pig back up real fast, then it jumped forward, stepping on Ernie's arm.

I could see by the expression on his face, he was hurt. When he tried to grab onto the top log of the pen to get out, his arm went limp. He was covered with mud so I couldn't see what was wrong. When he got out of the pen, he held his left arm to his chest and headed for the house.

Excited and wondering what happened, we followed him. When we got to the house I threw a bucket of water on him to wash the mud off. Standing there, holding his arm, all three of us stared at it. From the elbow to his hand, was a big curve.

Manny, with his nose almost touching it said, "Yeah, Ernie, looks like it's broke. I bet you're going to get a real good whipping when Mama gets back."

I could see that his arm was beginning to swell. Scolding him, I said, "I told you not to do it. Now, how are we going to straighten out your arm before Mama and Daddy get home?"

By this time, the shock wore off and it began to hurt. Looking at us, his eyes began to tear up then he started to cry. "Let's wrap it in the dish cloth and wait for Mama and Daddy to come home," I said, knowing there was not much we could do.

For the rest of the day, Ernie moaned and groaned. Every now and then we would open up the dish cloth and look at it. His arm got bigger and bigger then it began to turn blue

Each time, Manny walked back and forth with his hands in his pockets, looking at the ground, "Boy Ernie, I would hate to be you when Mama gets back."

The day seemed to never end. We kept looking down the road hoping to see the truck. The day turned into night. As every car that went by, we waited for it to turn in. Our eyes would follow it until it went out of sight then, Ernie would start crying again. Tired of waiting Manny went to bed.

At last we heard the truck coming. When Mama and Daddy drove up Ernie really started to cry loud. When Mama saw his arm, which was dark blue, she told Daddy they had to take him to the hospital. She told me to find something to eat, they would be back soon as they could.

It was way after midnight when I heard the truck drive up. I was anxious to see what they done to his arm to straighten it out. What I saw was a white cast. His fingers were sticking out and were blue and swollen. For the next two days Ernie cried and cried, his arm hurt so bad.

Then I woke up in the middle of the night and heard Daddy sawing on Ernie's arm with the hand saw. Daddy said the cast was too tight and he had to take it off.

It took weeks for the swelling to go down and the blue to fade off. His arm was never the same. It still had the curve in it and he had a hard time bringing it to his mouth. He never had the desire to ride those pigs again.

Ernie was 2 years older than me. He had thick black hair that always went to the right. He was lazy and would sleep in every chance he got. Ernie's arm kept him from using the axe and saw for any length of time. This suited him just fine!

Manny and I picked up our tools; the cross-cut saw (handles on both ends), two double bitted axes and a jug of Kool-aid. The morning was cool but the July sun would be beating down soon. With tools in hand, we followed Daddy through the woods.

Daddy walked ahead of us, looking at this tree and that tree. Stopping at one that caught his eye, lifting his wide brimmed hat back off his forehead, he sized it up and down. "This one will do." Pulling his hat back in place, he went on looking for the next one.

After picking five trees, satisfied, he said, "That will do for today. Tissie, check the best way to fall the trees so they don't get hung up." Just before getting out of sight, he looked back, "I'll call when lunch is on."

My job was to check, before falling a tree, to see which way it leaned and if the area was okay to fall it in that direction. If not, the tree had to be undercut and forced to fall in another direction. It was important not to fall the tree into another one and get it hung up. When this happens, we would just have to wait until the wind blew it down.

Getting started, we would clear the area around the tree far enough so, when we pulled back on the saw, we wouldn't get caught up in the brush. I would check the area where I wanted to fall the tree then center the undercut. With Manny on one side and me on the other, we would place the saw on the tree, I would pull back, then Manny would drag the saw to his side, back and forth, until the cut reached a third of the way through the tree.

Then, with the axes, Manny would stand on one side of the tree and me on the other. I would swing the axe and take out a chip about eight inches above the cut. As I drew back my axe to make another swing at the tree, Manny was taking out another chip. We would chop away the undercut, one chip at a time, him, then me, in rhythm.

When cutting the back of the tree, cutting it evenly with a

slight down angle to the undercut will fall it straight ahead. If it needs to be pulled to the right or the left, leaving a thicker side in the cut pulls the tree to that side. This was something I took very serious. Daddy knew it and depended on me to do it right.

When the tree started to crack, we would look up, making sure it was falling in the right direction. We would drop the saw and run in the opposite direction in case the tree kicked back off the stump.

When the tree was down and the limbs from other trees quit falling, we would take up our axes and start to chop off the limbs. Then we cut the tree into seven-foot-long logs, the length of the posts. At this time, Ernie would be clearing the way for the logs to be dragged to a place by the road to be split into posts.

When we were on the third tree, Daddy's call came for lunch. The only thing that saved us from the heat of the sun was we were in the shade of other trees and brush. Lunch time was our only break in the day. Being that it was in the summer it didn't get dark until late in the evening, so we worked until then.

Our drink of the day was Kool-aid. Manny and I had many arguments. He would want to take a break and have a drink. I wanted to get on with the work. He would sit down and tip up the jug.

"Manny. You just had a break. Come on. Get back to work!"

Grinning at me, he would say, "Go on, kill yourself. I'm taking a break."

I would get so mad, I would holler, "Daddy, Manny won't work!"

"Go ahead and holler he can't hear you."

It took all the strength I had to do the day's work and there were times I would be so frustrated at him, I would sit down and cry.

When I had a coughing spell, I had to stop working, sit down and cough holding my head. He used that to take a break. We would work awhile and he would say, "Hey Sis. Have a coughing spell so I can take a break."

Hollering only made me cough more. So, it got to the point if the job only took one of us, I would keep on working and paid no attention to him. I could tell when he was getting tired at the end of the day, he'd quit teasing me.

Ernie had been skidding the logs we had ready that afternoon. When he came for the last log he told us supper was on. Without a word, we walked back to the camp.

After supper, Manny was the first one to go to bed. I washed the dishes, put things away, sat with Mama and Daddy at the fireplace for awhile and went to bed. It wasn't until I went through my coughing spell before I went to sleep. Tomorrow, it would start again.

It was just breaking daylight when Daddy called us for breakfast. "Today we start splitting the posts. Eat, so we can get started. I will show you kids how to go about it. You will put in a tough day but I know you can do it."

After breakfast, he gave us several wedges in different thickness and both an eight-pound mall. Carrying our tools, Manny and I followed him to the area where the logs were. When Ernie brought in the logs Daddy had him place them side by side by the road.

Starting with the first log, he rolled it away from the rest. He took a wedge and a mall and began to show us. Where the log had a crack in it, he placed the thin wedge at the end, he then pounded it in until it was level with the log. When the crack opened, a thicker wedge was placed where it would fit then other wedges were pounded in following the opening. By the time he reached the other end of the log, it split apart.

Each half was split into 4x4 posts by placing a wedge on the end of the log, making a crack. Again, he followed the crack with other wedges. Each time the measurement of the post had to be 4x4 inches. After he finished the first half he handed the mall over to me.

"Manny, when Tissie drives the first wedge in, you put the

next one in. I want you kids to take turns pounding the wedges in. It will go faster and it will be easier on both of you."

Taking up the mall, Manny looked at me and smiled. *Damn!* I thought, *he's going to give me trouble.*

Daddy had one more instruction. "I want you kids to stack the posts, starting by the road. Lay ten posts side by side. On top of the ten, lay another ten crossways. I want 100 posts to a stack. That way, we can keep track of how many we have." Leaving us to the task, he went back to the camp.

When Daddy got out of hearing distance, Manny said, "Can't say we cut all the posts. Daddy had a hand in it." With a mischievous grin, he added, "Sis, just watching Daddy work made me tired, I need a break."

"Damn it, Manny, don't start giving me a bad time. I'm tired all the time." Picking up the wedge, I placed it on the end of the half log Daddy left and started to pound it in.

One post, two posts... ten posts. So, the morning went. The sun reached an all time high. Sweat rolled down our faces and our necks. I could feel the sweat roll down my back and my shirt stuck to it. Manny pulled his shirt off. Of course, in doing so he had to flex his muscles.

"Hell, this is easy," as he swung the mall.

Stopping for a minute, I scolded him, "Manny, we just started. We haven't worked a half day yet. Have you even given it a thought, 2500 posts?" He stopped, put down the mall and looked at me.

"That's two thousand five hundred posts!"

"Yeah and this is just the beginning, you smart ass."

Taking up the mall again, he said "Sis, don't think about it. Let's go ten by ten. Ten posts this way and ten posts that way and ten layers up."

Somehow, he touched my heart. Maybe, he teased me a lot, but telling me that made me feel better. We were a team!

At noon, we heard Daddy call. It was time for lunch. While

eating, Daddy told us we didn't have to go back to work for a few hours. He said it was too hot. Hearing that was music to our ears!

After lunch Manny asked me, "Sis, how about we take a dip in the creek?" Without waiting for my answer, he ran for the creek.

The creek was shallow so we laid down with our clothes on. In the heat, it was like taking a cold drink of water. Our break ended too soon. It was time to pick up the mall again.

Our work day went from the end of breakfast to high noon. Then after a few hours off during the heat of the day we'd work until it got too dark to see. Days of the week didn't matter. Daddy's call gave us the time of day. Each day faded into the next. *Don't count the posts...*

Falling the trees seemed like kids play compared to splitting the posts. Boy, did our tempers flare! Manny's breaks and my coughing didn't mix well.

He would take the Kool-aid jug, sit in the shade of a tree and tip it up, holding it there while looking at me from the side. Every now and then bubbles would leave his mouth and go to the top of the jug.

I would get so mad I would call out, "Daddy, Manny won't work. He keeps taking a break!"

"Manny, listen to your sister. Get to work and stop tormenting her!" he would call back.

Slowly, he would get up and pick up his mall, walking close to me, he would say, "Sis, if it wasn't for Daddy I would beat the shit out of you."

Narrowing my eyes at him, I would respond, "Just try it. Daddy isn't always around, you'll get your chance. Now, get to work!"

When we completed splitting the logs into posts that Ernie had drug in, it was time to go out and fall more trees. Daddy would go out and pick the trees that we had to fall. Manny and I took up our axes and the cross-cut saw and headed for the woods.

Ernie would harness up ole Sherry and drag them in. Falling

the trees and going back to splitting the posts didn't leave any time for a break for Manny and me.

Our work area was close to the road. Several times during the day, logging trucks would pass by, going up the mountain with an empty load and coming down with a full load of logs.

The road had about six to eight inches of loose dry dirt on it. When a truck went by a cloud of dust rose to where Manny and I could not see each other. When the dust settled, we would be covered from head to toe!

At first, we got mad at the trucks. Then, it got to be funny. As the day wore on, we would have streaks where sweat would run down our cheeks and necks. As the dust settled, our eye lashes would be white and blinking made little puffs of dust. Looking at each other, we would laugh. And, to make me laugh more, Manny would do a little war dance, shaking the dust off. It was funny to see him dancing around while the dust that shook off seemed to follow him.

Trying to be serious, I would get back to what we had to do, "Stop Manny. We have to get these posts out before the trucks come!"

"Hey Sis, lets count the posts and see how many more we have to split."

Leaning on my mall, "Manny, we have a long way to go so why don't we just keep splitting. That way, before we know it we'll be through. I don't like to think, gawd, we have one thousand more to go."

Standing there, giving it some thought, "Yeah, I like that idea. Okay, let's get on with it."

Splitting those posts was a grueling job in the hot sun. When it got too dark to see, it was time to go back to the camp. By that time, the eight-pound mall felt like it weighed fifty pounds.

Getting back to camp, we had to take our turn washing off in the creek before having supper. After washing the dirt out of my nose, I could smell the food cooking. It smelled good but when I started to eat, it made me feel sick. Then Mama and Daddy would start pleading with me to eat.

Each night I would go through my coughing spell. It was awful. Mama and Daddy would automatically lift their legs to let me pass to the end of the truck bed.

Daddy would say, "Tissie, if you keep that up you'll end up in some sanatorium."

I didn't know what he meant. When I would crawl back to my spot by Mama, she would hold me and pet my head, whispering, "Sissie, you'll be alright. Now, try to get some rest."

Somehow, I felt better when Mama held me. Petting my head with her rough hands from all the hard work for so many years, was soothing to me.

Working every day from sun up to sun down on the posts, trying our best to get them out soon as possible had its problem. It was not fast enough! No money was coming in and our food supply hit rock bottom!

Ernie would go out and hunt for a grouse. Now and then he would get one but it didn't go far between five people. Even Trixie was starving.

Daddy even took his turn hunting. When Daddy was growing up, he used to break horses to ride. His feet were stepped on several times by the horses and broke his arches. It pained him to walk very far so the hunting had always been left to Mama. Something had to be done!

So, sick as Mama was, she insisted that Daddy saddle up Cheyenne for her to go hunting. Helping her onto Cheyenne, she headed out at dawn.

Daddy told Ernie he had to work with me on the posts. He told Manny he had to go down to the neighbors, which was about two miles down the road, to see if they had some work for him.

"Take your pay in food and see if you can get some hay for the horses."

The neighbors didn't have a farm but they had a garden and

livestock. Manny spent several days working for them. I don't know what kind of work he did but he came home every night with vegetables, eggs and a couple times with a chicken. He also took the truck to get four bales of hay for the horses.

After Mama hunted for three days she came back with heart and liver hanging from her belt! When Daddy saw her and knew we would eat, he gave us kids the rest of the day off.

That night, Daddy sang as he cooked. The rest of us watched his every move. I had the table set long before he was finished. Ernie carried water from the creek for Mama to wash the blood off her hands. Trixie smiled every time someone looked at her. Our world was good again!

Hoping for the best, Daddy had built a drying rack to dry the deer when Mama first went out to hunt. He went along the creek and drug in dry brush used to cook the meat. Now, it was going to be put to work.

Before daybreak, Mama, Ernie and Daddy went up the mountain to get the deer she killed while Manny and I went back to splitting posts.

Because of the heat, the deer had to be taken care of right away. So, when Mama, Ernie and Daddy got back, Ernie made the fire under the drying rack while Daddy skinned the deer.

Making a place for Mama in the shade, Daddy put together a table for her to cut up the meat. Using two boards together, he placed a block of wood at each end. Sharpening her hunting knife, he put it by her side.

After skinning the deer, he handed Mama the first front quarter so she could start cutting it up for the drying rack. Ernie worked the fire while Daddy began to lay the cut pieces on the rack.

Later that morning, Manny and I began to smell the meat cooking. Manny said, "Now, I know how Heaven smells!"

This was one aroma that didn't make me sick.

Meanwhile, back at the drying rack, Daddy took over working

the fire. It had to be kept at a level not to burn the meat. When the meat was cooked on one side, he would turn it over. When he thought it was done, he would move the pieces where it would be in the smoke. The type of wood he used gave the meat the flavor.

Knowing the first pieces of meat were cooked, smiling, he gave one to Mama. With such love and pride, he stood there and watched her taste it.

Calling Ernie over to her, Mama told him, "Take several pieces to the kids while it's still warm. I'm sure they're hungry for some."

The summer wore on while Manny and I fell more trees and split more posts. The stacks of posts grew, one hundred per stack! The sun beat down on us and the dust plugged our noses. Manny no longer danced, he just shook the dust off.

Manny lost his humor when I gave him his breaks with my coughing spells. There were times I felt he worried about me.

Walking to the work area in the morning, he asked, "How you doing, Sis?"

"Manny, there are times I don't think I can get up in the morning. At night, I feel like I'm going to die. I have to make myself breathe."

"You know Sis, we have more than twenty stacks. When can I count them?"

Thinking about it for a moment, "I think it's Monday. Let's wait for five days then we'll count them. Okay?"

With a smile, "Okay Sis!" His walk quickened.

Watching him walk ahead of me, I felt somehow, we grew up this summer. Teasing me stopped and when the day ended, we walked back to camp without complaining. When the call came in the morning, we ate in silence, walked to the workplace, took up our malls and started to swing at the wedges. There were times we didn't talk to each other for hours. Other times, we would take a break and reminisce of the past or things we would like to do.

At such a time, Manny said, "Sis, I can't wait to start school.

What do you think about it?"

"I just wish that when we start school, we can go all year. I'm not sure what grade I'm in."

"I'll tell you one thing, Sis, I'll go to school as long as you go," he said.

Taking up my mall, "Okay, that's a deal."

On the morning of the fifth day, Daddy asked, as if he listened to our conversation from before, "Well kids, how close are we of hitting the 2500 mark?"

Sticking to my decision, Manny spoke up, "We plan on counting the posts at the end of the day."

"I hope you're close because the trucks plan on coming to pick them up next Monday. That gives you kids three days, counting today."

"Don't worry Daddy, we'll make it," I said.

Walking down to the work place that morning, I looked at the stacks of posts and wondered if I could make it to the end. My body felt weak and, always, tired. The only thing that drove me was my mind. I had to go on! It was as if my mind dragged my body along. At the end of the fifth day we had twenty-three stacks and thirty-five posts!

"Sis, we'll make it. If we have to use a lantern and work into the night, we'll make it!" Manny said, as he danced around.

Feeling the weight of it all, "Manny, you count the rest of the posts while we work. Don't tell me until the last one is split. Please," I begged.

Nearing the end, I could tell, because he kept looking at me with a smile. When it was time to start splitting another log, Manny came to me and took my mall. "Sit down, Sis. Watch me split the last log."

While he worked, I watched him and began to cry. *Oh, dear God, I made it through. If there was ever another order for posts, it will kill me.*

When Manny threw the last post on top of the twenty-fifth

stack, he came to me and reached for my hand. Pulling me into a standing position, "Don't cry Sis, we made it," he said, "I sure hope to hell they don't expect us to load those damn posts."

"Oh no, Manny I couldn't do it!"

"Don't worry Sis. If we have to, I'll do it alone."

On our way back to camp, I had a coughing spell. He stood by me as I coughed. When I spit up, there was blood.

"Oh my gawd Sis, I didn't know you done that when you coughed!"

"Yes, I've been doing that for a long time," I said, trying to catch my breath. However, by this time when I spit, the blood wasn't mixed with spit.

"Give me that mall." Taking the mall from me, "Sis, if I had known that, I would have split the posts by myself."

"Manny, please don't say anything to Mama or Daddy. With Mama being so sick, I don't want them to worry about me."

The next morning, two big trucks drove up. There were two men to a truck. The first truck backed up to the first row of posts. Two men got in the back to stack the posts while the other men from the second truck loaded the posts.

I watched them from the camp for awhile. Feeling tired and weak, all I wanted to do was lay down and die. I crawled into the back of the truck and laid down. Mama came to the back and asked me if I was alright.

"Yes, Mama. I just want to rest."

I don't know if any other trucks came. I didn't care.

The posts went for twenty-five cents each. I didn't figure how much it came to. I didn't care. All that mattered was Mama and Daddy could go and get something for us to eat.

In the heat of the day, I laid in the back of the truck with the canopy Daddy put over the back that shielded me from the sun. I thought of the past two months that seemed like it would never end. I listened to the sound of the posts being loaded onto the trucks.

In my mind, I could hear the mall hitting the wedge... ping... ping... ping... I felt my muscles twitch with each fall of the mall. I thought of Manny and how hard we worked. I thought of the times he made me laugh and how angry he made me. Through it all, we grew closer together. *Yes, he's my brother*. I felt like we spent half of our lives with the eight-pound mall in our hands.

The summer of 1951 was coming to an end. August 29th, my birthday, I turned 16. Oh, how I couldn't wait to be 16. Why? I don't know, it just sounded like a good year. I stood 5'1" and weighed about 95 pounds. I had pimples all over my chin and forehead. The cough I had could compete with anyone. The blood in my spit began to pale but the fatigue I felt only got worse. At night, after my coughing spell, I would lay down and wonder if I had the strength to take the next breath.

After the sale of the posts, Mama and Daddy had to go to town to buy gas and food. It was great to see how happy they were as they prepared to go. With our bedding in the back of the truck covered with a canvas, they headed down the road.

For us kids, it was time to get work done at camp. The boys gathered wood for the campfire, cleaned up the campsite and brought water for me to do the long overdue washing. The clothes had piled up and would take me two or three days to get done. I knew my knuckles would take a beating from the washboard but it would have to work through the callous on my hands from working on the posts.

After gathering up the clothes and looking at the pile, I thought, this will be child's play compared to the posts! However, my body didn't handle it quite that way. By this time, I went about my work a different way. I worked and when I felt tired or weak, I sat down and rested. In the past, I always felt like I had to keep going and finish what I was doing. Now. Right now.

In the late afternoon, the truck was coming up the road. We could hear the empty racks with the chain across the back end rattling long before the truck appeared.

THE POSTS

Pulling up in the yard, Daddy got out and went around the front of the truck to open the door for Mama. Helping her down, I noticed she held something in her arms.

"Tissie, come here, we have something for you," Daddy said with a big grin.

Excited, I ran to see what they had.

In her arms, Mama held a little black dog. Handing it to me, she said, "Sissie, we thought you would like to have a little friend."

It was love at first sight! She was a Chihuahua with one speck of white at her throat. We took to each other like long lost friends! I don't know of anything that could have made me happier. Holding her close, shivering, she buried her little head in my neck. Only one name suited her, Tiny.

Since winter was not far off and school would be starting, Daddy said it was time to prepare for the cold weather. It was time to set up our 16x16 army tent for us to spend the winter in. At least it had a floor and would be warmer than the back of the truck.

Sitting around the campfire that evening, Daddy set the plans. "Tissie, you can finish the washing tomorrow. The boys and your mama will go with me to get the tent. It will take us most of the day so have supper ready for us before it gets dark."

Early the next morning, after breakfast, the boys took our bedding off the back of the truck before leaving.

Excited about having our home to live in, I wanted to have everything clean. Although, making more work, I decided to wash all the bedding first so it would dry before night.

Trixie and Tiny got along great. Tiny shivered so much I made Trixie lay down and I put Tiny by her and covered them up. They watched me go about my work and every time I looked their way, Trixie would smile at me. I didn't know which one I loved the most. Even though I had to take time out to cough or rest, they brought happiness to my day.

In the late afternoon, I heard the truck coming. The back was piled high with the tent and the boys sat on top near the cab. The old truck seemed to labor as it swayed back and forth with the heavy load. A big cloud of dust rose as they went by our work area. I was glad when the dust stayed behind.

As the dogs went to greet them, I put the food out where they could fill their plates. It was still early enough to start working on setting up the tent after supper.

After I cleaned up the supper dishes and put everything away, Mama and I sat by the campfire and watched Daddy and the boys work on the tent.

Giving Mama a fresh cup of coffee, she said, "Sissie, I see you washed the blankets today. They needed it because of all that dust from the road."

"Mama, I can hardly wait for the tent to be up. It will be so nice. We can sleep in our beds and the cook stove will keep us warm."

"I only wish we were closer to the school bus stop. You kids wouldn't have to walk so far."

"That's okay, Mama, we can do it."

When it was too dark to work, Daddy and the boys quit for the night.

"Well, it looks like we have to spend the night looking at the stars," Daddy said while taking his place by the fire. I gave him a cup of coffee.

"If everything goes right, we might have'r up by nightfall tomorrow." Looking around the camp, "Tissie, better set out our bedding so we will have a place to bed down for the night."

"Daddy, you didn't see. I have the beds all set up for us behind the lean-to." He gave me a little half smile. His eyes and smile made me feel proud.

On the third day, we moved in. I loved standing in the middle of the room after the cook stove was set up, telling the boys, "Put that here. Put that over there." Even though everything went back into its original place, it felt good.

After the tent was up and everything moved in, Daddy said,

"Tissie, I know you love your little friend but she will have to stay outside with Trixie."

"But Daddy, she's so little and her hair is to short, she'll freeze to death!"

"Now Tissie, dogs are dogs, they belong outside. Enough said."

It really made me feel bad. I just couldn't stand the thought of Tiny being outside. She shivered all the time.

A couple of days later, Mama and Daddy had to go to town and, of course, the boys wanted to go. I had things to do and didn't want to go.

When the truck went out of sight, I got the hammer and handsaw and went to work. I sawed off the corner of the door just big enough for little Tiny to fit through. I cut a piece of canvas from the corner of a tarp and nailed it to the opening.

I took Tiny and pushed her through it. I went outside and pushed her back through it. Then, I put her outside and called from the inside. I tapped the canvas flap and soon she came in. I went outside and called her, she came outside. The job was complete!

That evening at suppertime, while we were eating, Tiny's little toe nails were clicking on the wood floor under the table.

Hearing her, Daddy told Manny, "Put that dog outside. We don't need her in here while we're eating. Put her out!"

Manny got up and put Tiny outside and sat back down.
Soon Tiny's little toe nails were clicking again under the table.

Looking under the table, Daddy said, again, "I thought I told you to put that damn dog outside!"

"I did." Manny said, while he got up and put the dog out again.

By the time he sat back down, Tiny's little feet were clicking again at Daddy's feet.

With his fork and knife in his hands, getting ready to take a bite of food, Daddy stopped. Slowly, he turned around and looked at the door. Turning back to the table, he put the piece of food that was on his fork into his mouth. Without looking at me, with the slightest bit of a grin, he said, "If it means that much I guess it's alright."

Before bedtime, Daddy told me, "It's alright for Tiny to be in the house since I can't do much about it now, but you better make her a bed to sleep in. I don't want her to be sleeping with you."

I took a small cardboard box and cut a hole in the side of it. I put a piece of bedding in it for her. I put it under my bed and let her know it was for her. But, when the light was blown out, slowly she crept out making sure her little toe nails didn't make any noise. She would stand up on her hind legs at the head of my bed. Being real quiet, I would reach, taking her under the arms, I would lift her up and put her under the covers. She would crawl down the side of me to my feet, turn around and come back up. She would then settle down in my arms. With the back of her head under my chin, she would take a deep breath and fall asleep. Gawd, how I loved her!

1943 – Age 8

"Daddy and I are going to town to get school clothes for you kids. I want you to stay at home so I can try them on you when we get back," Mama said while she had each of us step on a piece of cardboard and traced around our foot.

Curious, Manny asked, "Why are you doing that, Mama?" while he watched her trace around his foot.

"So I'll know what size shoes to get."

"You mean we have to wear shoes to school?"

"Yes, and you will have to wear good clothes and comb your hair."

"But Mama, I don't want to go to school and I don't want to wear shoes."

Ignoring Manny's frustration, "When you kids come home from school every day, you will have to change your clothes so they won't wear out."

Watching Mama trace Ernie's foot, I asked, "Where do you get our school clothes?"

"The church has a rummage sale now and then and they have lots of nice clothes and shoes. They even have coats. We'll buy some when it gets cold."

I liked the idea of new clothes and couldn't wait until they got back.

Getting ready for school the first morning was something to behold. For me, Mama bought boy's long underwear and long tan stockings that she pulled up over the legs of the underwear and pinned it at the top. The two dresses she got for me were the same style, they had long sleeves. My shoes were boys' high tops that laced around the ankle. Then she parted my hair down the middle and made two tight braids and tied a string at the end. After she was through, she wanted me to show Daddy.

Standing in front of him I felt weird, like I was entombed in clothing. With a smile on his face, Daddy said, "Myyyy, you look nice, Tissie."

Turning away from him, I wasn't so sure. One thing for sure, I will be glad to change out of these clothes when I get back.

Now, it was the boys' turn. They didn't look so different. Mama had cut their hair the day before. It made their ears look bigger and you could see skin through the hair until you got to the top of the head. That's where the change took place. Mama parted their hair on the side and slicked it down. They wore bib overalls and shirts that had long sleeves. Their shoes looked like mine.

Daddy took us in the truck the first morning to catch the bus. Getting out of the truck, Daddy told us to be good and listen to the teacher. He waited until we could see the bus coming, then he left us standing there looking like geeks and drove back to the house.

Looking at me, "Sissie, you look different", Manny said. Sweating from wearing so much clothes, I just snapped my eyes at him.

The ride to school was awful. The kids in the school bus kept *looking at us. I died a thousand deaths before we got to the school. I wanted to go back to the mountains where I felt safe, where I could hide behind the trees and do the watching.*

It was time to get ready for school. I'm not sure if we were expected or not. However, Daddy knew where the bus turned around, which was at the house where Manny worked for food.

Looking at Manny and me, Daddy said, "You kids better make a trial run to where the bus turns around so you will know how long it will take."

Ernie didn't make any attempt to go back to school. Mama and Daddy never pressed him about it.

Manny was all excited, "Come on, Sis. Let's run all the way."

It made me tired just to think about it. "No, let's just walk fast. I know I won't last if we run."

When Mama and Daddy went to town they had set the time on our old wind up clock with Daddy's warning, "Better keep this clock wound up so you'll be on time for school."

He looked at the time and gave it to me. "Take this with you and watch the time. Manny, you kids walk. It's too hard on your sister if you take it too fast."

Off we went! It didn't take long before I had to stop to cough and catch my breath.

"Gawd, Sis. We will have to count on you coughing or we will miss the bus." Manny said, after we had to stop for the third time.

"Don't get mad at me. I can't help it."

"Remember what I said. If you stop going to school I will quit too." My coughing had him worried.

"Don't worry, I want to keep going to school too," I assured him.

The trial run that day got us to the bus stop fifteen minutes late. After resting we headed back to the camp. We decided to start twenty minutes early on the first day.

On our way home Manny asked, "What grade do you think they

will put us in?"

"I'm not sure but I think we will be put in with the big kids."

Neither one of us knew the answer. The problem was, through our school years, we did not always start on the first day. Then we'd get snowed in during the winter and just never went back to finish the year. So, I guess it was up to the teachers to put us in whichever class. I wasn't sure how it worked, maybe they went by our ages.

Manny was put in the 7th grade and I was put in the 8th.

Going to school was a nice time for Manny and me. We would get up in the morning, eat breakfast and head down the road to catch the bus. At the end of the day, we would get off the school bus and walk home. It was fun to exchange stories of the day at school on our way home.

This one day, Manny was excited to tell me of his find. "Sis, I think I found a bike for us to ride to school. I'll check on it tomorrow. If it works out, I'll bring it home."

Sure enough, a couple days later, he wasn't on the bus. He rode the bike all the way home! It was dark when he got back but we practiced riding it up and down the road kicking up dust. Of course, Ernie had to take turns also. I think he sort of wished he was going with us.

"Just in case, we will start at the same time and see how long it will take," Manny said as he spun around the yard kicking up dirt.

The next morning I was all excited to be on our way. Manny held the handles bars steady as I climbed on. We wobbled a little bit before taking off down the road. It was great! But it didn't take long before the handle bars hurt the bones on my butt bouncing on the dirt road. By the time we got to the bus stop, I was glad to get off. Manny hid the bike in the brush before the bus came.

That night when we got off the bus, it was time for the ride home. After riding on the handle bars for a while, my butt couldn't take it. So, I told Manny I would walk instead. He insisted we take turns riding the bike while the other walked. That didn't last long. It was too hard on my legs to peddle up the road. Finally, we decided to walk the bike home.

Now, the next morning was a different day. When my butt couldn't take it anymore, I decided to have Manny ride on the handles bars and I would peddle the bike!

"Sis, you can't do that. I'm too heavy for you to steer the bike."

"I can do it!" I insisted. "Now, let me!"

"Well, don't blame me if we wreck," he said, as he climbed on the handle bars.

Holding the handle bars steady while he climbed on, I could feel his weight but I just knew I could do it.

The mountain road had weeds and gravel on the sides and the middle was smoother ground where the tire tracks went. Except for bumps and holes in the tracks, it was fine. The problem was staying in the track!

Going down the road, the bike began to pick up speed without me peddling and Manny forgot to tell me how to put on the brakes!

"Sis, you're going awfully fast. Slow down!" he yelled.

"Manny, I can't stop. How do I stop?" By this time, I knew it was too late.

It had rained the night before and at the bottom of the hill was a big puddle. This meant there was a hole in it and there was nothing I could do but go through it.

When we hit the puddle and the hole made the front wheel go sideways spraying water, mud, gravel and Manny along with it. I followed him! I landed on my stomach and skinned the side of my face and hands as I slid down the road.

I was so upset I sat up and cried. My face and the front of my clothes were covered with mud. My hands hurt. Manny got up and brushed himself off.

"Well, that takes care of the bike. The front wheel is bent." Taking the bike, he threw it off the side of the road. "Come on, Sis, we'll be late."

Still sitting on the ground crying and frustrated, "Manny, I can't go to school like this. Look at my clothes I'm all dirty."

He came to me and helped me up, "Come on Sis, it'll dry before we get there." Still crying I followed him. I was heartsick. I didn't want to ever see that bike again!

It was great to be settled after the long hot summer cutting posts. I loved going to school. I got the job of working in the kitchen serving food. I didn't eat very much but I loved the grilled cheese sandwiches. It was the first time I ever ate one.

I also got to play on the girls' basketball team. However, I had the problem of coughing and had to sit out most of the time.

Daddy circa 1920

Chapter 2

TAKE A DEEP BREATH AND HOLD IT
Age 16

It was about the end of October when the teacher told the class that we were going down to the Inchelium store to have x-rays of our chest. The Mobile Unit was parked there and everyone in the community was urged to have x-rays.

The teacher lined up the whole class and marched us to the store. Then we stood in line waiting for our turn. It took the whole afternoon.

Standing in line, looking at the Mobile Unit which was a white van, I remembered seeing it in Nespelem. It had been in the summer about two years before. Mama, Manny, Ernie and I had our chests x-rayed in that same van. I also remembered the letter that Mama received telling her that I had, *"possible trouble in my upper right lung."* Thinking about it for a moment... *oh well, it's probably gone.*

As the line got shorter and I got nearer to the van, I remembered the lady in white said I couldn't have buttons on my clothes. If I did, she could move them to the side. I felt my blouse. I was okay in that area.

Then it was my turn, I stepped into the van, the lady asked me to get up close to the black flat screen. She asked me to put my chin on the top and put my hands on my hips. She then pushed my elbows forward. She stepped behind a wall and looked over at me, "Okay, take a deep breath and hold it." Smiling, she excused me and asked for the next student. All the students waited until everyone took their turn, then we marched back to the school and took the bus home.

A week had passed and on the following Monday, the lady that was in charge of the kitchen called me aside and told me the County Nurse came and wanted to talk to me. "Take your lunch break now. She's in the kitchen at the table waiting for you."

1941 – Age 5

There were days that my fever got so high I would say funny things. My brother Ernie said I would roll my eyes around and told him I could see little animals running around in the house.

I got so weak I couldn't walk or sit up in bed. Mama had to carry me outside to go potty. She knelt and cradled me in her outstretched arms while I went potty. It was a beautiful, bright, moonlit night. The snow covered everything with smooth mounds that sparkled from the light. It was so cold that our breath came out in puffs of steam.

I laid my head back and looked up at the sky. The stars twinkled, "Oh Mama, look at the stars. Aren't they beautiful?"

"Yes Sweetheart. Look over there. That's the big dipper and over there is the little dipper."

Feeling the cold air on my hot body felt good. As she pet my head, my hair would come out.

The nurse was sitting there with her lunch in front of her, smiling at me when I walked in. "Hi Christine, I'm glad to meet you, please sit down, I need to talk to you." She seemed to be very nice. "My name is Janice."

Sitting down across from her, I wondered why she wanted to talk to me. I couldn't think of anything I had done for her to single me out. I was very bashful and it was hard for me to talk to anyone when all the attention was on me.

She must have realized this and asked me how I liked school, how many were in my family, where I went to school before, how old I was…

Sitting there, I had a hard time swallowing my food. I kept my head down and a lump started to grow in my throat. For some reason, I felt like I wanted to cry.

Reaching across the table, she patted my hand. "I'm sorry to upset you, but everything will be alright. I'm the County Nurse and it is my duty to make this visit. Remember the Mobile Unit that came to the store and all the school children came for x-rays?"

Nodding my head, I kept my eyes on the food on my plate. *Oh oh, here it comes. She's going to tell me I have trouble in my upper right lung like the letter said.*

Easing into the reason why she was there, "Christine, have you been coughing a lot?"

Looking up at her, *she knows! Oh God, something is wrong with me.*

Looking back at my dish, "Yes."

"Do you spit up?"

"Yes, and there's blood in it."

I began to realize this visit was serious.

"Christine, I'm sure there are times you feel very tired. Could you please tell me about it?"

"Yes, I can never get enough rest. And, there are times breathing is too much. And, I don't like to eat so I force myself."

The Nurse knew she had my full attention. She also knew it was time to get to the point of her visit. I noticed, this time, she had a hard time swallowing her food.

"All the things that have been happening to you and your chest x-ray tell us, you are a very sick girl. I cannot stress it enough. You must come with me today. I will take you to the hospital. Now." Leaning towards me, "Please Christine, you cannot wait!"

The first thing that came to my mind was Mama and Daddy.

No, I cannot just leave. I began to feel my heart beat faster. I wanted to get up and run out the door... *I have to go home... oh my God, she wants to take me away!*

Getting up from the table, I looked at her, "No. I can't leave. I have to go and tell Mama and Daddy. You got to understand, Mama is very sick and they need my help."

Reaching out, she grabbed my arm, "Christine, please listen to me. You have tuberculosis of the lungs." Putting her hand to her chest, "Listen, three-fourths of your right lung is covered and a third of the left. If you do not go to the hospital now, you have about six months to live. That's how serious it is!" she stressed.

Tuberculosis? I had no idea what the word meant. One thing I knew for sure, I was going home.

I saw concern in her face. Maybe if I went home I would not go to the hospital. "I already talked to your parents this morning and they agree that you are sick and should go to the hospital."

Still determined, I told her, "No matter. I'm going home first and talk to Mama and Daddy about it. I could never just leave without seeing them."

"Please, do the right thing and go to the hospital."

"If I go to the hospital, how long will I have to stay there?"

With the look of hope, she said, "I cannot answer that question. It will be up to the doctor after he has given you tests and medication."

"I'm sorry but I have to leave. I have to go home." I went outside and spent the rest of the day waiting for the bell to ring.

When the bell rang ending the school day, I was the first one in the bus. The other kids were laughing and running down the aisle, pushing each other out of the way of their favorite seat. I wondered if I was the only one that had to go to the hospital. Looking at each one, if I saw a sad face, the nurse visited them too. I saw no signs.

It was the first week in November and cold. Getting off the bus, breathing in the cold air made me cough. The bus driver held the door open for a few seconds and watched me. Maybe thinking I was alright, he closed the door and went on his way.

A drizzling rain and fog promised me I had a long, cold, wet walk home. Worried and thinking about the nurse's visit, I didn't realize Manny didn't get on the bus. I figured he decided to get a ride with one of his friends. However, it made me sad. I wanted to talk to him about my problems. I wanted to ask him if I should really go to the hospital. I knew he would be interested because he worried about me when he saw the blood in my spit.

Pulling my coat up around my neck to keep the cold out, I started up the road. Making the decision to go to the hospital and leave Mama and Daddy weighed heavy on my mind. Looking up the road that faded into the fog made me feel lost and lonely. Thinking about Manny, *why didn't he come home with me?* I needed to talk to him. We had gone through so much this summer I knew he could help me make a decision.

As I entered the fog, night closed in. I could feel the mist on my face and everything disappeared around me. I lost my sense of direction. If it wasn't for the gravel and mud on the road, I may have wondered off.

The dry dirt which rose in clouds every time a car or truck passed by this last summer had turned into mud. Every now and then, I would step in the mud and sink up to my ankles. I tried to walk on the sides of the road but after falling down a couple times, I stayed in the middle.

After about an hour, my feet felt like they were frozen. I kept my hands deep in my pockets and my shoulders high to keep out the cold. *Don't think of the cold, think of Mama and Daddy and the decision we have to make,* I said to myself. *It's more important.*

It seemed like hours had passed before the fog began to lift so I could see a few yards up the road. Once in a while, I would hear an animal scamper off. It was hard to tell how far I had walked due to the fog.

Suddenly, I heard something coming down the road toward

me. The fog was too thick to see so I stopped and waited for whatever it was to show itself. Out of the fog came my little dog Tiny! She started to jump up at me. I picked her up and soon Mama came into view.

I was so happy to see her, I ran to her and we hugged each other for a long time. She pets my head like she had done so many times before, with those beautiful rough hands.

"The nurse came to see us today. Your daddy and I worried about you all day. We could hardly wait for you to come home so I decided to come and meet you."

"I know. She came to the school and talked to me." Holding onto Mama, I felt like I couldn't let go and I began to cry, "Oh, Mama, I can't leave… I can't."

Gently moving me away from her, "Come, I made some biscuits for you. I knew you would be hungry."

Hand in hand, we walked the rest of the way home in silence. Each dreading the decision that lay ahead and what it all meant.

When we got home, the tent was warm and welcoming. Daddy and Ernie were out feeding and watering the horses. Before going into the tent, Trixie gave me a big smile.

Mama sat a chair in front of the cook stove and asked me to sit down. Kneeling down, she took off my shoes and socks that were covered with mud. She then opened the oven door, laid a stick of wood on it and had me put my feet on it.

"There, that will warm your feet."

"Oh Mama, you don't have to do that. I'm fine. You make me feel pampered."

"Sissie, I don't want you to get sick. It was really cold for you to walk home. Now, just sit there and warm yourself while I get something for you to eat."

I loved the smell of the wood burning in the stove and Mama's cooking. I loved watching her as she worked. Just looking at her, I knew no matter where she was it would be "home".

I thought of all the places we camped in the mountains. Mama and Daddy would set up the tent. Mama would take a few boards and make a table. They would make a lean-to and wrap a canvas around it to block the wind. Daddy would gather fir boughs and Mama would weave them for our bed. With the bedding spread out for us to sleep, it could snow or rain, no matter, we were warm. Knowing Mama and Daddy were near, we felt protected.

Bringing me out of my thoughts, Mama handed me a plate with two biscuits cut in half. In place of butter, she put bacon drippings on them. It was so good I had two more. Being that I didn't eat much, I felt stuffed. It really made Mama happy to see me eat.

When Daddy came in he was happy to see me. "Well, Tissie, how do you feel? We talked to the nurse today. It doesn't look good."

Mama poured him a cup of coffee. Sitting at the table, he looked at me for awhile. "You know, Tissie, now-a-days they just give you a few pills and send you home. So, don't worry about it until we see the doctor."

Looking into his eyes, I don't think he believed what he was saying. This old man had lived a long time and saw a lot of things in his day. He had mentioned "consumption" before and knew something about it. I figured if this was happening to someone else, he might have gone into detail of what he knew.

The room fell silent. Ernie sat at the table across from Daddy re-reading his funny books in the dim light of the kerosene lamp while the three of us stared at the flickering light around the cracks of the stove door. A decision had to be made and making it seemed so final.

Sitting in my lap, little Tiny snuggled closer to me. Turning around, I looked at Mama, "I'm 16 now and I have never killed a deer. Before we make any decision, I would like to go hunting and I don't want to come home until I get one, okay? Then I will go to the hospital."

Mama and Daddy looked at each other. I could see it relieved them and made them both happy. "When do you want to go hunting, Tissie?" Daddy asked.

"Tomorrow, if Mama feels like it."

It was then that Daddy missed Manny. "Where is that damn kid? I suppose he's with those yahoo's again. He should be here at a time like this. He seems to come and go as he pleases. That boy has no respect!"

I could feel Daddy's anger and it hurt me to see he was losing his grip on holding the family together. The outside world was pulling us apart in more ways than one.

Early the next morning, Daddy got up and made breakfast while Mama put our food together. "Better dress warm, Tissie. The nights are cold and there's no telling when you girls will be coming home," Daddy said while he whipped the pancake batter.

When breakfast was over, Daddy saddled up Cheyenne while Mama made up our bed roll. I was so excited I could hardly wait.

Shortly, it was time to go. Daddy had tied down the bed roll behind the saddle leaving space for me to ride. He divided our food into two sacks and tied them together with a short rope. He threw it over the back of the saddle, the bundles hung on both sides. He then attached Mama's gun scabbard to the left side of the saddle for her 30-30 rifle.

However, Mama liked to hold her gun across her lap, between her and the saddle horn, while riding. This way, if she saw a deer, the gun was quick to pick up and Cheyenne done the rest. He would turn to the right and stand still, waiting for her to shoot. She had him well trained.

I stood and waited while Daddy held the reins of Cheyenne and helped Mama mount. Cheyenne started to go around in a circle. Daddy had to calm him down for me to get on.

There were tears in my eyes as I adjusted myself behind the saddle. We were going hunting, just Mama and me! There was nothing in the world that could've made me happier.

Mama had to hold Cheyenne back, pulling on the reigns. He

held his head high and walked around. Daddy had to take hold of the bridle to steady him while he gave me my rifle, the 25-20.

Looking up at us, Daddy had a big grin, "Well girls, have a good hunt. Tissie, I hope you get that big buck that is waiting for you. I'll expect to see you when I see the whites of your eyes."

Reining Cheyenne towards the mountain, we were on our way! I put my arms around Mama's waist and laid my head on her back. The thoughts of the hospital were swept away. Nothing else mattered.

With my head against Mama's back I could feel her warmth and there was a strength about her that made me feel safe. I wanted so to hold on to this time with her. Only too soon, I became aware of the squeaking the saddle made with Cheyenne's every step and the gravel on the road he kicked up. Looking around, the day was clear and we were dressed for the cold. It could not have been a more beautiful day.

It took all morning traveling up the road that the logging trucks came down during the summer while Manny and I cut the posts. We reached the 23 Mile Campground in the early afternoon. Mama insisted we camp and do our hunting from there.

"We'll camp here and rest for now. It gets dark early so it's best we get an early start in the morning," Mama said as she helped me down from the back of the saddle. I was happy to hear that. I felt really tired.

The campground was used many times through the years by the people of this land. Mama and Daddy knew the country well. All that remained was the skeleton for tents that the hunters left standing only to be used again the next year. Someone had nailed a box on a tree for a cupboard. Boards were nailed together and attached to a tree that served as a table. In the middle of the campsite was a circle of rocks that formed a place for the campfire. An old car seat, with the springs poking out, sat against another tree. The cotton that covered the springs had been carried off by varmints long ago.

"Sissie, gather some limbs for the fire while I take the saddle off Cheyenne. I'll get something out to eat. You must be hungry."

Taking a pot that she had brought for coffee, Mama used it to get water for us while she watered the horse. I made the fire to heat the water as she staked out Cheyenne in a place where he could eat.

Mama had brought dried deer meat, coffee, bread and canned peaches for us to eat.

Sitting by the campfire that night was like Heaven. Just Mama and me! The reason that brought us here did not enter my mind. I could hardly wait until morning so we could go hunting.

After everything was put away for the night, we sat by the fire and talked about old times. There were so many places we camped and hunted through the years. Most of them were called "our home". It wasn't until we talked about the good times when us kids were little that Mama started to cry. I got up and sat close to her. We hugged each other for a long time. "Don't worry, Mama. We will go camping again when I get back."

Finally, we spread out our bedding and it was only until I got over my coughing spell that we went to sleep.

The next morning, we were up at daybreak. We didn't make a fire, we just had some meat and bread for breakfast. Mama saddled Cheyenne while I secured our food and bedding on top of the table.

Mama mounted Cheyenne and I handed her my rifle. She guided the horse to a stump where I could get on. After leaving the camp, we traveled for about a half hour. Stopping, Mama pointed to a mountain peak. "That is where we will hunt."

My mother knew the reservation like no one else since the main part of our food came from hunting. She knew the ways of the deer and where they gathered during the seasons of the year. The bucks were now in rut. Just listening while she explained, I got so excited. I wanted to go up there right now!

It took us a while to get to the foot of the mountain. "We will climb up so far and go on foot from there."

When the horse began to climb, I hung onto Mama. I felt so safe with her, she knew what to do all the time.

After climbing for some time, Mama whispered, "This is where we will stake out Cheyenne. We'll walk from here." Putting her finger to her mouth, she motioned for me to be quiet. "I want you to walk as quiet as you can and watch everything, the trees, bushes, logs and listen to every sound."

My heart began to beat faster. I had hunted with Mama before but she was always in the lead. This time, she followed me. I was the hunter!

Looking around, the woods came alive. I could see all. I could hear the sounds of the woods. I came to realize just how much sound my walking through the bushes made. When a bird flew up, I would jump. I could hear the flapping of its wing as it took to the air. Way in the distance, I could hear a woodpecker pecking on a tree. I could even hear its little feet holding onto the tree as it pecked here and there.

After awhile, we came to a clearing. Here and there were thick patches of trees and brush. Mama touched me on the shoulder. I looked back and she motioned for me to stop. There was a patch of brush to the left of us. Again, she motioned for us to go to it. Slowly, we went and stood behind it and scanned the hillside. Mama rolled a cigarette, lit it and handed it to me. She made one for herself.

We continued to watch for about a half hour. Suddenly, out from behind a patch of fir trees a big six-point mule deer buck trotted up the hill. He held his head with his nose up, his antlers lay back as if they were heavy. He headed for the wide-open hillside. He didn't seem like he was in a hurry. He was about 100 yards from us. I could practically count his whiskers!

I raised my gun and took aim right behind the shoulders and pulled the trigger. He kept trotting. I aimed again and pulled the trigger. He kept trotting! As he got farther away, I carefully took aim and pulled the trigger. Nothing happened. I watched as he went out of sight over the hill. I was stunned!

I looked over at Mama. "Oh Mama, what happened? I know I aimed in the right place. He's gone, Mama. He's gone!" Sitting down on the ground, "I lost my chance," I cried.

"Hand me your gun, Sissie. I don't think it was you." Taking my gun, she examined it. "It's the gun not you." She found that the hind sight was up one notch. This meant I was shooting above the buck.

Sitting there, I was sick at heart. "Mama, I will never get another shot like that again."

Putting her arms around me, she said, "Listen to me. When I was young, my mother told me that it is an old Indian belief, that the first deer you get should be a young one. Then, Sissie, you have to give it all away. This means that you will be lucky in hunting the rest of your life."

After giving it some thought, I felt better. Maybe the next one will be young and I will have to get one more to keep. I was ready to go on hunting.

We continued to go up the hill, traveling slowly due to my coughing. Nearing the top of the hill, we started to follow a deer trail. I started to cough really hard. I came to a log that lay cross the trail, too weak to go on. I laid down on the ground and hung my head over the log. I coughed until I had dry heaves. I felt weak and sweaty. When I spit up there was blood in it. I hid it from Mama. She sat down beside me and petted my head.

After the coughing subsided, I laid there with my head hanging over the log for a few minutes. I looked up at Mama with tears in my eyes from the strain of coughing. After catching my breath, "Mama, I can't go on. I don't think I have the strength to get up right now."

"Yes, Sissie, I know. Let's rest now." She pulled my head over on her lap. Cooing, she pets my head. The cool breeze dried the sweat on my brow, it felt good.

After about fifteen minutes, Mama got up and told me to stay there. "I want you to rest here while I go and get Cheyenne." Looking at her I could see the pain in her eyes.

It was not for the lost hunting trip. She knew I had to go to a place unknown to any one of us and there was no time to lose.

I laid there in the trail waiting for Mama. I was too weak to hold my head up. I could feel the breeze blowing on my back. In the distance, a squirrel began to bark at me or maybe at Mama. After about an hour, with my head on the ground, I could hear footsteps. Sounding like a large animal, I knew it was Cheyenne. I was still lying in the same position as when Mama left. Only dying would have relieved me.

Getting off Cheyenne, Mama came to me and pulled me into a sitting position. Brushing off the embedded pine needles from the side of my face, she handed me some bread and dried meat.

"Eat this, it will make you feel better." Looking at the food made me sick. I felt like throwing up. But to please Mama, I ate as much as I could.

"Do you feel like going now?" Mama asked.

The way I felt, there was no time that would be right because I never felt rested. "Yes Mama, let's go."

"There's a big log down the hill where you can get on easier," she said, as she helped me up.

Leading Cheyenne, we walked down the hill. It took all the strength I had to get on the log and onto the horse. With my arms around Mama's waist and my head on her back, we went back to the camp.

I stayed on Cheyenne while Mama bundled up our things and tied them on the back. It was late in the afternoon when we started down the mountain.

We traveled way into the night. Every now and then we would hear something run through the woods. Whatever it was, Mama or Cheyenne didn't seem to mind.

Coming off the mountain, the lower we got, fog began to set in. I could feel the mist on my face and I began to get cold. Mama had me put my hands in her pockets in front of her. I buried my face in her back and could feel the warmth from her.

After what seemed like hours, Trixie and little Tiny came to meet us. Knowing it was us, they didn't bark. When we got to the camp, Mama guided Cheyenne to the front door and Daddy came out to meet us. Taking the reins, he helped Mama off the horse. I slid off the horse into Mama's arms.

"You girls go in, there's coffee and some leftovers for you to eat." Without a word about why we came back so soon, Daddy led Cheyenne away to be fed and watered. I could imagine what he might be thinking when he took the saddle off. He knew it wasn't good.

Mama made me eat before going to bed. She went to my bed, rolled back the covers, I laid down and Mama covered me up. She kissed me on the forehead and petted my head for a few minutes. Little Tiny came and stood by, waiting for Mama to pick her up. She put her in bed with me. After making her way down to my feet, she turned around and came up and laid in my arms.

Daddy came in and I could hear him pouring himself a cup of coffee. Mama left me and went to where he was. Before drifting to sleep, I heard him ask in the Indian language, <How is she?>

The next morning, we started to get ready for the trip to the hospital in Nespelem. The mood in the house seemed better. A big decision had been made and it was time to carry it through.

I began to think about where we lived. How could I explain it to someone if I was asked? I don't think we ever had an address, I wasn't sure.

"Daddy, if I'm asked where I live, how can I explain it or tell them?"

Daddy was setting at the table with one leg crossed over the other, his head tilted back with his eyes closed. He had a cigarette in one hand and the other on his cup of coffee.

I'm waiting for his answer, instead, he just sat there.

"Daddy! Did you hear me?" A little half grin crept on the side of his mouth. "Daddy!"

"Well Tissie, you tell them, we live up Lynx Creek. The farther you go, the tougher it gets. We live in the last house."

I knew it was the best answer I would get. My daddy was a man of few words. I learned that when he gave an answer and you thought about it, it was all you needed to know. The message was there.

After kissing little Tiny goodbye and telling her to be a good girl and that she could sleep in my bed while I was gone, Mama, Daddy and I climbed into the old truck. As we passed by the place where Manny and I cut those posts, I felt a tug at my heart. Manny and I grew up there. Another chapter in our lives was just beginning. Sitting there by Mama as we headed down the road, I watched the trees go by and wondered, *where would it take us?*

After arriving at the Nespelem Hospital, we went into the waiting room. Not knowing we had to make an appointment, Daddy, Mama and I sat on the chairs and waited. Soon, the nurse at the reception desk asked Daddy if she could help him. Quickly, Daddy stood up, with his hat in his hand, told her we wanted to see the doctor.

"Do you have an appointment?"

"No Ma'am, the County Nurse told us to bring our daughter in."

"Sir, the doctor is busy at this time. If you could give me your name, I will make an appointment for you to see him." Looking at her book, with pencil in hand, she waited for his answer.

"Do what you will, Ma'am, we will just wait for him to see us today." Giving her his firm answer, he sat back down.

Realizing he had no intention of leaving, changing her tone, she asked, "Maybe, if you tell me why you need to see the doctor today, I will see what I can do."

Standing up, Daddy explained, "You see, my daughter here," pointing at me, "Had a chest x-ray this last month. Then, the

County Nurse came to see my wife and me. She told us she has consumption and if we don't get her to a hospital right away, we may lose her."

The look on the nurse's face spoke a million words! "Your name please, sir?"

"My name, Ma'am, is Ned McDougal." Looking in our direction, nodding his head at Mama and I, "My wife Isabel, my daughter Christine."

"Please sit down. I will get the doctor." Not wasting any time, she disappeared through a door behind the desk.

Sitting back down, Daddy had a half grin, "I take it they don't like to hear that word."

Seeing her reaction and Daddy saying that, I wondered, "Gosh, Daddy, is what I have that bad?"

"Tissie, they think they might get it. Don't worry, a few pills and you'll be alright."

Within a few minutes, the doctor and the nurse came into the waiting room. Quickly, Daddy stood up and reached to shake hands with the doctor. "I'm sorry to barge in like this but we live a long way from here and couldn't come back."

"That's just fine. I'm glad you came. Please, sit down."
Smiling at me, the nurse asked me to follow her.

The doctor watched as the nurse led me into a hallway by a side door. "I need to talk to you and your wife. Please, come into my office," he said.

Down the hallway a few feet, the nurse opened a door to a little room and handed me a white gown. "Remove your clothes and put this on. It ties in the back. I'll be right back," as she quickly walked away.

Looking at the gown, it made me feel self-conscious. I was afraid someone might see me. I didn't like having just this little thing on and with the back wide open!

When the nurse came back, she had on a white gown that went down to her ankles, a white cap that tied in the back and a mask.

Oh, and rubber gloves! All I could see was her eyes. It looked really strange to me.

She handed me a paper sack, "Put your clothes in this. I will be giving it to your folks. Please leave it in the room and come with me."

After stuffing my clothes in the sack, I followed her down the hallway in my bare feet, holding my gown closed in the back. I looked back to see if any one might be coming up the hall.

She took me to a room that had an x-ray machine in it. Standing me before it, she placed my arms to my side, put my chin on top of the screen and told me to wait while she stood behind a half wall.

Looking at me over the wall she gave the order, "Okay. Take a deep breath and hold it... okay, you can breathe now."

With the x-ray over, she asked me to follow her. We went down this long hallway. At the end, she stood by the door while I caught up to her.

"This will be your room. Get into bed and the doctor will come and see you a little later."

Everything was white, the walls, the bed, the side stand and the nurse! I didn't understand why I had to go to bed, I didn't plan on staying. But, as I climbed into bed, I thought, *Mannn, something is wrong, this means I'm staying!* Looking around, *Hey, the paper sack!?* Then I remembered, she said that she was going to give it to Mama. My heart sank!

The bed I sat in was hard and the sheets were stiff and cold. I waited for Mama and Daddy to walk through the door. The minutes dragged on and on. I started to get worried. Different nurses came in and out, all covered in white gowns down to their ankles, white masks and rubber gloves. One nurse put a name tag on the foot of my bed. When other nurses saw my name, they would say hello. Some wore glasses, which would move up when they smiled.

After what seemed like hours, the doctor came in. "Well, hello

Christine. How do you feel?"

"Where is my mama and daddy?" I asked, getting ready to get out of bed.

"Now, now, young lady, you have to stay in bed. Your mother and father already went home. They will come back to see you tomorrow. We will be running tests on you and we will work on getting you well," he explained.

Anxious, I asked. "How long will I have to stay here?"

Not meeting my eyes, he said, "It will take time. I will look at your x-ray and take a few tests and see what we will have to do. Right now, I want you to rest and take the medicine we give you."

"You don't understand, Mama is not well and I have to go home."

Looking me straight in the eye, with a firm voice, he said, "The best way you can help your parents is to get well." Turning to leave, "I will see you tomorrow."

The following afternoon, Mama and Daddy came to see me. They brought me an apple and an orange. "Daddy, don't buy me anything. It costs too much and they give me more food than I can eat."

"Have they been giving you any pills?"

"Yes, Daddy, it's like you said. Maybe I can go home right away," I said with a smile.

It bothered me later because Mama began to cry. But then, she was on the verge of crying since the nurse visited them at home.

There were so many questions going around in my head that needed answers. The nurses that came into my room would be covered from head to toe in white. When they left the room, they would remove them and leave them on the floor at the door. When I finished my meal, they would take my tray and leave it on the floor by the door. Sometimes it would sit there until the next meal. *Why?*

The days passed. Time dragged on. My bed was hard and I longed to be at home. I wondered if little Tiny was sleeping in my bed. I was glad I cut the hole in the door. This way, I knew she would be inside where it was warm. I wondered if Manny kept going to school. I wondered if the kids missed me at school. I wondered if Mama felt any better.

There wasn't a clock in my room. I couldn't see where the sun was to get a sense of time. Nurses came and went. The doctor came and went with no answers, just the same words every day, "How are you today, Chris?" People passed by my room and looked in. I didn't know who they were. Nurses came with pills and stood there while I took them. I felt lonely and forgotten. The white room had nothing to look at. It was as blank as each day that passed which seemed to never end. One week...two weeks....

Then, at the end of the second week, the doctor came in unexpectedly. He was all excited. "I have good news. You will be taking a long trip." Smiling at me and patting my foot, "There will be an ambulance leaving at one o'clock this afternoon. It will be taking you to Tacoma!"

My heart fell. Leaning forward in bed I thought, *Tacoma? I don't know where Tacoma is. Why am I going to Tacoma?*

"I can't go. Mama and Daddy are coming to see me tonight and I have to be here."

"Christine, it is important that you go to the hospital in Tacoma. They are equipped for your type of illness. The doctors there have the type of medication you need to get well."

Oh my gawd, I can't leave?! I have to go home! What is he saying? My heart was sick and my nerves were on edge, "How long will I have to stay there?"

Avoiding my eyes, he said, "I'm not sure but, I would say about three months. It all depends on your case."

Three months! I could not leave Mama and Daddy for three months! I did not like the way he wouldn't look at me. *Somehow, he doesn't want to tell me the real truth. But what was it?*

Coming closer, he patted my hand, "I know I haven't been able to tell you what to expect but I'm not a specialist. The doctors in Tacoma will know how to treat your illness. Many patients have gone there and gotten well."

"If I go now, Mama and Daddy will be so upset if I'm not here this evening when they come," I pleaded, "I have to see them." Leaning back on my pillow, "I can go on the next ambulance."

The gentle tone in his voice changed, "Listen, Christine. A little baby swallowed a button which is lodged in its throat. The ambulance has to take the baby there today. It cannot wait."

"I'll wait. When will the next ambulance go there?" I asked, as I slipped down in my bed and pulled up the covers.

Annoyed, he said, "It could be a month or two months. It all depends on when an emergency comes in that has to be taken there."

Seeing the expression on my face, he knew he had won the battle. Standing there, he waited while I thought over the situation.

"Okay, I'll go. Tell Mama and Daddy where I went and how long I will have to stay." Sinking farther down in my bed, I turned my head away from him, feeling helpless.

Trying to make me feel better, he said, "I know you will be happier there. You will have roommates and someone to talk to. I admire you, you made the right decision." Smiling at me, he turned and left.

Laying there looking out the window, I wondered if I made the right decision. *When will I see Mama and Daddy again? Three months is a long time.* I wondered how I would get back after I'm well. They didn't have the money to come and get me. *I don't think they even know where Tacoma is.*

In the middle of my lunch, I saw the ambulance back up to the backdoor which was by my window. Two men got out and went into the building.

About an hour later, the nurse came in with a white bathrobe and socks. I had nothing to pack, not even a comb. My clothes were given to Mama and Daddy. Talk about having nothing, everything I had on belonged to the hospital.

The nurse left and came back with a wheelchair. Handing me a mask, "Put this on and keep it on during the trip."

Putting on the robe, I got into the wheelchair and hooked the rubber bands on the mask around my ears. Turning me around, she wheeled me outside to the side door of the ambulance, told me to get in and left. I felt like a piece of luggage. *I guess I wasn't there long enough to make a friend.*

Chapter 3

CUSHMAN INDIAN HOSPITAL

It was November 29th, 1951. A date that was easy to remember, it was my brother Manny's 15th birthday. As the ambulance pulled out onto the highway and began to pick up speed, I watched out the window as the countryside passed by. I had no idea where Tacoma was and wondered what it would be like. I was glad I only had to stay there for three months. The doctor was right, the only way I could help Mama and Daddy was to get well. But I still worried how I would get back home afterwards.

The two men in the front seat didn't talk to me, only to each other. I didn't see the baby. I figured it was in the back.

1941 – Age 5
With the camp built, it was time for Mama and Daddy to cut wood. Now, us kids were free to roam the countryside. Exploring Frosty Meadows took us all summer.

One thing that was new to us at the meadow was the cars that went by. It didn't happen often but it really drew our interest. When we heard a car coming, us kids would hide in the bushes or behind a tree and watch it go by.

The only thing we heard Mama and Daddy say when a car went by was, "They look like white people," or "They look like

Indians." If there were more than two people in the car, they said, "Looks like a bunch of white people," or "A bunch of Indians." We didn't know what it meant. We never wondered who we were.

For a while, there wasn't anything to see but traveling along at a speed I wasn't used to, we soon passed over mountains and through towns. The lights from buildings and cars looked beautiful. I had never seen so many. And the cars, they looked so new. I saw a few people walking on the streets. It seemed like every town we passed through got bigger. Sitting there, I couldn't wait to get to the next town.

It seemed like we were traveling on flat ground for a long time, then we began to go into the mountains. The lights of the ambulance passed over snow piled high on the sides of the highway and on the trees. It reminded me of home. There were so many curves in the road it made me wonder if I could ever find my way back.

Reaching the top of a large mountain, we began to descend. After traveling for some time, I caught a glimpse of lights beyond the trees. It meant we were coming to some towns. It made me happy to finally see something. Going around a curve, it was like the trees parted and opened up a sight that caught my breath. A sea of lights! The lights twinkled and covered the land for as far as I could see. I was amazed!

Sitting there with my nose glued to the window of the ambulance, I stared at the scene. Then, before I knew it, we somehow faded into that sea of lights. When it happened, I didn't know, but we were now part of it. I felt disappointed.

Leaning back, I watched the buildings go by and highways that intertwined. The cars all seemed to be in a rush to get there, wherever they were going. And somewhere in the many signs above the highway, I saw a sign that read Seattle.

Feeling the direction of the ambulance, I felt like we were going south. Soon we were on a highway where the driver didn't have to stop so much. After what seemed like an hour, the driver took a left turn off the main highway. He made several stops and turns. I was glad he knew where he was going, I was completely lost.

Sitting on the edge of my seat, I watched as the driver turned into a driveway that looked larger than most of the side streets we passed. Up ahead, I saw a large open green field that was lit up by surrounding lights. To the far left, where the field sloped up, a large pale orange building stood, the biggest I had ever seen. Lights on the ground shone onto it which made the building stand out against the dark night sky. It was five stories high. The first, second and third floors rose up and tapered off at the fourth floor. The fifth floor was even smaller. On the top of the building was an American flag that moved with the wind. I was in awe at the sight!

As the ambulance slowly entered the driveway and before turning to go on the road that went behind the building, I saw a large sign that read "CUSHMAN INDIAN HOSPITAL". I sank back into the seat. Oh my gawd, I'm here! That big building looked so majestic and important and I was going in there!

Going around the back, we went under a canopy and stopped. It wasn't long before a nurse came out pushing a wheelchair. Behind her, two other nurses came out, one on each end of a stretcher on wheels. They were all dressed in white. The nurse with the wheelchair came to me and asked me to get in it. The "baggage" had arrived.

Without a word, the nurse pushed me through two large doors entering the basement of the building. The sign above read "ELEVATOR". There were buttons on each side of the doors. She pushed one, we waited, soon one of the doors opened. Pushing me in, she turned the wheelchair around and faced the open door. Pushing another button marked "2", the door closed. The elevator went up and left my stomach in the basement.

When the elevator opened, the nurse wheeled me out onto the second floor. Straight across from me was a long table that had several articles on it. Fluorescent lights shone on them. I learned later, that type of light sanitized the mail going out.

To my left was the center desk. The nurse wheeled me to it and talked to the nurse behind the desk. Looking around, I saw a long hallway with the letters above it marked East Wing. Behind me was South Wing as I faced North Wing. When the nurse finished talking to the nurse behind the desk, she wheeled me down the North Wing hallway.

I felt like I was in another world. Everyone seemed so serious and didn't have anything to say to me. I could hear the nurse's footsteps behind me moving at a fast pace. Halfway down the hallway she slowed down and stopped at the door where the number above it was 231.

With a quick turn, she wheeled me in. Looking around the room I saw six beds. The center bed on the right was empty. Everything, walls, beds and the gowns the five patients wore, were white. As the nurse pushed me up to the empty bed, all eyes were on me. I felt awful. It was even worse when the nurse handed me a gown and told me to put it on. She then asked for the one I was wearing. She wanted me to change here, right in front of all those strangers! I just died when she said, "Take them all off." I done everything I could to keep myself covered while I changed.

The bed may have looked inviting after the long trip but it was stiff, cold and hard. The sheets were so tightly tucked under the mattress while being made, they pressed down on my toes and it hurt.

All during the time I was trying to get settled, all ten of those eyes watched every move I made! Glancing up every now and then, I tried to pretend I was alone.

After about ten minutes, the nurse came in and asked me if I was hungry. I told her the last time I ate was at noon. "I'll get you some crackers and milk."

The room was so quiet you could hear a pin drop. When the nurse gave me the crackers and milk, I'm sure they all could hear me chewing. When I drank the milk, I could hear it go all the way to my stomach. I kept my eyes on the cracker as I put it in my mouth. I looked into the glass as I drank the milk trying hard to avoid those eyes. It reminded me of Trixie. She loved to watch anyone while they ate, watching each morsel of food as it entered your mouth.

Boy, I was really glad when the nurse came and took my glass and said, "Lights out."

I laid awake a long time and wondered how long it would be until I could go home. I thought of the three months the doctor told me I would stay here and it seemed like forever. I worried about Mama and thought of the work that had to be done. She couldn't wash clothes or help Daddy. The boys seemed to be gone all the time. *How can they survive without help?*

I felt so alone and small in a world far away from Mama and Daddy. Rolling over in bed, I dried my tears on the stiff sheets. *Oh dear God, get me well soon, I just have to go home.*

The next morning I was awakened by the clatter of bed pans, water pitchers and basins. The matrons, as they were called, were passing out each of these items to the patients. Catching me off guard, I jumped out of bed and started to help them. Just then, the nurse that came in to pass out medication saw me rustling back and forth. Leaving her cart, she quickly made her way to me and grabbed me by the arm, "What are you doing? Get in your bed this minute!" With those eyebrows above the mask almost together, she led me back to my bed. Scared to death, I got into bed, slid down under the covers and looked up at her.

Grabbing my pillow out from under my head, "You won't be needing this for awhile. Now, I will tell you what you will need, REST! If you want to get well you will need rest, rest and more rest. Do you understand me?"

I was so scared I couldn't talk, all I did was nod my head.

"I'm not finished yet. I want you to lay flat on your back and when you eat, roll onto your side, the tray will be on the bed in front of you. Now, there is the bed pan. Laying on your back, lift your butt and slide the bedpan under, do your job and call the matron. I'm sure you will learn how to clean yourself." Making herself clear, she turned and went back to her cart and continued to pass out the medication.

After she left, I looked around and all those eyes were on me. Laying on my back, I looked at the ceiling and closed my eyes. *Mannn, where am I?*

Making her way around the room with the cart, she got to my bed and gave me a little paper cup with a tiny orange pill in it. "This is a vitamin. After you have tests, the doctor may prescribe other medication for you." Looking down at her cart, "I'm sorry for scolding you but it is important for you to understand that you need rest. The doctor will give your pillow back when he feels you're well enough. And, I'm sure, at that time you will be able to sit up in bed during meals." Smiling at me, "You may even be able to look at books."

Finally, after the breakfast trays were given out, the room cleared out, leaving us to eat our meal. We ate in silence. Every now and then, I glanced at the other patients.

Across from me, to my left, was a gal that was dark, fat and ugly. Her cheeks were puffed and pocked. She had black thick straight hair. Her bangs were cut off straight above the eyebrows. Her hair was then cut off at ear level. She sat up with her legs crossed, Indian style, and leaned forward while eating. I had a feeling she wasn't happy with the world. It was hard to tell how old she was. Her name was Dotty.

The girl straight across from me laid down while she ate. She seemed to be about 25 years old. She wore black rimmed glasses and there was a sadness about her. Her name was Thelma.

Across and to my right, this gal was something to look at. She was skinny. Now, I mean skinny! Her eyes looked like dark holes and her teeth seemed too big for her skeletal face. I could see her scalp through sparse hair that stood up on her head like a little monkey. Her elbows and hands looked big with sticks for arms. I noticed that after she smiled or talked, the creases it made took time to fade. I couldn't guess how old she was but even in her state, she seemed happy. Her name was Helen.

On my side of the room to my left was a lady about 40 years old. She had to have been a beautiful woman at one time. I learned later, when she was young, she was in a car accident. She had a terrible head injury. Her face on one side was pulled down and she couldn't completely close her eye. Her ear was also pulled down and pugged. Her jaw had been broken and she didn't have any teeth. It made her talk out the side of her mouth. Scars zigzagged the side of her head and damaged nerves caused that side of her face to droop. I instantly liked her. Her smile and the look in her eyes showed kindness. Her name was Martha.

To my right, by the window, was a gal about 35 years old. She had light brown hair and skin that looked like porcelain. She wore glasses and her whole manner seemed fragile. She gave me a feeling that she had resigned herself to "whatever". Her name was Gladys.

The room seemed quiet most of the morning. Dotty got out her handwork, remained sitting and began to click her crochet hooks. Martha laid on her side, facing Dotty, coughing now and then. Helen laid on her back watching me. Gladys laid on her back and looked out the window. I looked to see what she was looking at. I saw several seagulls flying against the wind.

I looked over at Martha, she was smiling at me, "Hi, I'm Martha. What's your name?"

"Chris. Where are you from?" I asked, glad to have someone to talk to.

"I'm from the Spokane Reservation."

"You are? I'm from Inchelium!" I was so glad to know someone so close to home.

Looking over at Gladys, Martha said, "This is Chris. She's from my part of the country!" She spoke as if I was a long lost relative.

"Hi, nice to meet you."

Forgetting that I had to lie down, I sat up. "Hi, I just came from Nespelem. I'll be here for three months."

It was like the flood gates were opened, I began to rattle on about how sick Mama was and that I had to go home soon as I could. In the middle of what I was saying, I looked around and all the girls were staring at me. They were not smiling.

In a quiet voice, Gladys asked, "Who told you that you would be here for three months?"

Feeling weird, I felt like I said something wrong, "The doctor at Nespelem. He told me that the doctors here had pills that would get me well so I could go home soon."

By this time, she raised herself up on one elbow and leaned towards me. "Chris, listen to us and you will know. I've been here, in this bed, for the past 18 years."

"Yeah, my name is Dotty. I've been here for 8 years."

"I'm Thelma. I've been here 4 years."

"I'm Helen. I was here for 5 years and left before I was well. That was two and a half years ago. I've been back six months. They brought me back on a stretcher. I was on my death bed. Lord knows when I will ever leave again. Sorry, Chris."

Stunned, I looked over at Martha. She had tears in her eyes. "Sorry Chris. I've been here 7 years."

Slowly, I began to slide down in bed. I began to pull the covers up to my chin. My mind went blank. I tried to think but I couldn't. It was like time had stopped. Someone had hit a bell and the echo blanked out everything else.

Lunch time came... supper time... lights out. Staring at the ceiling that soon disappeared, the floor lights lit my way through space. I felt like I was tumbling with nothing to hang onto. I was going nowhere. I felt like I was fading away. *How can I not have a tomorrow?* Everything... my dreams... my hopes... my life, disappeared into nothing. The sound of carts, bedpans, pitchers and

"Good morning girls," brought me back to earth.

Looking at the girls, I thought of what they said. I felt like I lost a battle I was expected to win. Everyone is looking at you and are wondering what you are feeling. The room is quiet. They are wondering, are you going to cry or give an excuse?

I could do nothing but look back at the ceiling. *Yes, this is real. I'm here and I must try to accept it. But, does Mama and Daddy know? Did the doctor tell them the truth? Is that why Mama cried when I said I would be home soon? I was told if I didn't go to the hospital I would die in six months. Is this what Mama and Daddy believe, I may never come home? Daddy said he knew something about people who had consumption. He never said what happened to them. How much do they know?*

The days began to pass. One day was the same as yesterday. I hear rustling in the hallway, soon the door opens. The matrons come in with the bedpans, pitchers of fresh water, basins for us to wash our faces. Beds are wound up for those that had permission to sit up. The nurse comes in with medication, makes her round and goes to the next ward. The doctor comes in with a nurse following him. He stops at each bed with his usual, "Good morning, how are you feeling today?" Answers are the same, "Fine." Sometimes the answer is, "I have a pain." He looks at the nurse, puts an order in, then moves on.

Big carts come down the hallway, stop at our ward and the matrons bring in the food trays. After some time, it comes back and our trays are picked up. We lay there, waiting for the hours to pass. Some patients are lucky and receive mail. Some stare at the ceiling while others look out the window. Tick, tick, tick the hands of the clock slowly move.

"Hey, Chris. Ask the doctor if you can have earphones." It was Martha.

I looked at her, puzzled, "Earphones? What are earphones?"

She smiled at me, "Just ask him for earphones then I'll show you how to use them. Okay?"

I could hardly wait for the doctor to make his round and was excited to have something to look forward to.

When the doctor walked in, I tried to look pitiful. I asked him if I could have earphones. He looks at the nurse that was following him with her cart, d"Please, see that Chris gets earphones." She looked down at the notebook on the cart and writes it down. It seemed like forever before they left the room. I had a hard time holding back my emotions. I was so happy I wanted to scream!

It wasn't until after rest hour before the nurse came in with my earphones. She plugged it in the wall outlet and, before handing it to me, said, "The music is turned off during rest hour and when the lights are out at night." Handing the earphones to me, "Enjoy the music."

Before she was four steps away I had the earphones on. Closing my eyes, I began to hear the music. Oooh, I was in Heaven! The minutes and hours just flew by. Before I knew it, the matron was tapping me on the shoulder, it was time to eat supper. I kept the earphones on during the meal. There wasn't a song I didn't like, it didn't matter how many times I heard it. After what I lost, I felt life was good to me.

After supper, I closed my eyes and waved my hands to the beat of the song like the leader of an orchestra. That was the next thing to dancing!

I'm moving my hands to the music when it shut off. Opening my eyes, I looked around. The lights were off, it was time to sleep! *Damn.*

"Hey, Chris." Martha got out of bed and came to me. "You can talk to other patients on the earphones like this." Taking my earphones, she held one ear pad to her ear and the other to her mouth. "Listen in one and talk in the other. It's that easy."

I did as she instructed. Holding the ear pad to my ear, I could hear voices. Patients were talking to each other. After listening for a while, I wondered how they knew who they were talking to.

"Martha, how do they know who to talk to?"

"Just listen for a while and you will hear someone you might want to talk to. Then get their attention, however."

The first night I listened. I heard one guy I thought I would like to talk to but after listening for awhile, I fell asleep.

The next morning, I grabbed the earphones and put them on. The music! Life was so good! It sure made laying flat on my back tolerable. I paid no attention at what went on around me. I told the girls, "They can take everything away from me but leave me my music!"

I sort of lost interest in listening to the voices on the earphones. Their voices seemed to blend together and the one that interested me ended up mixed with the others or left the line altogether.

Bath day! I just couldn't get used to someone else washing me. Oh, how I hated it. But, there she was, with her pan of warm water.

1943 – Age 7
Mama reminded us kids, "Be sure to clean up the dishes and give the baby her bath. And, don't stray too far from the house. Jolene is too small to be left alone."

After they left, I sat the dish pan on the bench and washed the dishes while Ernie wiped them. Standing on a block of wood, Manny put them in the cupboard. When all was finished, the boys went out to play while I gave my little cousin Jolene a bath.

I took the stove lid off and sat the tea kettle on the open flame so it would heat fast. I then sat the dishpan on the floor with cold water in it. When the tea kettle started to boil, I poured it in the water that was in the dish pan until the temperature was just right. I undressed Jolene and sat her in the dish pan.

Minding my business like most "mothers", Ernie burst through the door. "Sissie, Sissie, there's a grouse on that big tree. Where's the 22 shells? Hurry!"

Dropping everything I was doing, I ran to the old Singer sewing machine and started digging through the drawers. Grabbing several shells, I ran out the door right behind Ernie who already had the gun. Running to the edge of the yard, Ernie stopped and took aim.

Looking up to where he was aiming, I saw this grouse sitting on a branch in plain sight. I quickly made the Sign of the Cross, put my hands together, closed my eyes and said, "Please God, let him get it. Hail Mary full of grace...." When Ernie pulled the trigger, he missed the shot. The grouse flew up the creek and into another tree. It wasn't long before the three of us were sneaking up on it. There it was, sitting on a branch.

Again, I started to pray, watching him take aim, I closed my eyes and waited. Ernie missed the shot making the grouse fly further up the creek. Every time we came up on the grouse, Ernie would aim and I would pray.

Forgetting all about Jolene sitting in the dishpan at the house, I followed the boys up the creek. It wasn't until we got hungry and saw the sun reach the mountain that we looked at each other and shouted, "Jolene!"

Running as fast as our legs could carry us, we headed for home. When we got to the house, before going in, we could hear the truck coming down the mountain. With the fear of God in us, we ran in the house. At first, we didn't see Jolene. When we found her, she was under the kitchen table lying on her back. Holding the tea kettle on her stomach, she was sound asleep.

The tea kettle was black with soot and was all over Jolene from head to toe. The worst of it was on her stomach and face. There wasn't any water to try and wash it off. I shouted, "Manny, take the bucket and get some water!"

By this time, Ernie is trying to make a fire in the cook stove but he can't get it started due to the shakes. To make things worse, Jolene starts crying and I couldn't stop her. When the door opened, Mama stepped in and looked at us. Ernie was standing by *the cook stove with a burnt match in his hand, the stove door was open and inside was a pile of sticks half burned. His eyes were large and unblinking as he looked at Mama.*

I was standing by the kitchen table with the wash rag in my hand. My hands and the rag were black from trying to wipe the soot off Jolene. My eyes were black from wiping the tears away, knowing what lay ahead.

"Okay, young lady. Give me your arm." Wipe, wipe. "Okay, give the other." Wipe, wipe. She pulls the sheet down to my waist, swish, swish, flop, flop. "Now, turn on your side while I wash your back." She washes my back to my butt. Now, she heads for my feet. She pushes up the sheets above my knees. I'm ticklish so we have a time with my feet. Standing up, she lets me know bending over was hard on her back.

Now, she hands me the cloth and tells me, "I washed down as far as possible and I washed up as far as possible, now, you wash impossible."

Now it's time to change my bed. What an ordeal.

"Okay Chris, roll over to the other side of the bed." She pulls the sheets out from under the mattress and throws it over me. Then she remakes half of the bed. "Okay, it's time for you to roll back on this side." She then pulls the rest of the used sheet off. She pulls the clean sheet tight and with a snap, tucks it under the mattress then makes a firm fold at the corner.

Now, I'm lying in the middle of the bed flat on my back. She takes the folded clean top sheet and whips it around until it unfolds, leaving the square creases caused by the folds. Lifting the sheet, she throws it in the air guiding it towards the bed. When it settles, it's perfectly in place. She does the same with the blanket.

My eyes follow her as she straightens the sheet and blanket over my chest. Not knowing what to do with my arms, I hold them close to my sides. Now she heads for the foot of the bed. With a snap, she jerks the blanket and sheet making sure they are straight.

At the corner, she lifts the mattress, makes a fold and jams it under the mattress. Going to the other side, she does the same. Now my toes are flattened down like a toe dancer.

Done with me, she goes on to the next patient, leaving me like I've been put in a body cast. The sheets are stiff and cold and the mattress feels like a concrete slab. I'm thinking, *just when I softened up those sheets, damn.* It didn't help not having a pillow! *There must be a way to fix this, hmmm...*

The matron went to the door and said, "It's time to rest, girls." I couldn't wait until the door closed.

I stood up in bed and danced around, stomping my feet. I began to pull up on the sheets, loosening them up. I stomped my bed until I wore myself out before laying back down. All this time the girls are watching me.

"What the hell are you doing?" Dotty scolded.

Smiling at her, I said, "I'm feathering my nest. What the hell does it look like?"

At the end of the second week in December, two matrons came in carrying boxes. Following them, the janitor came in with a fir tree. He took it to the window and placed it on a stand, making sure it was in the center. With a big smile, he wished us a Merry Christmas and left.

1942 – Age 7
"Come on, you kids. We're going to stop for awhile and visit with some friends of ours."

People! Oh my gawd. All we have to do is see people we don't know, us kids are thinking. Getting out, we saw a house that looked like a big long box with smoke coming out of the chimney and different colored lights strung along its roof. Pushing us along in the deep snow, Mama and Daddy knocked on the door of the strange house. A man opened the door and was happy to see them. They exchange greetings with, "Merry Christmas!" and asked us to come in.

The house was small but they had chairs, a table, a cook stove, pretty dishes and beautiful covers for their beds. They even had pretty, flowered covers for the windows. It all looked so nice and new but strange.

A small fir tree sat in the corner and had a lot of things hanging on it. There were red, blue, white and green lights strung round and round it. On the branches were long silver strands that glittered and moved every time someone walked by. A little boy sat on the floor and was playing with a toy train that went around in a circle on tracks. Now and then he would give us a sideways glance as if to say, "See what I have?" Under the tree were different sized boxes. They were all wrapped in beautiful paper, some with images on them, others with stripes, all had bows on them. It was beauty I never seen before.

The man gave Daddy some whiskey and the woman gave Mama some coffee. They talked like they knew each other for years and were having a gay time. All the time, us kids are huddled behind Mama and peeking around at the boy while he showed off with the train. If we didn't look at him he would stop and look our way. When we would look back at him, he would start playing again. The woman gave us kids some candy and cookies. Instead of eating them, we stuffed it all in our pockets.

Finally, it was time to go. Everybody said goodbye and wished, "Merry Christmas and a Happy New Year." When we got back to our house and us kids went back to bed, Ernie said to Mama, "Maybe he has a new train but I bet he doesn't have bean shooters like we have."

"Yeah," I said, "And he just sits there and watches the train go around in a circle. We can run through the mountains!"

Manny sticks his head out from under the blankets, "I kinda liked that train."

The matrons opened the boxes and began to take out different colored lights on a wire. They began to wrap it around the tree. Plugging the end into the light socket, the lights came on. It shone red, green, blue and white. It was beautiful! Oh, this is how they make a Christmas Tree!

They began to add different colored balls and shapes of ornaments. At the end, they hung thin strands of silver thread-like fringe. I was in awe. I couldn't take my eyes off the tree. The tree seemed to be alive and the fringe sparkled and moved with the slightest breeze. Later on that evening, the matron came in and called, "Lights out. Have a good night." It made me sad. I just knew it would look beautiful in the dark.

By the end of that week, beautiful boxes wrapped in different colored paper with bows on them began to fill the area around the tree. At mail time, a matron would come in with another box or two and call out the name of the patient it was for and she would place it under the tree. I wondered where the boxes came from.

By the middle of the second week, three days before Christmas, the presents kept coming. Everyone had their name called several times. My name was never called. I felt embarrassed. The girls began to look at me. I wanted to die!

I put on my earphones but all I heard was Christmas music. I took them off and pretended to sleep. There was no place I could hide, there was no place I could look, those eyes were on me. *If only I knew where those presents came from I would understand.*

The day before Christmas, Mrs. Hanson, the nurse, came in and joyfully called out my name, "Chris. This is for you!" Giving me a big smile, she put it under the tree.

It only made things worse for me. I didn't want pity. I didn't want their gift. I didn't want anything, ever! I couldn't help myself, covering my head I began to cry. To make things even worse, she came to me and patted me on the shoulder.

"Now now Chris, things will be alright."

I wanted to shout for her to get away from me. The visitors that came to see the other patients never really left an impression on me. But now I understood it was friends and family that sent all those presents. I had no one. My heart was sick.

From the day I arrived and found out what lay ahead of me, I had done everything to drown out the loneliness, the worry, and to accept my fate. But, with Christmas and watching the other patients being remembered by someone, I felt lost and forgotten.

I was glad when the call, "lights out" came. Tired of lying on my back, I turned on my side and began to think about those presents. I knew no one from home would be sending me a present. Mama and Daddy don't have any money so they couldn't send any. My brothers don't think of anything like sending me something or even coming to see me. Living back in the mountains, I didn't have any friends, so that takes care of that.

The only two people that would give me the last bite to eat was Mama and Daddy. I began to realize that they would never forget about me. Knowing they thought of me every day was the best present I could have. I fell asleep feeling their love.

I woke up Christmas morning feeling better and smiled at the girls. They were surprised and smiled at each other. To let them know I didn't resent their presents, I asked with interest, "When are you gals going to open your presents? I want to see what you got."

"Oh, we can wait until this evening." Dotty answered, without interest.

"Maybe, you can wait until tonight, but I want to open the presents after breakfast." Helen told her, with a frown.

"How about... after rest hour?" Martha said, then quickly added, "Everybody for after rest hour, raise your hands." Dotty was the only one that held out.

I enjoyed watching the girls open their presents. They received new robes, bed jackets, anklets to keep their feet warm under the cold sheets, combs, brushes, hair pins, candy, cards, writing paper, etc. Everything a person would want in a hospital. I was glad for them and it filled my whole afternoon. It was like I went shopping without buying anything. However, I did envy Helen for the earrings she received and Martha for the ring she got.

In the middle of giving out the presents, the matron handed the small package to me. The present was odd shaped so it couldn't be wrapped as nice as the others. But of all the presents opened that afternoon, the single one I received took everybody's attention. They watched as I started to unwrap it. They acted like I was unveiling a precious gem. Slowly, I pulled off the ribbon then peeled back the paper. It was a bottle of Jergen's lotion!

Their eyes quickly went to my face to see how I felt about it. Holding it up, I said, "Oh my, just what I wanted!" Opening the bottle, I poured some in my hands and rubbed it on.

I think they were disappointed. If they only knew, I never had any type of lotion in my life. I was happy to receive the present. My skin felt so soft and I actually had something to put in my nightstand. Now all I needed was a toothbrush.

The next morning, I looked at the Christmas tree. It looked dead. Somehow the excitement was gone and it looked like it had a bunch of junk on it. It was sad to think, just hours ago, everyone was happy, the tree glistened and the presents sparkled with beautiful paper and bows. Now, looking around me, the girls were back in the same old routine. The gifts were tucked away and may not be looked at for some time. Looking at Dotty, I knew she would never wear that frilly bed jacket she received.

Oh well, back to my earphones, but not before I greased myself with the Jergen's lotion.

Three days later, during rest hour, I had my earphones on listening to the voices with my eyes closed. Suddenly, someone grabbed my hands. It startled me. Opening my eyes, it was one of the matrons. She put her finger to her mouth, wanting me to be quiet.

"I have a big surprise for you. I'm so excited! Right after rest hour, when everything is done, I'll bring it to you." Keeping her finger to her mouth, she left the room.

A surprise for me? I wondered if she made a mistake. Maybe it was for one of the other girls. I didn't have to keep down my hopes because I didn't expect anything.

Back to the earphones. I was still trying to understand those voices. This time I thought I would try to talk to someone. Putting one ear pad to my mouth and the other to my ear, I called out.

"Hey, can anyone hear me?" The talking went on. "Hey. My name is Chris. Does any one of you guys want to talk to me?"

Over all the other voices, he answered. "Chris. My name is Howard. Yes, I would like to talk to you."

I got so excited, pulling the ear pad away from my mouth, "Martha. That guy I told you about. You know, the voice. He's on the line!"

She had been facing me and listening to me talk. I knew she wanted me to find a friend. "Don't talk to me, talk to him. Hurry, you might lose him."

When I put the ear pad back to my ear, the music came on. Rest hour was over. *Dang it!*

After the regular routine was over, the matron that came in during rest hour rolled in a big box on a dolly. With a big smile, she came to my bed.

"Merry Christmas, Chris. This is for you!"

Surprised, I sat up in bed. "What is it? Are you sure it's for me?"

"Yes. Look, it was sent before Christmas. It was overlooked downstairs and it was brought to our attention. Let me see who it's from."

She looked at the address. "It came from the Inchelium School."

Inchelium School? I barely knew anyone from school. I went there for such a short time, it's a wonder anyone remembered me. For some reason, I wanted to cry. Maybe I didn't just disappear without anyone noticing. I was so overwhelmed by the thought, I laid back down and looked at the ceiling, "They remembered me!"

"Now now, Chris. You just lay there and I will open the box and take out the presents." She began to work on it.

Dotty stopped crocheting. Helen stretched her neck, "Oh, Chris, I can't wait to see what you got!"

The matron began to take the things out of the box one by one. There was candy, Christmas cards, cookies, writing paper, just everything one could imagine. In the end, she brought out a black and white Panda Bear. It was small but it stole my heart. I took it and held it to my breast. That little bear sat on my nightstand for years.

When it was all over I'm sure I received more presents than anyone. However, I began to give away presents to the other girls. It turned out to be the best Christmas I ever had. I not only received, but those kids and teachers in Inchelium gave me something to give.

That night, I didn't listen to the voices, I held the little bear in my arms and thought of the brief time I spent in Inchelium. *One day I will go back.*

CUSHMAN INDIAN HOSPITAL

Chapter 4

TAKING THE CURE

Three months! The time I would have been able to go home if what the doctor in Nespelem told me was true. *Well, here I am. I've been lying here, flat on my back, all this time.* I wondered how much progress I made.

I put on weight, felt good, I didn't cough like I used to, and I had been taking 42 pills a day. The doctor also ordered a streptomycin shot that I received twice a week. Every Tuesday and Friday it was, "Bottoms up." Every one of us would turn over on our stomach. The nurse would come by, pinch the cheek of our butt, jab us with a needle, then let it burn.

But, *this damn bed!* The back of my head must be flat from the hard mattress and my butt started out flat and I'm not sure that mattress helped any. I decided to see if the doctor would give back my pillow. *I got the earphones, now I'll ask for the pillow.*

The next morning when the doctor made his rounds, I asked for the pillow. "I'm sorry. I didn't realize you didn't have a pillow." Looking back at the nurse, "See that she gets a pillow." He looked at the chart he held, giving it some thought. Then he ordered an x-ray and a sputum test. "We need to run some tests," he added, then moved on to the next patient.

Tests! Maybe... maybe. No, I better not hope. These girls had tests, many tests through the years, and they're still here.

After lunch, when the matron came to close the door for rest hour, she gave the pillow to me. I mean, that was the highlight of my day!

Oh, the pillow felt so soft. I'm hugging my pillow when I looked over at Helen. She's getting out of bed! All of us watched her as she laid on her stomach and slowly slid off the bed, hanging on to the sheets. Standing on the floor and holding onto the bed, she began to walk around the bed. She had this big grin, feeling proud of herself. She reminded me of a toddler just learning to walk.

When she got to the head of the bed on the other side, she started to come back around. Trouble started when she tried to get back in bed. She didn't have the strength to pull herself up. After several attempts, she began to cry and sat on the floor.

I felt so sorry for her, I quickly got out of bed and ran to her aid. I never touched anyone that was so skinny. Her arms were like sticks. I helped her to stand up. I held on to her around the legs and pushed her onto the bed.

Going back to my bed took all the strength I had. Getting into bed was another thing. I made a couple attempts then I sat on the floor. I figured I would rest for a while then try it again. Martha wanted to help me but I told her I wanted to sit on the floor just because I hated that bed!

When I finally got back into bed, before covering up, I looked at my legs. I had no muscle. When I tapped it, it shook like jelly. My arms were the same! *Man, no wonder I got so tired just getting out of bed.* I decided I had to do something about it.

Every rest hour and when the lights were put out each night, I exercised. I would lift each leg several times. Then lying on my back, I would make like a butterfly, waving my arms and legs back and forth. It didn't take long before I was prancing around the room during rest hour.

Dotty began to get on my case. Sitting there with her legs

crossed Indian style, clicking her crochet hooks, "One of these days you're going to get caught."

"Yeah, tell me, what can they do to me?"

Keeping her eyes on her crocheting, "You'll see. They have their ways."

Ignoring her, I went to the window and looked out. There was that big green field I saw when we drove up in the ambulance. Man, I couldn't believe how many seagulls were out there. The field was about the size of two football fields and it was white with the birds!

The paved road, coming from the street, completely circled the field. On the right, a doctor's house I was told, was near the entrance. On the other end was another big house where some nurses lived. Way in the distance, I could see the town of Tacoma.

Stretching my neck, I could see those big steps leading up to the entrance of the hospital. Everything looked so big, it made me feel small.

Looking up at the clear blue sky made me smile, *one day I will walk down those steps. Mama and Daddy will be waiting for me in that parking lot.* I could just see Mama smiling up at me. I could see Daddy's white hair shining in the sun. Closing my eyes, "Yes, one day...."

"What are you thinking about?" It was Gladys.

I didn't realize I spoke out loud. "Oh, nothing", I went back to my bed. One morning after breakfast, the nurse came with a wheelchair, handed me a white robe and mask and asked me to get in the chair. "It's time for you to have an x-ray."

It felt good to get out of bed and "go somewhere". She whisked me down the hallway. On the way, I got glimpses of patients in the other wards. They also looked as I passed by. When we got to the elevator and waited for it to open, I looked down the East Wing and saw guys looking out the door of their wards. I noticed one or two had robes on that had red, white and blue stripes, others were in white PJs.

The x-ray room was down in the basement. Going down in the elevator gave me that strange feeling in my stomach. Leaving the elevator, straight ahead of me was a long hallway and to my right was the entrance where the ambulance came and dumped me off. Going to the left, the nurse took me to this small room that had a big machine in it.

Sober faced, she prepared everything and had me stand up against the flat screen. With my hands on my hips, she pressed my shoulders closer to the screen. She disappeared behind a half wall which separated us. Peering over it, she told me, "Take a deep breath...hold it." She ducked down, "Now you can breathe."

Job done, I'm back in the wheelchair and on my way back to my room. Now I'm telling you, there is no small talk. We're all business!

That evening the nurse came around with the medication and gave me a small bottle. "Whenever you cough up sputum I want you to spit it in this bottle."

Looking at the bottle that had my name on it, "What's sputum?" I asked.

"When you cough up, mostly in the mornings, spit it in the bottle." Feeling that I understood, she left.

Martha leaned over to me. "Chris, it's when you cough up crap. You know, boogers."

"If you don't, you will have to have spaghetti for breakfast," Dotty spoke up, not taking her eyes off her handwork. But I did detect a grin. Coming from her let me know it wouldn't be pleasant.

"Martha, is it all that bad?" I asked.

"Chris, don't worry about it. It will be a long time before you might have to have the spaghetti."

The next morning, after the usual routine, the nurse came in right after breakfast. She came to my bed, pushed up my pajama sleeve, dabbed it with a cotton swab containing alcohol. Holding up a syringe, she squeezed out a drop of solution from the needle and jabbed me in the arm. Oooh, it burned.

"I will be taking you to see the doctor in half an hour." Giving me a quick smile, she left.

"I wonder what they're going to do to me now?" I asked Martha.

"Don't worry. In a few minutes, you won't care."

Sitting up in bed, Helen said, "Chris, lay there, close your eyes and enjoy the ride."

"Yeah. Maybe you'll shut up for awhile," Dotty grumbled.

Gladys rolled her head towards me. "Don't worry Chris, you'll be alright. It's part of the cure. I'm sure the doctor will explain it to you."

I began to feel calm and warm. I closed my eyes and took a deep breath. I didn't feel like talking to anyone. My body felt light as a feather. I no longer felt the covers on me. Before I knew it, the nurse came back with a wheelchair.

She helped me get out of bed and into the chair. Every move tickled me. Sitting in the chair, I laid my head back and closed my eyes. All the while, I was smiling. The nurse wheeled me out the door and down the hall towards the center desk. I loved the feel of the breeze blowing in my face. It was like, *I don't want this to ever end!* The sway of the wheelchair tickled me. Then, all too soon, she whisked me into a room. Coming to a stop, I opened my eyes.

I saw two stretchers side by side with about four feet between them. Each had bags with liquid in them and numbers showing the amount. They hung on poles with tubes coming down. At the far left, there were two screens on the wall with lights behind them. I could see images of lungs on the screens.

Two doctors stood by the stretchers waiting for me. Like the nurse, they were dressed in white with white head coverings and masks. One had black horn rimmed glasses. I hadn't seen him before. The other one was Dr. Salli, the doctor that made daily rounds on North Wing. I recognized him because he had bushy black and gray eyebrows and was short and fat.

The nurse pushed me up to the first stretcher and helped me stand up. Both doctors lifted me onto the stretcher, laying me on my back. They were on each side of the stretcher looking down at me. I saw the horn-rimmed glasses move up slightly, letting me know the strange doctor smiled.

Dr. Salli explained to me that I was going to have a procedure called a pneumoperitoneum. They were going to use air to collapse my lung which was supposed to allow it to heal.

The doctor with the horned rimmed glasses introduced himself as Dr. Kulla as he put a little pillow in the small of my back, making my stomach stick out. He pushed up my pajama top and lowered my pants, leaving a space below my ribs. In the meantime, Dr. Salli attached a large syringe to one of the tubes coming from a bag. It had a needle attached to it that looked to be about six inches long.

With a regular syringe with a small needle attached, Dr. Kulla wiped an area right below my right rib with alcohol. To numb the area, he stuck me with the needle, making me flinch. The doctors stepped away and talked about the images on the screen while the nurse stood by and watched.

A few minutes later they came back and with one on each side of me, they began the process. With my belly pouching out, Dr. Salli took the large needle and inserted it under my rib, upwards, at a slant.

Both doctors seemed to know when it was in the pocket of my lung. Their eyes moved to the bag as Dr. Salli counted off the cc's. All this time, I never felt a thing.

When the job was done, the doctors helped me back into the wheelchair. I giggled as the nurse wheeled me down the hall. Laying my head back, closing my eyes... *oooh yes*

When the nurse helped me into bed, it tickled me all over. Talking to no one in particular, I said, "Mannn, I could do this again."

"Oh, you think so? Just wait until it wears off," Dotty said to kill the joy.

Lying on my back, I didn't bother opening my eyes. With a smile that stayed on my face, I fell asleep.

It wasn't until the evening meal before I woke up. Man, I didn't feel good. When I tried to move, a pain jabbed me under my collar bone. There was pain with every breath. I wanted to take a deep breath but the pain was too great.

The matron tried to roll me on my side to eat but I couldn't move, it hurt too much. "Oh, I think I'm going to die," I groaned.

Feeling bad for me, she called the nurse. "She may need something. She's in a lot of pain." I motioned for her to take the tray away.

The nurse came back with a syringe and gave me a shot. Slowly I faded away, only to wake up hours later begging for another shot. This went on all night.

The next morning, I didn't want to eat because I had to move. The pain was so great and my lungs begged for air but I could only take short breaths.

Without asking for another shot, the nurse came in and repeated the procedure from the morning before. A half hour later, she came back with the wheelchair. By this time, the pain had lessened. She helped me out of bed and into the chair. Down the hallway we went. But this time, I wasn't joyful. I guess there was pain but I didn't care. I hung my head and closed my eyes. All I felt was the wobbling of the wheelchair. It didn't matter much where she took me.

When the wheelchair stopped, I didn't open my eyes or lift my head. The doctors picked me up and put me on the stretcher. Like a rubber doll, they put me in the position they wanted. I didn't bother to see what they were doing.

In the process, I felt a dull pain deep inside that seemed to grow. Like inflating a balloon, the rubber stretches as it gets bigger.

I don't remember being taken off the stretcher or going down the hall. The matron called for help to lift me into bed. The pain brought me back to my senses. Looking at the nurse, I begged, "Give me a shot. I… can't... breathe!" I labored with each breath. "Hurry… please!"

"Chris, it's too soon to give you a shot. I'm sorry."

To hold down the pain, I had to lay flat on my back, without a pillow, and try not to take a deep breath. But my body was begging for air! When I tried to take a deep breath, it was like being stabbed in the upper right side of my chest with a hot poker. The pain went to all parts of my body and made me stiffen out.

All during the night I felt like I was in the deepest part of Hell. I was slowly suffocating. I kept the emergency button in my hand. When I was sure I was going to die, I pressed the button. If it was time to have another shot, the nurse brought it in and gave it to me. If it wasn't, she sympathized with me.

The next morning, when I thought I couldn't stand anymore, the nurse came in again and gave me a shot. A half hour later, she came back and helped me into the wheelchair. Only this time, when she lifted me up into a sitting position, I lost consciousness. When I came to, I was back in my bed, begging for a shot.

The days came and went. When the doctor came by, I rolled my head back and forth, mouthing, "No… no," gasping for air. I couldn't cry, it made me need air. The only way he knew I was crying was the tears rolled down the sides of my face.

On the third week, mercifully, the treatments stopped. The nurse came and told me the doctor wanted to see me in his office. Climbing in the wheelchair, I wondered what the next move would be.

Both doctors were in the office. Dr. Salli explained that they ended the treatments because I had lung adhesions that caused me so much pain. They were going to use a different way to collapse the lung called a pneumothorax. I left the office with their promise that they won't let me go through that again.

About six weeks later, I started the trips down the hall to that stretcher and that big needle. This time, the doctor laid me on my side and had me put my arms over my head. He put the pillow under my side, which spread my ribs apart. About six inches below my arm pit, he inserted the needle. After several minutes, he pulled it out. The job was done. The pain wasn't as bad and the shots helped me through it.

The routine began. Every Monday and Friday the matron would come with a wheelchair. I would get in and she would wheel me down the hall where I would wait in line.

First, several patients would go in this little room that was dark. Both doctors were there and they would be covered with thick rubber aprons, gloves and goggles. Dr. Salli sat on a chair in front of a large screen that was connected by an arm coming from a big machine. He guided the screen by holding onto handles on both sides. It was called a fluoroscope.

The patients in the room lined the wall waiting for their turn to go behind the screen. When they stood behind it, their whole insides could be seen. I could even see their heart beating. After the x-raying was over, we formed two lines waiting for our turn on the table. Each doctor worked a table.

At first I wanted to be the last one in line, dreading the needle. After thinking about it, waiting only prolonged the fear. So, after the x-ray was over, I would make my way to the front of the line so I could be the first one on the table.

One day the matron brought in a screen on wheels, the type with gathered material on a frame that is used to shield a patient from sight. She unfolded it and pulled it around Thelma's bed.

Curious, I watched as the nurse and matron kept going behind the screen attending to Thelma throughout the day. Then a stretcher was brought in and taken behind the screen. Soon, with the nurse on one end and the matron on the other, they wheeled her out.

Whispering, I asked Martha, "What happened to Thelma?"

"She's pregnant."

A baby! I didn't know she was pregnant. I thought about it for a while. Trying to be even quieter, "I thought she was here a long time. How come she's having a baby?"

Smiling at me, "She went out on a pass."

Two days later they brought her back. Later on, in the night, I could hear her crying. It really made me feel bad. I wondered, will she ever be able to be with her baby. It was never said whether she had a boy or girl.

For the next two days, the matron came in and went behind the screen. After a few minutes, I would smell vinegar.

"Hey Martha, what are they doing with vinegar?"

"They're giving her a douche."

"A douche? What's a douche?"

"One day you will find out, Chris. I can't explain it to you." She covered up her head, ending the questions.

Once a week, a lady would come in with books on a cart. She would ask if anyone wanted something to read. The ban had been lifted so I could read in bed. I knew nothing about books other than school. Picking out a book was beyond me.

Seeing my puzzled look about picking something, Helen called me. "Hey Chris, ask if she has the book, *Knock on Any Door*. I think you'll like it."

The lady looked the cart over and picked it out for me. Handing it to me, I saw that it was real thick. Opening it up I noticed the printing was real small. *Man, I'll never get through this!*

After mentioning it to Helen, she asked, "Why? Are you planning on going somewhere soon?"

Snapping my eyes at her, I settled down to start reading. It didn't take long before I was hooked. I fell in love with the main character, Nicky. My eyes traveled over the words in slow motion, afraid to miss a word. When I got to a word I didn't know, I would ask Martha. After awhile, I noticed it irritated her so I just skipped those words.

I read through meals. I read through rest period. I read while I sat on the pot. The only thing that stopped me was when they put out the lights.

Lying there one night, thinking about Nicky and what was happening, I wanted to keep reading, *Damn! There has to be a way. The floor lights!* Sitting straight up in bed. *Yes, the floor lights!*

I flipped over on my stomach and hung my head over the side of the bed and looked around to see where the light was. It was on the wall right at the head of my bed. Perfect! It had a frosted glass over the opening. *Yeah, there is a way to fix that.*

I had a spoon that was left on my bed one day and I put it in my nightstand. I got out of bed, took the spoon and crawled under the bed. It didn't take long before I had the glass off. I grabbed my pillow and blanket.

Looking at me with a frown, "What the hell are you doing, Chris?" Martha asked.

"I'm going to read under my bed. What does it look like?"

"Gawd, you do the damnedest things."

"A man's got to do what a man's got to do," I said as I crawled under the bed.

I folded the blanket to make it as soft as I could and put my pillow in place. Opening the book to the marked page, I began to read until my back couldn't stand it anymore. I put the glass back in place and crawled back into bed. It was the only time that my bed ever felt soft. The next morning the matron had to wake me up. However, I was back under the bed that night. I kept it up until I finished the book.

I was so sad when the story ended. It just broke my heart when Nicky got the electric chair. He started out as an altar boy and died in the electric chair! Gosh, how could he have gone so bad? But I still loved him.

I expressed my feelings to Martha. "Oh, Chris. It's just a story someone wrote. Don't take it to heart."

"Yeah, but it probably happened to someone."

"Girl! I'm picking out the next book for you to read. I'll make sure it ends happy!"

The next day when the lady with the books came into our ward, Martha quickly asked for the catalog. "Give it to Chris. It has a lot of pictures. It will give her something to dream about."

For the rest of the day my eyes poured over all the beautiful things! I never saw so many things a person could buy. It never occurred to me that a catalog was for ordering things. At home, we used it for toilet paper. Now, I looked at it in a whole new light. The part that interested me the most was the dresses and shoes. However, there was only one dress I liked the most. It was light blue, had little cap sleeves, fitted to the waist with a narrow belt. From the waist, it flared out and ended above the ankle. It had small flowers sprinkled over the entire dress and was sheer with an underskirt that matched the color of the dress. Oooh, it was beautiful! Then I had to pick out just the right shoes to go with it.

Looking over the shoes, I picked out a pair of little white shoes. Satisfied, I asked Thelma, showing her the dress and the shoes, "What do you think? Do they go together?"

Looking at what I showed her, "Yeah, yeah. Looks great." I knew she wasn't interested.

During rest hour, I got up and went to the window. It was a beautiful sunny day. I looked at the seagulls, then at the steps leading the front entrance. Again, I pictured myself leaving the hospital and going down those steps.

Only this time I was wearing the little blue dress and the white shoes. They made a clicking sound with each step. Down in the parking lot, Mama and Daddy were waiting for me. Mama smiled and I saw tears in her eyes. Seeing me, Daddy took off his hat and his white hair glistened in the sun.

It saddened me because I couldn't get past the scene. It kept starting over and over. I knew I had to keep it alive. The day had to come no matter how long it took. *I WILL walk down those steps.*

Breaking into my thoughts, Dotty sitting cross-legged in her bed, crocheting, "Why do you keep going to the window? You got some kinda problem?"

"You know Dotty, when I first went to the window there was a lot of seagulls, now there isn't but half the amount. I noticed we have chicken every Sunday. What do you think?"

"You make me sick. It's like you to think of that," she grumbled.

"It was just a thought, Dotty. Just a thought."

Before the week was over, I just about wore the pages out of the catalog. It was time to give it back to the lady.

I tried to read other books but nothing captured my interest. It was time to go back to my music. But, during rest hour when the music turned off, I just had to get out of bed and run around the room. I would run and slide to the door, turn around, run and slide to the window. Dotty was the only one that objected. I didn't care.

Other times, I would go to the window and see a bunch of seagulls in an area, I would try to count them but they always messed me up by flying up and coming back down. Since they all looked alike it was hard to see who got counted. Then I would look at a seagull flying against the wind. I tried to see how long I could keep my eye on it. Problem was I had to blink. I was never sure it was the same one.

Even though the rest hour was two hours long, there were times I almost got caught out of bed. I would hear the carts coming down the hall, nearing the door. I would run and slide up to my bed, jump in and act like I just woke up.

"You keep that up gal, you'll never get well," Dotty said.

"Oh yes I will. You've been sitting in that position for so long, I wonder if you'll be able to stand up," I spat back.

During one rest hour, Martha motioned for me to come to her

bed. Even though my bed was next to hers, she wanted to whisper to me. "Listen. I know how you can see the guys on East Wing and talk to them."

I looked at her with my eyes big as saucers, "How do you talk to them?"

Laying back and acting like she had something special to tell me, "Now, it's not easy as you may think. First, you have to get across the hall from our door. The door to the bathroom is right by the nurse's desk. You have to make sure no one is in the hall before sneaking across. Then, there's getting back without being seen.

"Now, this is how you talk to the guys. You make letters with your fingers. This is 'A'. Hold the tips of your pointer fingers together, put the tips of your thumbs together. Make the 'b' like this, hold your pointer finger straight, with the other, form the 'b' at the bottom."

We spent the remaining time practicing, talking to each other forming the letters with our fingers. I loved learning something new and exciting. Now, all I had to do was get across the hall. I could hardly wait until the next day.

Soon as the door closed for the rest hour, I sat up.

"Wait until the coast is clear," Martha cautioned. "Listen at the door. You will be able to hear when someone is walking around. When it is quiet, look out to make sure. Then make a dash across the hall."

I was so excited I could hardly stand it! I took a deep breath, got out of bed and tiptoed to the door. I put my ear on the door and listened. I could hear movement. I looked at Martha, she put her finger to her mouth to quiet me. I waited. Then I could hear footsteps heading up the hall. Slowly, I opened the door and peeked out. No one was around. I stepped out and closed the door behind me. I looked up and down the hall and hurried across to the bathroom. When I went into the bathroom, two other girls were already there. Looking out the window, I saw several guys at the windows on East Wing making signs with their fingers.

I watched for a while, then I noticed that one guy pointing at me and writing, "Pretty smile." I didn't know who he was talking to. He kept pointing at me.

"Me?"

"Yes. Name Ernie. Yours?"

"Chris."

"Never see before."

"Here 1 year."

"Here 10 years."

"Where from?"

"Montana. Where from?"

"Inchelium."

"Never heard of it."

Worrying that I might have a hard time getting back to my room, "Have to go." I waved to him.

"Talk tonight on line."

I was the last one to leave the bathroom. I was a little slow forming my letters. Waiting at the door, I looked both ways. No one was around. I made my way back to the ward.

Of course, I had to tell Martha all about it. "Martha, he's going to talk to me tonight. His name is Ernie. He said I had a pretty smile. Can you believe it?" Getting into bed, I slowly slipped under the covers with a dreamy look on my face and sighed.

Martha groaned, "Oh, what have I started?"

Lying there gazing at the ceiling, "You made my life exciting that's what you did. And, I believe life is what you make it."

That night, Ernie and I talked into the wee hours of the morning. The next morning the matron had to wake me up for breakfast. I slept most of the day and didn't have the strength to get out of bed during rest hour. I started to get my days and nights turned around but I enjoyed doing it. I'm sure my ears began to "cauliflower" holding the ear pads so tight to my ear in order to hear.

One afternoon, after listening to her complaining for several days, Dotty mumbled to herself about the patient down the hall. "I think something has to be done about that woman next door. She has to use an oxygen tank and she smokes. One day she is going to blow us to Hell."

"If it's got you worried, tell the doctor," Helen told her.

"Yeah, I think I will. When I die, I want to be buried whole."

"Listen Dotty, don't worry. If she blows us up, I'll tell the doctor to make sure to find your hole and bury it."

Boy, she sure got mad at me. "Why don't you keep your mouth shut," she spat at me.

The other girls found it funny and held their hands over their mouth or pulled the covers over their head.

Several weeks later, I went on one of my regular trips to have the pneumothorax treatment, when I returned, Dotty was gone. It was never said whether she moved to another ward or went home. It was not unusual for a patient to leave without word. The matrons or nurses went about their business as if nothing changed. No one asked any questions, leaving me to wonder. However, it made me feel bad. I really missed her because she grumbled about everything and it amused me.

I pictured her being pushed down the hall in her bed, a matron on each end, sitting Indian style and crocheting, not missing a stitch. There were times I would hear her needles clicking as she kept crocheting after the lights were turned off. I never saw anything she made. Oh well, such is life.

Several days later, the matron came in pushing a wheelchair with an old lady in it. She was so cute. She was short and fat. I found out later that she came from Alaska and her name was so different, Olinga.

She smiled all the time. Maybe because I was the youngest in the room, she kept her eye on me. She didn't understand the English language and I watched as the matron and nurse tried to explain to her, "This is your bed. This is the wash basin. This is how you wash your face."

The real fun came when they tried to explain to her how to use the bedpan. She sat in bed and looked at the bedpan and saw what they were trying to get her to do. Shaking her head "No", she got out of bed, took the bedpan from the matron, sat it on the floor, straddled it, pulled down her pajama bottom and squatted. She gave me a big toothless grin.

After several attempts, they gave up and left her to do as she pleased. After that, every time she needed to use the pot, she would hold the bed with one hand, her PJs with the other and squat over the bedpan.

1941 – Age 6
One day Mama went hunting and took Ernie with her. Daddy had to go to Blacks Meadow to get hay for Sherry and Cheyenne. That left Manny and I and, of course, Trixie. We were on our own. The chipmunks and squirrels took to the tops of the trees.

After going over familiar ground, we decided to venture into new territory. Making a circle around, we got back onto the road below our camp. Excited, we skipped down the road. Going around a turn we saw a tent on the side of the road. Not used to seeing other people, we jumped into the brush and peeked around the trees and watched the camp. On the other side of the road was a saw just like Daddy's and they had logs ready to cut. No one was around. After we were sure no one was home, we slowly made our way to the camp.

We stood by the tent and listened. Maybe someone was inside. Everything was quiet. The door of the tent was tied in two places. Splitting the door of the tent between the ties, I peeked in. There was bedding, boxes and camping gear. Before deciding to go in we looked around the camp and down the road and listened. When we were sure, we lifted the bottom of the tent and crawled under.

In the boxes was food! They had "ready-made" bread in a bag, something we never had or saw before. Then, we found a jar of jam. This really made us aggressive! Standing up, we started to go through the boxes and to our surprise, candy! Then there was peanut butter, something else we never had before. Sitting down, I opened the peanut butter while Manny opened the jam. We found out the peanut butter tasted better if we put the jam on the bread too. We ate two peanut butter and jam sandwiches. This had to be the best day of our lives. Those sandwiches! The candy! We ate until we were sick.

Looking sick, "Sissie, I don't want any more." Throwing down our half-eaten sandwiches, we filled our pockets with candy.

Leaving the tent, we looked around, making sure there was still no one around, then headed for the saw. We pushed the dolly up to the end of the tracks and took turns riding it down to the saw. After several rides, it jumped the tracks and was too heavy to put back on.

Running to the saw, Manny said, "Let's cook." He picked up a small bucket and started to pour saw dust into the 50-gallon barrel of water that served as the radiator for the saw. Excited, I took a stick and started stirring the pot.

Looking around, Manny found some oil, "Sissy, this will make it taste good," he starts pouring it in. Smiling, he looked into the barrel and watched as the black oil mixed with the yellow saw dust. Then he figures it needs some dirt. The mixture gets so thick I couldn't stir it anymore. By this time, it's getting late and the sun was reaching the mountain, we had to head home.

Walking up the road, I said, "Boy that was fun but it made me tired. You put too much dirt in it."

"Yeah, we really had fun but I liked the peanut butter and jam the best. I wish Mama and Daddy would get us some."

Digging into our pockets, we took out the candy we saved. When we looked down at Trixie, she smiled. We gave her some. Watching Trixie eat the candy, I said, "We should have given Trixie the sandwich you couldn't eat."

"Yeah, we better eat all of the candy before we get home. If Mama sees it we will sure get a whipping."

When we got back to our camp no one was home. We decided to look for something to cook. We opened the grub box and looked through it. We found the cocoa and remembered when Mama made us a cup, it really tasted good. So, we decided to make some.

First, we had to make a fire. After it was going good we got a frying pan out and poured water in it and sat it on the fire. Manny poured in the cocoa while I stirred it. It began to get thick. I took a spoon and tasted it, it was awful. I gave Manny a little taste.

Making a funny face, he said, "I think Mama puts salt in it to make it sweet."

Thinking about it for a minute, "Yeah, I think it will." I poured some salt in then tasted it. "Oh, it is terrible!"

Manny went to the grub box and started taking things out trying to find something else to sweeten the cocoa. At that moment, we heard voices. Holding our breath, we listened. It's Daddy! Oh my gosh, we had to hide our cooking! Then we heard a strange voice. They were on the road but hidden behind some bushes. Peeking around the bushes, we saw a stranger talking really fast and in a scolding voice to Daddy. We saw Mama and Ernie coming up the road from Blacks Meadow.

It wasn't long before all three were listening to the stranger rant and rave. We couldn't hear what he was saying but we knew he was mad.

Looking at Manny, I said, "Looks like trouble. We better hide the cocoa. That will really make Mama mad if she sees it."

Running to the campfire, which was dying, I grabbed the frying pan with the cocoa mixture. With Manny at my heels, we ran around the back of the teepee and he held up the canvas and bedding while I slid the frying pan under it.

Next, it was important to put everything back in the grub box. With Manny on one side and me on the other, we started to throw everything back in the box but it was too late!

Mama was walking up the hill to the camp and she didn't look happy. She went straight to the tree where a washing basin sat on a block of wood and where Daddy washed his face and shaved every morning. On the tree hung his razor strap.

Olinga and I became friends. We could not talk to each other but our hand signals were understood. Boy, did we get into trouble.

During rest hour, I would wave to her, she would wave back. It wasn't long before she was on my bed. I would do "Patty Cake" with her, then one day she came with a deck of cards. Oh, how she loved to play cards. We played Steal the Pack and Rummy. We would laugh whenever one of us won and clap our hands together. Martha had to warn us to be quiet several times.

One rest hour, Olinga sat looking at me waiting for a signal to do something. This time, I got out of bed, stood in the middle of the room and motioned for her to join me.

I had her stand by me. I rolled up my sleeve and motioned for her to do the same. I rolled up my pant legs, she done the same. I tied my PJ in a knot at my waist, she done the same. Then we began to dance. Holding hands, we went around and around. It may not have been any kind of real dance but we had fun.

This went on for several days before we got caught. We began to giggle too loud. Before we knew it, the door opened and the nurse walked in. I made a flying leap into my bed leaving Olinga standing there wondering what happened. When she saw the nurse, she ran for her bed. Without saying a word, the nurse left the room closing the door behind her.

The next day the doctor gave me a scolding. When he left the room, Olinga and I looked at each other. She had a twinkle in her eye. She knew we would do it again.

Every now and then, I would sneak across the hall and visit with Ernie. Olinga wondered where I went and wanted to go. I had to make her understand she couldn't go. It made me feel bad when she got a sad look.

One rest hour, Olinga and I were dancing when the nurse walked in again. This time, she scolded us and sent us to our bed. After rest hour, she came to my bed and asked me to give her my pajama bottoms.

Surprised, I said, "No!"

With hands on her hips, "Come on, Chris. Give them to me."

"No!"

"If you don't give them to me I'll get help and take them off of you."

Holding on to my pants, "No you won't!"

She turned and left.

I quickly tied the strings of my pants in several knots.

She came back with two matrons. The matrons stood on one side of my bed and the nurse on the other side.

"Okay. It's up to you. You either give them up peacefully or we take them."

Looking at the three of them, I knew they meant business.

"Okay, okay. I'll give them to you." I tried to untie the strings but the knots were too tight. Working at it for a while, I gave up.

The nurse looked at the strings and saw the problem. She told one of the matrons to get a scissors. After cutting it off, I took my pants off making sure I was covered and handed them to her.

"Now be a good girl and stay in bed. We want you to get well."

All this time the other patients were watching. They started to laugh at me. It felt awful laying in bed naked. The sheets felt like ice against my bare skin. Even though I was covered up, I still felt like someone might see me.

I covered up my head and tried to think of a way out of this. *Pins! Yes, I need pins.* Leaning over, "Gladys, do you have four safety pins?"

Smiling at me, she opened the drawer of her nightstand. Looking around in it, she came up with a small package of pins and handed it to me.

I crawled deep under my covers. I pulled my pillow under the sheets with me. Working at it, I soon had the pillowcase off and put it on like a four-corner diaper. I pinned it on each side, at my waist, then at the top of each leg. Coming out from my covers, I smiled at Gladys and handed the package back. The girls were watching me, wondering what I was going to do.

Jumping out of bed, I twirled around, showing off my handy work and got back into bed before getting caught. The next rest hour, Olinga and I were at it again!

The next bath day, the matron didn't know I had my pants taken away, so she brought the regular change. I was back in business.

I started making several trips a week to the restroom across the hall. Ernie and I had fun talking. Then he asked if he could visit me.

I had no problem talking to him across the "air", but to come and see me at close range scared me. I told him I would think about it.

1941 – Age 6
This was the first time I knew we had a half-brother. Allen was 17. I don't know how he found us. I just remember him being at Saddle Camp. He left before winter because he slept outside and we only had one tent.

Allen introduced us kids to the "bean shooter" which was not good news for the squirrels and chipmunks. He asked Daddy if he had an old inner tube he could use. Daddy gave him one that was beyond use. Allen had us cut it in half inch strips. We were so excited. The three of us kids went to work following his instructions. Next, we needed one inch square leather for the pocket.

When all was ready, we followed him through the brush looking for just the right size and shape branch for the "Y" handle. Back at camp, he had us cut notches on the top of the "Y" where we could tie the rubber bands to.

Then it was practice time. We had to look for small rocks to use for the "bullets" which was placed in the leather pocket. Allen sat an old coffee can on a stump about 40 feet away. The rest of the day we practiced trying to hit the coffee can. After that, we challenged each other to see who could shoot the best.

The three of us kids always wore bib overalls and from the time we got up in the morning, our bean shooter was in our back pocket and the rest of our pockets were full of rocks. We could hardly wait for breakfast to be over so we could go hunting. It didn't take long before you couldn't find a chipmunk or squirrel around our camp.

The most exciting thing was when Daddy asked us to put our bean shooter to good use. Smiling at us, he said, "Why don't you kids see if you can bring home a grouse for dinner. I'd love to have chicken!"

Those were magic words! It was a new challenge and we had a lot of practice. Then Daddy had to instruct us where to hunt for grouse and brush pheasants. The grouse could be found along the ridges and the pheasant along creek beds.

Before heading out, he warned us, "Watch the sun and head back before it's too late." Hunting grouse and pheasants was not as easy as chipmunks and squirrels. It took a lot of hunting before we came home with a bird. We had to learn to sneak up on our game. Most of the time we came home empty handed.

I can't tell you how many times we broke our bean shooters. It was common to see one of us kids stretching the rubber band on the "Y" while the other tied a string around it. You could find strips of rubber and string under our pillows. You wouldn't find crumbs in our bed, it would be rocks that were all about the same size.

Daddy had made this go-devil. It looked like a big sled and was pulled by the team of horses. We used it in the winter and summer. When we needed wood, we would hitch the team to it and load it with wood or anything else that had to be moved.

One day Daddy asked Allen to take the go-devil and get some wood for camp. The tree that they fell was a distance down the road. Allen hitched the team to the go-devil. He called to me and asked if I would like to go with him. I was so excited because I thought he was wonderful and I just knew he liked me best. After we got out of sight of our camp he asked me to sit on his lap. It surprised me! I never sat on anybody's lap before. It made me feel special.

After awhile, he stopped the horses and said he had to "take a leak". He went to a tree, unbuttoned his pants and, in plain view of me, began to do his job. When he was done, he turned around, letting me see his "thing". Slowly, he put it back in his pants. Smiling at me, he walked back, sat on the seat and pulled me back onto his lap.

Getting back to the room I asked Martha, "Ernie wants to visit me. Should I let him?"

"Why do you even ask? You know you will like it."

"But, he might think I'm ugly. I might disappoint him."

Rolling her eyes, "Maybe, he will be ugly and he'll disappoint you."

"Okay, okay. I'll think about it."

Before turning over to sleep, Martha said, "Chris, the only time it matters is if you plan to marry him."

Oh gawd. I started to toss and turn trying to make up my mind.

I stayed away from the window and the earphones for a couple days. Then, I decided to listen to the voices. Ernie came on and started to call my name. It took awhile before I answered.

"I didn't hear from you. I hope I didn't upset you."

He sounded so nice and concerned, it touched my heart. "No, you didn't upset me. I just had to take a trip around the room. I just got back and here I am." I tried to make him laugh.

He sounded real serious, "Where did you go?"

"Gawd, Ernie. I'm teasing you. Anyway, see if the doctor will let you visit next week."

The following week, on visiting day, I stayed in bed during rest hour and wondered how I could make myself pretty.

"Martha, what can I do to look nice for Ernie? He's coming today, you know."

"Oh, Chris, you look nice already. I'll give you some lipstick to put on. You can put some on your cheeks too but not too much. Here, I'll do it for you."

She got out of bed and sat on mine. Closing my eyes, I held up my face for her to do her trick. She traced my lips, filled them in and lightly rubbed my cheeks with the color from my lips. She fluffed up my hair, leaned back and checked me out.

"There, you look just right."

"Are you sure? It's not too much?"

"No, no. He just might ask you to marry him!"

"I wished I could sit up when he's here," I said with a frown.

"Ask the Head Nurse. She might let you since it's the first time you had a visitor." It gave me hope.

When rest hour was over and after the regular routine, the Head Nurse came in with the medication. I asked, looking pitiful. "I'm having a visitor and I was wondering if I could sit up during the visit? I've been here almost a year."

When she looked at me I saw a fraction of sympathy in her eyes. "Yes, I'll have the matron wind up your bed and I'll ask the doctor if you can sit up twice a day and during meals." Writing it down, she went on her way.

I could have screamed! Then I felt guilty for running around all the time. Rolling my head over, I looked at Martha. Looking pitiful, "Oh, I feel so weak."

"Oh, shut up, you weasel!" She tried to hold back a smile.

A few minutes before visiting hour, the matron came in and wound up my bed. As the bed slowly went up, I acted fragile and weak. I looked over at Martha and she grinned at me.

Waiting, my heart pounded. Finally, a wheelchair with Ernie in it came in the door. The matron pushed him up to the side of my bed. He wore a striped robe and a mask but I could see that he smiled. "Hi," he said, reaching for my hand.

Ernie was a tall man. Slender in build and he had black hair that was beautifully groomed. He had olive skin that looked smooth and his features were strong. I would've loved to have seen his smile. I would guess his age to be 25 to 30. He had the kindest eyes and, ooooh, his voice was like velvet!

I had a hard time knowing what to do or say. "Hi, I'm glad

you could visit."

"This is the first time I visited anyone since I've been here," he said. By this time, with both hands he held mine.

I kind of wondered if that was true but my heart went out to him anyway, it still made me feel special. "That's a long time. I'm sorry. You should see more people."

"Yeah, I know. But it wasn't until I saw you at the window. Your smile never left me, I just had to visit you and see you up close."

Man, I felt like shrinking down in bed! I pulled my hand away from him.

It really upset him when I pulled my hand away. "Oh, Chris, please. You're as pretty as I pictured you to be. Now, I will not be able to wait until I can visit you again."

He told me a little about himself. We talked about the hospital and the different things we liked. The hour ended all too soon.

As the matron pulled him backwards away from my bed, he asked, "Will I be seeing you soon?" He motioned with his head towards the bathroom window.

I nodded, yes.

When he left the room, the girls let me know how they felt by "Ooooh"... "Ahhh"... "He's so handsome!"

"Martha, did you look at him? Really look at him?" I asked. Man, I felt like getting up and dancing. I swooned the rest of the day.

The days and weeks passed. We talked at the bathroom window. We talked on the "night-line". He visited me several times. However, we never talked about tomorrow or yesterday. We lived for today. It was all in innocence. He had been here for such a long time, he knew it was the only way. I followed his lead and enjoyed the moment.

Then one night, he told me on the nightline that he wanted to visit me soon. He sounded serious and didn't want to talk any farther. He came the following visiting day.

"Chris, I wanted to let you know, I'm having an operation next week."

I couldn't believe what he was saying. "Why? What kind of an operation?"

He laid his head on my hands as he held them. "It means I will be leaving. I may never see you again."

I asked again, "What kind of an operation?"

"One of my lungs will not heal so the doctor decided to take it out," he said in anguish.

"Oh, my God. Do you have to?" I asked, feeling his pain.

Looking up at me, "Chris, I've been here over ten years. The lung will not heal! I feel it's the only way to be able to live even for a few years."

"Did the doctor tell you of the chances you have with one lung?"

"He said people live long lives with just one lung. I will just have to be careful not to catch pneumonia."

Feeling sad, "Ernie, are you going to take that chance?"

"Yes. I decided to roll the dice."

With the visiting hour ending, he asked. "Can I hold you this last time?"

With tears in my eyes, I said, "Yes."

He got up from the wheelchair and came to my bed. Bending over, he took me into his arms. He whispered his love for me and held me tight. The matron had to tap him on the shoulder before he let go. I fell back into bed like a rag. My heart was broken. I buried my face in my pillow and cried. That special kind of happiness was gone. Now I had to try and find a way to forget.

The next week, two nurses wheeled him down the hall and into the single ward across the hall from my room and next to the bathroom. It was called the recovery ward.

Just for a second, I saw him. After that, the door was closed. I never saw him or heard from him again. I waited and waited. I wondered if he made it through the operation. I wondered if he went home. Then Gladys told me when they had that type of an operation, they were sent home because they were free of the TB bug. That eased my mind, but I couldn't help but wait to hear from him.

The days passed, then weeks. I was heartbroken. I no longer went to the window. I no longer listened to the voices. I cried in the night. The songs on the earphones only made me sad.

I no longer danced during rest hour. Instead, I went back to the window and thought about home. I looked up to see where the sun was and wondered what Mama and Daddy were doing. I wanted to go home. The urge would be so great I wanted to scream! Then I tried to think about the dream of going down those stairs to Mama and Daddy waiting for me, but I couldn't.

Somehow, something happened to me. I tried to think of home but nothing was clear. It was like a record that was played so much you didn't want to hear it again.

I watched the seagulls flying around, others on the ground fighting with each other for space, and still others walking around looking stupid. I figured this is life and I better get used to it. *Ernie is out there in another world. He knows the score. It might be years before I leave here or maybe never. He never said, "I will wait for you." He knew better and he can't come to visit, he might catch the bug from me. It would put his life in danger. After all, he just has one more chance.*

I was in deep thought when Gladys asked, "Are you all right, Chris? You haven't been yourself these past weeks."

"Yeah, I know. But, I think I got things figured out. I just have to accept it."

I went to the window by her bed and leaned against the sill.

"Gladys, how can you do it? You never talk about your family. You don't have any pictures around. You lay there and look out the window. I know you think about things. I never see or hear you cry or laugh. How?" At the end of my question, I wanted to cry.

She looked at me and I saw a glint of a tear. "Chris, I've been there. I went through it all. I've cried, I've begged God. But, it's a funny thing, I can't do anything about it and I can't give up. Why? Because I'm living. I'm alive. The only way I can give up is to leave the hospital. To leave is to die."

Her answer shocked me. I never thought of it that way but she had time to think about it. It was close to 20 years for her. She never had visitors, though I didn't either. I didn't know her story. I felt ashamed for crying since she went through the same thing.

Maybe, that's my answer. My past is fading away, my tomorrows cannot be dreamed about. I have to go back and live in this room, in this bed. Mama, Daddy, the boys, now Ernie, is the past.

"Gladys. Don't ever give up. Your day will come."

"Chris, I want to let you know, you have made me happy. You're young and with your attitude you will get well."

Even though I felt bad for Gladys, she taught me a lesson. The thought of going home was lost.

The days and weeks passed and the spark went out of me. I watched as visiting hours came and went. I took notice who received mail and who had visitors. I listened as Helen coughed and spit up. I heard Thelma cry in the night. I watched as Gladys lay on her back and looked out the window. I saw her eyes follow a seagull. When it went out of sight, she looked at another.

Martha, on the other hand, had a wonderful husband. He visited her every week on visiting day. He held her hand and I saw the love he had for her. However, the car wreck she was in and the terrible head injury caused her to have bad headaches. When one came on, she went under her covers and stayed there for days. The nurses loaded her up with pills. I watched the lump she made on the bed and I felt bad for her. I missed her and couldn't wait until she stuck her head out.

Olinga lay on her side looking across the room at me. She felt my sorrow. Feeling bad for her, I would go to her bed during rest hour and play cards with her but the joy and excitement was not there like before. She would take her fingers and pull down on the sides of her mouth and point at me, shaking her head. I knew she wanted me to be happy. I let her know I would try.

One night after the lights were turned off, I lay there and thought of home. It had been over a year since the ambulance dropped me off at the back door. I wondered how much improvement I made. I wondered why the doctor even made his rounds. Nothing ever changed.

1944 – Age 8

It ended up taking us two and a half days to fall the trees, cut them into blocks and load the truck with a cord and half, making ready for the first load to go out.

With Trixie, Manny and I riding on top of the load, Ernie in the front seat with Mama and Daddy, we headed for home. Needless to say, we were tired.

When we got home and pulled up into the yard, we couldn't believe our eyes! Several of the sheep were standing around with blood pouring down from their throats! Dogs from the neighbors had come to our house and attacked the sheep. Three sheep were already dead.

The remaining sheep had to be put down because they were standing there bleeding to death. Everybody cried but Daddy. He swore while he went into the house to get the gun. The rest of us went into the house. We couldn't watch but listened to the shots.

When Daddy came into the house, he said, "The sheep will have to be taken away before they start rotting. Yeah, it's a sad day. A man can't have anything these days."

This night was different though. Laying there with my eyes closed, I saw red flashing lights behind my eyelids. I opened my eyes wondering what was happening. The room was flashing red. I looked to see where it was coming from. The light on the wall above Gladys's bed was flashing in groups of three, giving the S.O.S. signal. The signal is also seen by red lights flashing above the door of the ward and at the nurse's desk.

When I looked at Gladys, she was up on one elbow, facing me. She held the button in one hand while blood poured out of her mouth and nose. In a matter of seconds the door burst open and three nurses came running into the room. One of the nurses had a syringe and quickly gave Gladys a shot.

It wasn't long before the doctor came in. We watched as he checked her over and gave orders to the nurses. As they quickly wheeled her out of the room, there was not a sound from the rest of us. I wondered, *are they praying for her or for themselves?*

Christine Cassano

Chapter 5

SPAGHETTI FOR BREAKFAST
Age 17

Seeing Gladys hemorrhage put fear in me. I tried hard to stay in bed although I did make trips to the window to watch the seagulls and daydream. I took time and played cards with Olinga. It made her happy and I felt good about that. And, Martha and I spent time talking. She knew so much of things I never heard about.

I listened to the music but the joy wasn't there. After what happened to Gladys, I didn't want to know any more about the TB bug. It just depressed me. I decided to get back on the earphones. I spent several days listening to the patients talking and making dates to visit each other. Then on visiting days I would watch the door and see matrons pushing a patient down the hall, keeping the date.

One night while I was listening, I decided to enter into the nightline. "Hey, out there. Does anyone want to talk to me?" I listened for an answer. I called again. The talking went on with no answer. "Hey. My name is Chris. Tell me yours."

"My name is Howard. I haven't heard you 'on-line' before."

I remembered this guy's voice from the first time I listened to the voices. Excited, holding the earphones so he couldn't hear, "Hey Martha. I just got a guy by the name of Howard on the line."

"Tell him hello for me," she said, sounding bored
"Howard, I've been around awhile but not on the line."
"What floor are you on?"
"Listen, Howard. I've got the bug. If it scares you, hang up."
"Wait, all that doesn't matter. I would still like to know you."

I'm thinking, if he doesn't care, what the heck, "Okay. I'm on the North Wing. Where are you from? You know, before you came here."

"Alaska. Chris, I could tell you a lot more if I can visit you. What room are you in?"

1946 – Age 11
Towards the end of summer, Mama, Daddy and Allen took a load of wood to town. When they came back Mama was really upset. Something had happened while they were gone but no one said anything. Daddy wasn't his jovial self. He would sit at the table, having his coffee, and look as if he was thinking about something. It really bothered me. However, we worked together in the woods and everyone went about their job without a word. When the next load was ready to deliver, Allen stayed at home.

After Mama and Daddy left, Allen was in a sour mood. Avoiding him, I started to cook supper. During the meal, he ordered the boys to get their chores done before dark. After we ate and I started to wash the dishes, he told the boy's to, "Get a move on." They were only too happy to get out of the house.

After the boys left, he asked for another cup of coffee. As I was pouring his coffee, he asked me to have a cup with him. When I went to get a cup for myself, he said, "You know Sissie, you're such a pretty girl and I admire of how you care for the family."

Catching me off guard, I suddenly felt bashful. No one ever said I was pretty or admired me. It was a feeling I've never had before. When I went to the table, he got up and gave me a hug. Taking the cup from me, he asked me to sit down. When I sat down he took my hand, "Sissie, you're the only girl for me and I care for you very much."

No one had ever said things to me like that. I became aware of myself and it made me feel weird. I didn't know what to do with myself but sit there with him holding my hand.

When the boys came in, he told them to go to bed. Since the boys and Allen slept in the tent behind the house, that left just Allen and me in the house.

After they left, he got out the cards and we played for a while. He let me win every hand. As the evening passed, every now and then, he would reach over and touch my face and tell me how soft my skin was. I began to feel special, like he really cared about me.

Realizing it was getting late, he told me I better go to bed. I slept in a single cot in the room where Mama and Daddy slept. After gathering up the cards and cups, I went to bed.

I heard him blow out the light and he came to my bed and sat down. I was facing the wall when he bent down and kissed me on the cheek and began to rub my back and neck. All the while, he's repeating how he cared for me, how hard I worked, how I was the only girl for him, how soft my skin was and added, he couldn't get me off his mind. Listening to him, I fell asleep.

The next morning when I woke up I looked over at Mama. She was sitting up in bed with her cup of coffee. She wouldn't look at me. Something was wrong. Really wrong! She never did treat me like this. Something must have happened when they were in town.

"Mama, are you alright? Is there something wrong?" I asked, feeling awful.

Without looking at me, she motioned for me to leave the room. Getting up, suddenly there was a big lump in my throat. When I tried to swallow, it hurt. What did I do? Why is she mad at me? Mama never acted toward me like this, it made my stomach feel sick. It had been a long time since I had a whipping or a scolding. This anger was different. When I went into the kitchen, Daddy seemed okay.

Smiling at me, he said, "I let you kids sleep in today. We put in a good day's work yesterday. Today, we can rest." He had breakfast ready and asked me to call the boys.

Later on in the day, when everyone else left, Mama asked me, "What did Allen do to you last night?"

I didn't know what she meant. "Nothing. What do you mean? Why do you ask me a question like that?"

Then I thought of the things Allen said to me the night before. It made me feel ashamed.

"I believe you. But, when we got home last night he was laying in bed with you, if Daddy had come in he would have killed him!" She began to cry.

Boy, he isn't wasting any time! "Wait for a minute." Taking the earphone away. "Hey, Martha. Howard wants to visit me. Should I let him?" I whispered.

"Yeah, I would like to look at something new once in awhile." After answering, she turned her back on me.

Getting back on the line. "231. Howard, you're kinda rushing me."

"Listen Chris, this time is as good as any. I'll see you tomorrow."

Before I could answer he was gone. Man, he wasn't going to take no for an answer! Then I got to thinking about it, *tomorrow isn't visiting day. Boy, he'll be surprised when he gives it a thought.*

The next morning, I worried maybe he will come this afternoon. I asked Martha. "Do you think he will come? You know it isn't visiting day."

"You never know, he just might come anyway. You better be ready," as she handed me her mirror.

During rest hour, I kept looking in the mirror. Gawd, I looked awful. "Martha, could I use your lipstick? Maybe, you better fix my face again. Please."

She gathered up the potion from the nightstand, sat on my bed and began her magic. Leaning back, she looked at me. "Now, you look just right."

"You sure it's not too much? Is it like you did before?" I laid back and looked at myself in the mirror.

"No, it's not too much and yes, it's like before. It makes you look fragile and weak. You're getting good at playing the part, you know," she said with a grin.

After the routine was over and the medication passed out, I waited for the regular visiting hour time. I expected to see him, if he came, in a wheelchair.

I watched the door. Then a man walked in, stood and looked around the room. His eyes stopped on me! I think my heart missed a beat. He looked around for a chair. Picking one up that was by the door, he walked straight to me and sat it by the side of my bed. With confidence, he said, "Hi Chris," as he sat down.

I was glad I was laying down because my knees were shaking.

Howard was tall, a bit thick in build. He had short black wavy hair. He wore black horn rimmed glasses, an expensive looking wrist watch, a beautiful gold ring with stones in it. If he took off that damn striped robe and put on a suit and tie he would have been perfect as a business man.

He didn't waste time. He took my hand and held it firm. I was used to seeing rough working hands on a man but his hands were smooth and soft.

I was trying hard to get control of myself. "How did you know who I was?"

Smiling at me, "Because I knew you would be pretty."

Needless to say, he took my breath away.

I found out he was a musician and had his own band before he got sick. He planned on putting his band back together when he was released. Also, he was a skilled artist. I guessed his age at 35. His father was a pastor in his hometown of Ketchikan, Alaska.

I was in awe. He seemed so sure of himself. He knew what he wanted to do. The fear of never leaving the hospital wasn't in his vocabulary. He lived for tomorrow! It made me happy just to listen to him talk.

But, there was a question in the back of my mind. I just had to ask, "How come you could visit me when it isn't visiting day?"

"Oh, that. I have TB of the kidneys. I don't spread the bug so I come and go as I please in the hospital."

I was so impressed. For him to even look at me made me feel special. Then he asked me, "Do you like music?"

"Oh, yes. I listen every day, all day! I can't live without my music."

"I'm glad to hear that. In a few weeks, I will be the disc jockey for the hospital. The patients can send in requests for whoever they want and I will play the song. The station will be upstairs on the top floor."

Then, he added. "I've been working with the main office to get televisions for the wards. I think it is about time. But, it will take time before each ward will have one."

After we talked for awhile, he looked at his watch. "I'm sorry but I have an appointment. I will be talking to you soon."

"Howard, will you do me a favor? Don't just drop in on me. Let me know when to expect you. After all, I may not be at home," I said, trying to look serious.

"Okay. I'll remember that." Kissing my hand through the mask, he left.

Holding my limp hand up that he had kissed, "Oooh, did you see that, Martha?"

"Yeah, yeah, you got the man's attention. And, I did like the change of scenery."

Later, we talked on the nightline and he began dropping in for short visits. Each time bringing me little gifts like candy, fruit, books and flowers.

During those visits, I saw the other side of him. He was gentle, loving and kind. He made me feel so special. At his age, he probably had many girlfriends but here in the hospital, it was just him and me. Yet his dreams went beyond the hospital. He told of places he would like to bring me, people he wanted me to meet. Things he wanted to give me.

He assured me, "I know my parents would love you. Chris, one day you and I will be together. If I leave first, I will be waiting for you."

The more he talked to me about "us", I worried. I tossed and turned at night thinking about him. *He has so much, he gives me so much, he lives in a big city, his father is a pastor…*

I thought of the catalog and all those beautiful clothes and shoes. I don't have anything. Heck, I got excited just looking at that damn catalog and I would not feel right for him to give me things like that! I'm from a world he knows nothing about. I couldn't imagine him in the mountains or me in a big city. And, meeting his parents in their big beautiful house would scare me to death! I just know I would run the other way if I had to face something like that.

Howard made me forget where I was. I had trained my mind to live in this bed and in this room. Now, he dared me to think beyond. I must learn to accept it as a dream and go along with it. One thing I knew for sure, I could never fit in his world. If he really knew me and where I came from, I wondered what he would do.

Pushing the food around in my plate, I made my mind up. I will play the part and dream about tomorrow with him. I will keep his dream alive. After all, how could I make him lose hope?

I began to think of the good things he had done for me. He gave me someone to think about, someone who cared about me. He made me feel good about myself and I no longer felt alone.

One day, when he came to visit me, he told me The Request Hour would be starting the following Friday evening.

"When I start the program, the first request will be for you. I will start with our song and sign off with it. Be sure to listen." Telling me this, I knew he was excited to start.

When Friday came, I received a note from him, it read:

Dearest Chris,
Don't forget to listen tonight, our song, *I'm In the Mood for Love.*
Love you,
Howard

I handed the note to Martha. "Read this. Love is on the air!"

Taking the note, I watched her eyes going over the words. "Yeah, I know, I've been watching."

With my earphones clamped on my head I listened as the radio music shut off and Howard came on the air.

"Good evening. This is Howard. I'm happy to say that we will be having The Request Hour for the patients each Friday from 8 to 9 PM. Send your requests in no later than noon on Fridays.

"My first request is for Chris in room 231. *I'm In the Mood for Love* by Frankie Laine."

I never heard the song before. I listened to the words! *Oooh, how romantic.* I just knew I was in love!

When the hour ended, he said good night to me and played the song again. My heart melted. With that song, he told everybody in the hospital listening that he was in love with me! That night, I fell asleep with a smile on my face.

Howard made my days and weeks pass by fast. The attention he gave me made me happy. However, I never let my guard down. Now, with Howard in my life, I never let myself think beyond the next day. What happened to Gladys in the bed next to me, reminded me what could happen. And the sight of Helen, with her skinny body and with strands of hair that stood up, kept me in check.

Whenever Howard walked into the room, my eyes would follow him as he picked up the chair and came to my bed. He would take my hands and, with his mask on, kiss them. He was always concerned about me and asked if there was anything I wanted or needed. It was always up to him because I never knew what to ask for. Really, I didn't need anything.

One day, during rest hour, I had a feeling of loneliness so I got out of bed and went to the window. I looked out at the seagulls. They filled the green lawn, making it white, leaving a green rim. It was a sunny day without a cloud in the sky. A pale blue-gray haze hung over the city.

I wished I could go out there and take a deep breath. I wanted to run down the middle of all those seagulls, making them fly up, getting out of my way. When they settled down, I would run back through! I just knew it would be fun.

Looking up, the building hid the sun. I wondered what Mama and Daddy were doing. *Are they still living in the same place? Are they okay? Are the boys helping them?*

Now that I was in a hospital, I wished Daddy would take Mama to the hospital. Maybe the doctor could get her well. But I knew it would never happen. Daddy would always say, "When you go to the doctor they want to cut on you."

The ache in my heart never left. It was there just under the surface. I wished I could go and see them. Even for a little while. Just to see how they are doing and to tell them that I am happy. To give them hope I will be coming home one day.

I remembered back to the day that seemed so long ago, when the ambulance took me away. I pictured Mama and Daddy coming to see me that afternoon only to see an empty bed. They didn't let me say goodbye. It was like cutting off sound, leaving silence that had no end. I reeled through space with no connection. It took me awhile to find my place in that bed and in this room. *Yes, I'm okay now. I've found ways to be happy.*

Hearing the sound of activity in the hallway, rest hour was over. Feeling a bit melancholy, I went back to bed.

After supper, the Head Nurse came in and told me I wouldn't be able to have breakfast in the morning until after I had a gastric.

After the nurse left Martha said, "Now you will know what having spaghetti for breakfast is."

"What are they going to do to me?" I asked.

"You'll find out," she said, smiling.

"I know I'll find out. Please tell me, what are they going to do?" I begged.

"Listen, Chris. I couldn't do it justice if I explained. But you will live through it, I promise."

I worried half of the night. I couldn't imagine what having spaghetti for breakfast could mean or what it was.

The next morning the nurse came in with a wheelchair. She handed me my robe and mask then off we went. It always felt good riding in the wheelchair with the breeze in my face. And no matter what, I had to look into the other wards as we passed. When we got to the elevator, she pushed the arrow pointing down. Then, when we were inside, she pushed the B button. Arriving, she wheeled me into a little room and pushed me up to a table.

On the table in front of me was a bowl of water with ice cubes and a coiled-up hose in it. Looking at it, my eyes got big as saucers. *Mannn, am I supposed to eat that!?*

In the mean time, the nurse put on rubber gloves. "Now, Chris, this is what I'm going to do." She pointed at a red line on the hose. "I'm going to put this tubing through your nose and down your throat. I will push it in until I reach this line then suction some fluid from your stomach which will be tested."

She's going to stick that up my nose?! I looked at her, wild eyed, "You gotta be kidding!"

"Come on. It really isn't all that bad," she assured me.

"Have you had this done to you?" I asked.

"No, but many patients have had it done without any problem."

Backing up the wheelchair, "I don't know about this. I've got to think about it first… could you… maybe put me to sleep?"

Pushing the chair back to the table, "Now, Chris, don't give me any trouble. Let's give it a try. Okay?"

I looked at the coiled-up hose for a while. I noticed she was losing her patience. Cringing, I said I'd give it a try.

With a sigh of relief, she picked up the hose. Bending over to get a good shot of my nose, she stuck it in my right nostril. "Now, when it gets to the back of your throat take a deep breath. This will open your throat and keep you from gagging."

I tried but when it got to the back of my throat, I gagged and the damn thing came out my mouth!

Pulling it out, "Chris. You're not trying. Let's do it again. This time, follow my instructions."

Closing my eyes, I lent her my nose. Again, I gagged and it came out my mouth! I gagged again as she pulled the hose back out.

By this time, I'm mad. I pushed myself back from the table. "I can't let you do that again. My nose hurts. In fact, the inside of my nose feels raw."

"Chris, this has to be done. The contents in your stomach must be tested. Please, let me try it in the other nostril."

"I have to think about it for a minute." I stared at the hose.

The room was silent while I thought about what I had to do. I knew I couldn't get out of it. "Okay. I'll do it myself. You leave me alone and I'll call when I get it down my throat."

Giving me a worried look, "Are you sure you can do this yourself?"

"I'm sure going to try. But, I think I can do it."

When I heard the door close, I wheeled myself up to the table. I sat there for a minute looking at the hose. Feeling like I was ready, I picked up the hose with both hands. I put my elbows on the table on both sides of the bowl. Hanging my head over the bowl, I stuck the hose in my mouth. I pushed it back as far as I could, just before gagging. I held it there for a second, concentrating. Then, I took a deep breath. At that moment, I pushed the hose down my throat. I kept pushing the hose in until I came to the red line. Without gagging, the job was done.

I called out for the nurse. When she came in she had a look of concern until she saw the hose in my mouth, she gave me a big smile. As she sucked out the contents from my stomach, she said, "I'm sorry for getting upset. Now, I wish it was always this easy. I must say, you really surprised me."

After I took the hose out, I told her, "After this, I won't mind having spaghetti for breakfast."

When I got back to the room, the girls began to tease me. "How was the spaghetti? Did you enjoy it?"

Acting proud, I got back into bed. "As a matter of fact, I done it all by myself!"

Sitting up in bed, Helen said, "I don't believe it!"

"I sure did. I sent the nurse out of the room and done it myself. If you don't believe me, ask her."

When the matron brought my breakfast, she wound up my bed. While I ate, the girls stared at me. After awhile, Martha said, "Yeah, I believe it. After living beside her all this time, I believe it."

The following week the nurse came and took me to have an x-ray. When we got into the elevator, we had to wait for another patient who was going for an x-ray also.

When we got to the basement, the nurses pushed us to one side and left. We sat there waiting. I looked at the entrance where the ambulance drives up. The door was open and I could see the green lawn. The sun and lawn looked inviting. It had been almost a year and a half since I touched the ground.

1940 – Age 5

It was a beautiful sunny day. The little meadow looked green and the leaves on the poplar trees along the edge of the meadow fluttered in the breeze. The tall grass along the little creek mimicked the leaves, swaying in ripples as the breeze passed over. It was so inviting, we left the mountains to the squirrels and chipmunks.

We played along the little creek all day. The frogs couldn't get away from us quick enough and the butterflies stayed well out of our reach but we chased them nevertheless. Trixie ran back and forth barking. The sun got so hot we took all of our clothes off and laid in the creek and splashed water at each other.

Trixie had enough. She went back to the camp, laid down in the shade and watched us. We started to run up and down the creek. Along the way, we came onto this rattlesnake. He was real long and had several links to his rattler. Looking around, each of us found a stick and ran back to where he was.

Picking him up with the end of the stick, Ernie threw him up in the air towards the creek. We each took our turns throwing it around. The snake would coil up, shake his rattler and jump at us. We tormented that poor thing for about an hour or more until he couldn't jump anymore and just laid there. Our excitement wore off as well. We stood there looking at the snake.

Then I got an idea. I grabbed the snake by the back of the head and wrapped it around my waist. The boys, with their eyes wide open, backed off. Holding the snake, its mouth wide open, I looked at them with a mischievous grin. Letting out a scream, the boys started to run yelling, "Stop Sissy. We're going to tell Mama on you!"

I got between them and their clothes and made a hissing sound, "I'm going to get you... I'm going to get you!"

Wrapping their arms around themselves, "Please, Sissie. The mosquitoes are eating us up, please!"

Each time I said, "I'm going to get you," they would scream. After taunting them for awhile, I asked, "Okay, are you going to tell Mama on me?"

In unison, "No, we promise." I couldn't have trained them better. I tossed the snake into the creek. I noticed he moved a little so I figured he would crawl away after he rested up.

Looking over at the other patient. "I don't know about you but I'm going outside." I got out of the wheelchair and made a run for the door. She didn't waste any time. By the time I got outside, she was right behind me. We ran out on the lawn, laid down and rolled around. Then, we heard shouts from the building. Patients from the North Wing and the guys from East Wing hung out the windows and hollered, "Bring us some grass."

Another patient shouted, "Bring us some dirt."

It didn't take long before the two nurses came running out, "What are you girls doing out here? You know you shouldn't be doing this." They practically drug us back in. All the while, we're laughing.

When I got back to the room, I proudly said, "You can't believe where I went?" They didn't see us since room 231 was on the front side of the building.

Helen got all excited, "What did you do this time?"

"I went outside and rolled around on the grass!"

Martha had her back to me, she quickly turned over and looked at me. "How were you able to do that?", she asked.

Acting smug, I made motion like I was brushing the grass off, "Oh, it was easy. The nurse left me and this other patient alone. The door was open so we strolled outside. That's all there was to it."

"Gosh Chris, I want to go with you next time," Helen said, feeling the excitement of going outside.

"Who knows, Helen, I might get the feeling one day to go outside and I'll just walk down the hall and out the door." Thinking about it, after I had said what I would do, *hmm... I like that idea.*

The following week when Dr. Salli made his rounds, he stopped at the foot of my bed and his mask raised up, letting me know he was smiling at me.

After a second or two, he said, "Chris, it's time for you to pack your bag, we're moving you to South Wing. You've given three negative tests. Now be a good girl and stay well."

I sat there and stared at him. *South Wing?! That means I'm well!* I watched his mask move but I didn't hear what he was saying. All that went around in my head was, *South Wing! I'm well, I'm well!*

When the doctor and nurse left the room, everyone was silent. I couldn't stand it. I jumped out of bed and wound the bed back down. Getting back in bed, I crawled under the covers and cried. I had mixed emotions. I was happy my "tomorrow" finally came but I was leaving my friends behind. What would be their fate? Would their tomorrow come? *Oh, my God, make them well too.*

Right after lunch the nurse came with the wheelchair, it was time to go. Trying hard not to cry, I got into the wheelchair. As the nurse turned me around, I waved to the girls. "Hurry up and get well. I'm lonesome for you even before I leave."

All that I owned sat on my lap as the nurse wheeled me out the door. In the background, I heard faint goodbyes. It broke my heart to leave room 231. I had made friends that would stay in my memory forever. They taught me so much. Most of all, how to live with my illness and how to live in my bed. I laughed and cried with them. I hoped I left something behind also.

When we passed the center desk and headed down the South Wing, patients stood at the door of the wards and watched me. It made me feel strange. I couldn't wait until we got to my new room.

About half way down the long hallway, the nurse turned into a ward on the left. It had four beds, one was empty. Pulling up to the bed, the nurse took the things off my lap and put them in the nightstand. She pulled back the covers and asked me to get in.

I felt a bit bashful as I got into bed. My three roommates watched every move I made. I knew the nurse and felt somewhat attached and didn't want her to leave. To avoid the eyes, I began to straighten things up on my nightstand.

"Hi, my name is Jamie. What's yours?" Her bed was across the room on the left. I noticed she had a cast on one leg. I guessed her age about 18. She had long dark brown hair and was very pretty.

"My name is Chris."

The girl straight across from me gave me a big smile, "My name is Ann. Did you come from North Wing?"

"Yes."

Ann had short light brown hair and a wonderful personality. She went on to explain, "The reason I asked is like Jamie, she has TB of the bone and didn't have to go to North Wing. It's only if you breathe the bug."

"Hey, you guys. I have to introduce myself too. My name is Pat. I came from North Wing too. I spent three years there and have one more month to go before I go home."

I guessed Pat to be about 22 years old and Ann, about 20. It was wonderful to be in a room with girls close to my age. There was a light feeling in the room. They talked and laughed and acted like what I imagined a sleepover was like.

Hearing Pat say she was going home in one month, I wondered how long I would stay. I asked Pat, "How long did you have to stay here before going home?"

"It's like this. When you're on North Wing and you give three negative sputums, they move you to South Wing. Then they test your sputum each month. If the tests are negative, you can go home in three months!"

That night I could not sleep. *Oh man, in three months I can go home!* I wished I could tell Mama and Daddy, they would be so happy. I haven't heard from them all this time. I prayed Mama would be better. We moved so many times through the years, I wondered where they were living now.

I pictured things as they were when I left. The army tent by Lynx Creek. The doggy door I cut in the corner of the door, I wondered if little Tiny was still using it. I thought of Sherry and

Cheyenne and Trixie. I wondered if Daddy was still cutting wood. *Do they have enough food?*

I tossed and turned. *How will they find me?* I wondered where they could get some money to come and get me. *I know, I'll write them a letter... no, I'll wait until I have two weeks left. That way, they won't have to wait so long.*

Just thinking of Mama and Daddy coming to get me, the dream came back. This time, it was clear. I pictured myself walking down those front steps with Mama and Daddy waiting by the car. The sun is bright. I can see Mama looking up at me, smiling. When Daddy sees me, he takes off his hat and looks up at me. His hair is as white as the seagulls that are crowding the lawn behind him.

As I walk down the steps, I feel like I've done something great, like a soldier walking out of a battle field. The only thing that would be missing, the little blue dress and the white shoes that would've clicked with each step.

My Daddy never hugged me but the look in his eyes and the tone of his voice, caressed me with his love, *"Tissie, I'm glad you're well. We need you. It's time to go home."*

Mama takes me in her arms and holds me tight. She pets my head with those rough hands that never ceased to calm me. I can just hear her voice, *"Sissie, we waited so long...."*

I can see Daddy sitting at the table, his eyes are closed, he's leaning back, one leg over the other, with a little smile. Mama is making those special biscuits because I'm coming home. The kerosene lamp on the table is giving the room a soft glow. The tent is warm and my bed is waiting.

I buried my face in my pillow to muffle my cry. *Mama, Daddy, I'm coming home!*

My eyes were puffy the next morning. I was happy but, for some reason, I wanted to cry. I felt like I wanted to just let it out and get it over with.

"Chris, I know how you feel. It's been a long time but give it some time and you'll feel better." It was Pat, she heard me crying in the night.

I took the napkin from my tray and buried my face in it and cried. This time I didn't care who heard me.

"Listen Chris, the time will pass fast."

Jamie broke up the seriousness, "Hey, Chris. You know, you guys don't have to ride in the wheelchair anymore. We're up patients. We can walk to take a shower or to the doctor's office and even to have x-rays. Only, with my leg, I can't walk far so they have to take me in the wheelchair. Otherwise, I just hobble around here."

Ann had even better news, "I know what will make you happy, Chris. I won't tell you now but wait until rest hour."

I got so excited I could hardly wait until the time came.

Just before lunch, a patient came to the door. She had a little stuffed dog. She said "Hi" to everyone. Then she saw that I was new, "Hi, my name is Gretta and this is my friend, Snazzy McJazzy."

She was short and cute. I figured her to be about 14 or 15 years old. She talked for a while with the girls, then before leaving, she asked, "Will I see you girls later?" making a motion with her head towards the room across the hall. All the girls looked at her and smiled, nodding their heads. I knew something exciting was about to happen.

After lunch, it was time for the rest hour. The girls waited for about ten minutes. Jamie got out of bed and hopped to the door on one foot. The cast on her leg didn't seem to hold her back. Slowly, she opened the door and looked up and down the hallway. She looked back at us then whispered, "Okay, the coast is clear. Come on, let's go."

The rest of us jumped out of bed and ran to the door. By this time, Jamie was knocking on the door of the ward across from ours. The door opened and she disappeared inside. The rest of us looked both ways before running across the hall.

It was also a four-bed ward. The patients didn't waste time for introductions, they were all hanging out the window. All I saw were their backs. I made my way to an opening and looked down. They were talking to the guys on the first floor.

After watching for a while, I saw them passing notes, candy and different kinds of food back and forth by tying it on a string. There were a few things on the ground that had come untied.

I wondered where Howard was. He didn't know I got promoted. I hoped someone would get him for me. I asked Pat if she would ask the guy she was talking to, if he would go and find Howard for me.

When she asked him, he looked up at me and said, "Oh, so you're the one that has Howard talking to himself. I'm glad to meet you. Wait there, I'll go and get him."

It didn't take long before Howard stuck his head out. "Chris. Is it really you?"

"Yeah. I just moved to South Wing yesterday. Guess what? I will be going home in three months! I can hardly wait."

"I'm so happy for you but I'm going to miss you. I hope you won't leave me behind for long." I saw sadness in his eyes.

"Don't feel bad, Howard. We have three whole months before I leave. Who knows, the doctor just might tell you that you will be going home in three months. Or, maybe you will leave before me." I tried to make light of the subject.

He looked at the others sending different things up and down on the strings. "Chris is there anything you want?"

I thought for a while, "I can't think of anything."

"Come on. Think of something," he coaxed.

I watched the others and saw what they were giving. I felt a little mischievous and thought I would ask for something that I figured he couldn't get. "I know what I would like. I'm hungry for watermelon."

He gave me a big smile, "Okay, if that's what you want I'll have it here tomorrow!"

I'll be damned. He's going to get it!

All too soon we had to go back to our room. Crawling back into my bed, I thanked the Lord for all my good fortune. *I'm on South Wing, I have Howard, and I'm in a ward with these girls.*

A couple days later during rest hour, Pat asked me if I would like to go to the movies.

"Movies? Where? How can we go to the movies?" I asked, all excited.

"Just wait and see. We'll take you to the movies tonight. It starts at 10 o'clock."

Just to keep me in suspense, the girls wouldn't say anything the rest of the day about how they did it but talked about the movies they saw.

That night after the lights were turned off, Pat said, "Okay, it's time. Follow us and bring your blanket."

Each girl got out of bed, grabbed their blanket and lined up at the door. Pat was in the lead. She slowly opened the door, looked down the hall and made a run for the double doors at the end of the hall. When she disappeared into the ward, Jamie looked both ways and hobbled down the hall. The rest of us took our turn. The end ward housed six patients and a big TV set! Thanks to Howard.

By this time, Pat was behind the TV hooking it up to the nightlight socket. In the meantime, other patients from different wards crept in. Some had their pillows instead of blankets. By 10:00, we had a full house.

Hoping everyone that planned to come was there, two girls from the ward laid blankets along the floor in front of the doors to hide the light from the TV so the nurses couldn't see it from the hallway or the center desk.

It was Showtime! Pat went through the channels until she came to the one with the movie. Then, all of us settled back and watched the movie.

Everyone had to be real quiet because the sound was turned

down low. After awhile, someone would snore. You would hear several, "Shhh!"

Although I was tired when we got back to our room, I asked Pat, "When will we be able to go to the movies again?"

"A different movie comes on each week on that channel. So, next week we'll go to the movies again."

"Next time, could you show me how to hook it up? Because you might leave before I do and someone needs to know how."

"Okay, I'll also show you how to turn to the movie channels."

That night, I counted my blessings. I might have been in the hospital but I was happy. I wished I had always been in this room. I loved the girls. I had friends, real friends! We talked and laughed. No one was sick. If they were, they didn't show it. I knew I would miss them when I went home.

I had been on the South Wing about a month and a half. We went to the movies each week and we hung out the window every rest hour. The days just flew by and I loved it.

I talked to Howard every night on the nightline and at the window. He came to visit me every other day. The girls teased me.

"Oh, he likes you!"

"How did you meet him?"

"Did you know him before you came here?"

I came back with, "Oh, we're just friends."

"I don't think so."

Ann looked at me, with a smile, "I think he's in love with you."

"Oh, you girls stop it. I'm not the only one that talks to a guy. Look at all the other girls and guys hanging out the window and talking on the earphones," I said in defense.

Pat had to put in a word, "Yeah, but what I can see, he's one love sick puppy!"

I had enough. I covered my head with my pillow.

A week later, when I got on the nightline, Howard wasn't

there. When I hung out the window, he didn't show up and he didn't come to visit me. It made me feel bad. I wondered what I might have said that offended him.

Then the following week, when I went to the window he was there. He asked me to drop a string, he had a note for me. As I lifted the note up, he said, "Take the note to your room before reading it. Give it a lot of thought before answering. I'll be waiting."

Walking back to my room, I wondered, maybe he's going home. Maybe he's having an operation. Maybe he doesn't want to talk to me anymore. I wound up my bed, got in, leaned back and tore open the envelope. The note read:

Dearest Chris,
All these past months, knowing you, I've fallen in love with you. I've given it a lot of thought. This past week I thought of everything, your illness, mine, and there is no other answer. Will you marry me? I know it is far in the future but I need you and hope we can be together.
Love,
Howard

After reading it several times, making sure I understood its meaning, I held the note to my chest, laid my head back and closed my eyes. *Oh my gawd, he IS in love with me. What will I do? What can I say?*

That night I tossed and turned. I couldn't sleep. I tried to think about him but couldn't. I tried to think about going home, I couldn't. *Man, I've got to stop this!* I tried to get my mind back in order.

Mama and Daddy... I've got to go home. There is no other way, they need me. As long as Mama is sick, I will never leave them. Then, if she gets well, how could I ever leave them alone? It will haunt me for the rest of my days. I can never be happy knowing they are by themselves back in the mountains.

Howard… If I told him about Mama and Daddy I don't think he can understand. He would have to see them and where they live. He could never understand my kind of life but he can understand why I can't leave them.

Then, there is love… What is falling in love? I have no idea what I feel. I know I like him a lot. I liked Ernie. He had told me he loved me but I thought of it as telling a friend.

This has to be given a lot of thought. Howard is sick and he might be in the hospital for years, or die here. How can I say no when I'm leaving? It would break his heart. How can I say no and have him lose hope? I had to find the answers to my questions.

For the next week, I wrestled with the questions. I didn't go to the window or on the nightline. When the girls asked me why, I told them I didn't feel good.

It was during breakfast when it came to me. *I'm still here in the hospital, who knows about tomorrow?* I remembered back in the beginning when Gladys taught me to live for today. *That's it! I'm still on the train, I'll ride it to the end! We'll live for the moment!* It was like a weight had been lifted off my shoulders.

The Good Lord gave me the answer just in time. After the breakfast trays were picked up and the medications handed out, Howard walked in. He picked up a chair and sat it by my bed. Sitting down, he took my hand and kissed it. "How are you? Have you been sick?"

Feeling a bit bashful, I said, "No." Leaning forward close to his ear I whispered, "You asked me to marry you and you don't even know how tall I am. You've only seen me in bed and at the window."

Smiling at me, he got up, moved back the chair, took my robe and handed it to me, "I'll take care of that. Here, put this on and come with me."

I didn't waste any time, I got up and put on my robe. "Where are we going?"

Taking me by the hand, we went to the door and looked down the hallway, nurses were going in and out of wards pushing carts. Matrons were going back and forth passing out towels and water. The hall looked busy and I was afraid to get in trouble. Howard said, "Come on, no one will notice."

We walked side by side down the hallway, passing by everyone. No one took notice, like he said. We passed the center desk and headed for the elevator. He pushed the down button. I held my breath, waiting. The elevator opened and two people got out. We stepped in and I thought the door would never close. We were alone in the elevator. Howard looked down at me and smiled as he squeezed my hand. He pushed the "B". When I looked up at him, he said, "I think you are just right." My head came up to his chin. Pulling me to him, he held me close as the elevator went down to the basement.

I was familiar with the basement. I had to tell him, pointing to the hallway, "I went over there in that little room and had spaghetti for breakfast." He laughed and asked me what it was. It almost made him gag when I explained it to him. Since he had TB of the kidneys, he didn't have to go through that.

Taking me by the hand, we went out the side door. We followed the building around to the South side. The yard sloped up to almost first floor level. The lawn was beautifully manicured. We walked up to the top of the little knoll. It was a beautiful day, there wasn't a cloud in the sky and the sun felt warm.

Still holding my hand, Howard pulled me to him. Now, holding both hands, he looked down at me and said, "I wanted to tell you in words. I love you and want to marry you. Will you marry me?"

"Howard, I'm afraid. I don't know what love is. And, there is so much you don't know about me."

In a soft voice, he said, "Chris, nothing else matters. Right now, it's just you and me. Please, give me an answer."

I laid my head against his chest, his words rang in my ears,

'It's just you and me.' I must live for today for his sake because I'm going home "tomorrow".

Lifting my head, I looked up at him. "Yes, I will marry you."

He took me into his arms and kissed me. It was my first kiss and I thought my heart was going to jump out of my chest. Then we held each other tight.

It was then that we heard clapping and yelling from the windows of the hospital. The patients were hanging out the windows and waving. I heard one of the guys say, "I thought you would never kiss her!" Then, out of nowhere came another patient with a camera and asked to take our picture. We sat on the lawn while he worked his camera.

The patient with the camera told us we caused so much excitement, we might get caught. It was time to go back. I left Howard in the basement and made my way back to my room.

The girls really teased me. "We watched him kiss you."

"Has he asked you to marry him yet?"

"Be careful he means business."

I didn't tell the girls that Howard had asked me to marry him. Somehow, I didn't feel right about it. I guess it was hard for me to make plans for tomorrow or even to just think about it. I had brainwashed myself for so long that I couldn't think ahead. Even when the doctor told me I was going home. The dream lasted for a short time. There were times I tried to think about it but my mind would go blank. It was easier to think about the here and now.

For so many months Howard had made me happy and I hoped and prayed we could go on as before. I didn't want to talk about tomorrow.

Christine Cassano

Ernie and Mama

Chapter 6

THE WHEELCHAIR
Age 18

Every Tuesday and Friday, it was "bottoms up" right after breakfast. I would turn over on my stomach, the nurse would pull down my PJ bottom, pinch my cheek and jab me with the streptomycin shot. It always burned so I would lay there until the pain faded away.

After some time, when I received the shot, my lips and tongue would feel real thick. It wasn't noticeable to others but I felt it. So, the next day when the doctor made his rounds, I told him. He ordered a capsule to take after each shot.

Boy, that capsule put me in another world! It would put me in a deep sleep. When the nurse made her rounds to take our temperature after rest hour, she couldn't find my heart beat! She had to shake me and make me sit up to find my pulse. I think, if rest hour was any longer, rigor mortis would have set in.

After I realized what it would do, I saved a capsule to take if there were nights I couldn't sleep. When I told Pat, she scolded me. "You could die in the night, girl!"

Smiling at her I said, "Whenever you can't sleep at night let me know, I'll fix you right up."

When the doctor next made his rounds, he asked the usual question, "How do you feel today?"

I usually never had anything to say but, "Fine." However, this day I told him, pointing at my right side by the collar bone, "I feel a little pain right there."

He took his stethoscope from around his neck and pulled up the back of my PJ and listened. He listened to my chest. "You're just fine," and went on his way.

The next day, we went through the same thing. "Chris you're going to have a lot of aches and pains. You're just fine."

I had been on South Wing for two months and I had one more month to go. I began to worry about getting home. I decided to wait two more weeks before writing to Mama and Daddy. I figured it would give them enough time to get some money for the trip. And, I didn't want to forget to tell them that I didn't have any clothes to wear home.

As each day drew nearer for me to be released, I began to get anxious. It had been so long since I saw my family, I wondered if they changed much. I wondered how much I changed.

I thought about what I would do when I got home. I would clean the house, cook for Mama and Daddy, and I would bring in the wood for the cook stove. I wanted to make life easier for them. I knew Mama would fuss about it but I would insist. I wanted to hear Mama laugh like she used to. I wanted to see that little grin on Daddy's face. I wanted to hear Mama call me Sissie. I wanted to feel her rough hands caress my head. I wanted to hear Daddy call me Tissie. *Oh, dear God in Heaven, it's just one month away!*

The next day the nurse came and told me it was time for the last chest x-ray and I had to have spaghetti for breakfast the next morning. I couldn't wait to get to the x-ray room and the spaghetti didn't taste bad! They were the last tests I would have to take. All I had to do now was wait.

The following Friday, a matron came in during rest hour and tiptoed to my bed. She held her finger to her mouth, wanting me to be quiet. She whispered, "Make yourself pretty. You have visitors waiting to see you after rest hour."

THE WHEELCHAIR

Sitting up, I asked her, "Who is it?"

She just smiled at me and tiptoed out the door. She closed the door then opened it up a crack. Giving me a big smile, she closed the door again.

Laying back down I wondered, who could it be? I had been here almost two years and no one visited me. I didn't think anyone knew I was here. I was sure everyone had forgotten I was alive.

My roommates even got excited for me. I combed my hair and asked if anyone had some lipstick I could use. I was so excited I could hardly wait until the door opened.

Finally, I heard rustling in the hall. The door opened and the nurse came in followed by a matron with fresh water. The nurse gave me my pills. I took them and waited until they left.

I got out of bed and went to the door and looked down the hallway. It was busy with matrons and nurses going back and forth passing out medication, water and mail. I tried to look past them.

Way down the hall, this side of the center desk, I saw these people. They looked dark in clothing compared to the white walls and the nurses. There were four of them and they walked slow, side by side. As they got closer, there was a familiarity about them, their walk, their size. The older man hung onto the woman's hand as she leaned into him, needing his support.

I waited, watching. Then, I knew! It was Mama and Daddy and the boys! I didn't wait anymore. Forgetting my robe, I ran down the hall dodging everyone in my way like a football player heading for the goal line screaming, "Mama, Daddy!" We hugged and cried and hung onto each other like it was the end of the world and we wanted to die together! I kept asking, "How did you find me?" over and over. I felt lost for so long. Now, I knew there was a way home.

1945 – Age 9

One day Mama and Daddy went to town. They left early in the morning before us kids got up. It was unusual because they didn't take a load of wood with them. It was late when they returned.

The next day, I had been working at the saw and when I came home Mama was sewing some clothes. I asked her what she was making. Looking up at me with tears in her eyes, she said, "I have to go to the hospital and have an operation."

I almost fell down, "Why, Mama? Why?" I could hardly believe what she was saying .

"I have a tumor in my right ovary and it has to be taken out." Wiping away the tear that rolled down her cheek, she went on sewing.

She never did go to the hospital and her suffering continued. The reason she was sick and the need for an operation was never mentioned again.

I noticed Mama looked thin and her eyes were hollow and showed her pain. There was a weakness about her. Around her head, she wore a red and black head band. It was a handkerchief folded into a strip which she wore when she had pain in her head. I realized she was still sick, only worse than when I left.

Daddy, of course, was always thin but I felt he could have more weight on him. When he talked, his voice sounded low, like he had something in his throat.

The boys were men. Their voices were lower than I remembered but they looked good. However, Mama and Daddy looked like they went through some hard times. Like I knew, I had to go home and help them. The boys spent too much time away.

Daddy had a surprise for me. He handed me a bag, "Tissie, we brought you some clothes from home, it's in the bag. Go and put them on, we're taking you on a vacation for ten days!"

"You mean, you're taking me out of the hospital?"

"Yes. We already talked to the doctor. He told us we had to have you back in ten days because of your treatments."

Taking the bag, I told them, "Wait here, I'll be right back."

I ran to the room and started to take off my PJs. "Hey, you

THE WHEELCHAIR

girls. I'm going out on a ten-day pass. Can you believe it?"

Ann said, "Yes, we were watching you and your family."

"Oh Chris, you almost made me cry," Jamie said, wiping her eyes.

"Enjoy yourself, Chris," Pat said. "We'll keep your bed warm while you're gone."

It felt weird to put on clothes and shoes. The clothes they brought were the same ones I wore to the hospital in Nespelem. The sack was probably the same one I stuffed them in. When I was dressed, I threw my PJs on the bed, waved to the girls, "See you when I get back."

Running back to my family, I took Mama's hand and Daddy's. The five of us walked down the hallway, took the elevator down to the first floor and out the front door.

Those ten days were the happiest days of my life! We took the ferry across to Bremerton and stayed with my "aunt" and her family. I'm not sure how I was related to her because we called all people my parents knew, "Auntie" and "Uncle". They were really nice people and made us welcome.

We talked way into the night. There were times we cried and laughed. We went swimming and walked the beach. We went to the zoo in Seattle and window shopped. We went on picnics and played in the sun.

All too soon it was time for me to go back to the hospital. On the way, we planned what we would do when I was released. Daddy told me they moved back to the little log house at 13 Mile and they had added a room for the kitchen. It really excited me, now I had a house to take care of!

We arrived back at the hospital at 10:00 on the last day of my vacation. The lights would be turned off but it didn't matter to me. I enjoyed the last miles with my family.

When we stopped in the parking lot, Mama just couldn't bring herself to go in with me. "Sissie, it's like ripping my heart out to see you go. Let me say goodbye now."

Mama and I hugged each other for a long time. We both cried as if we were parting forever. "Mama, it won't be long now. I'll be released soon and I can come home for good. Take care of yourself and Daddy. Mama, I love you with all my heart."

I said goodbye to Manny, "Take care of Mama and Daddy. They need you and Ernie. I will be coming home soon."

Daddy and Ernie went with me. As we walked up the steps, I looked back and waved to Mama and Manny.

These steps that I dreamed about so many times were taking me back into the hospital but the feeling was good. When we got to the top, I stopped and looked down at the parking lot. Everything looked so different than how I pictured it, but it was night. I thought to myself, *it will be in the daytime when I leave, then it will look like my dream. When the day comes, Mama won't be crying, she will be smiling like I pictured her.*

Daddy and Ernie walked me to the elevator and I pushed the button. Daddy took off his hat and hugged me. Ernie and I said goodbye. The elevator opened and I stepped in. As the door closed, Daddy tipped his hat to me.

When I stepped out of the elevator, the smell of the hospital met me and reminded me of the time I spent here. I missed the fresh air of the ocean and the sun that browned my skin during those ten beautiful days. God knew I needed it because it never rained and the clouds stayed away so the sun could smile down on me and my family.

My heart felt light as I walked down the hallway to my room. Two or three nurses went about their work as I passed by. One nurse with her head down looked up at me as I passed and gave me a half smile.

By this time, it was about 10:30. I slowly opened the door to my room and stepped in. It was quiet. The girls acted like they were sleeping but I had the feeling they were awake.

I took off my clothes and put on the clean folded PJs that were laid out for me when the bed was changed. Quietly, I got into bed.

THE WHEELCHAIR

It was strange, I expected a lot of questions but there was no fanfare. Laying there, I wondered what happened. After awhile, I heard someone crying. *Maybe someone died.* I was familiar with the reaction so, with the thought that they would tell me in the morning, I turned over and went to sleep.

The next morning, tired from my vacation, the matron had to wake me up. The basins were passed around, medication was given out and the breakfast trays came.

All this time, the girls avoided my eyes. Being a bit tired, I let it pass but I figured someone has to talk and let me know what the hell is going on. I didn't have to wait long.

About half an hour after the breakfast trays were picked up, a nurse came into our room pushing a wheelchair. She came straight to my bed. *A wheelchair? Why? A wheelchair? Is it for me? We don't use wheelchairs on the South Wing! Why?*

"Chris, the doctor wants to see you in his office. Please, get in the wheelchair."

I sat in my bed and looked at the chair. I knew what it meant. Something had gone wrong, really wrong. They're sending me back to the North Wing. I began to feel numb. It was like the sound was sucked out of the room and the girls were holding their breath. I knew they were waiting to see my reaction. If I closed my eyes I knew I would float away.

The nurse gave me time to collect my thoughts. I sat there and stared at the wheelchair. Somehow, I couldn't think. My mind went blank. Like a robot, I got out of bed, put on my robe, walked past the wheelchair and headed down the hall. The nurse followed me, begging for me to get into the wheelchair, "It's doctor's orders, please!" I kept walking.

The doctor's office was on the North side, next to the center desk. I walked past the desk and went into the office. Both doctors were there waiting for me.

The nurse followed me in with the wheelchair, "I'm sorry doctor, but she wouldn't."

Looking at her, Dr. Salli waved his hand, "That's okay." Then, turning back to me, "Have a seat, Chris," he said, pointing to the two chairs sitting in front of the desk.

I sat down. I didn't have to ask any questions, all I wanted to hear was the verdict.

Dr. Kulla began to explain, "Chris, I'm sorry to give you the news about your last chest x-ray and the sputum test. It came back positive. I'm afraid we will have to send you back to the North Wing."

Dr. Salli went to the box on the wall with the light behind it. The images of my last chest x-ray were on it. I saw circles drawn on the negatives in a red marker.

Pointing to the circles, he explained, "This is where the germ broke out and it seemed to spread fast because it didn't show up on last month's x-ray."

Dr. Kulla, with a tone of sadness in his voice, explained that they would stop the pnuemothorax treatments and wait for the air that was put in my lung cavity to be absorbed by my body before they would make the next move. And, I would continue taking all medication.

I had heard all I wanted to hear. I got up and asked. "Is my bed ready?"

Dr. Kulla closed his eyes and nodded.

I turned and went past the nurse with the wheelchair, heading for the North Wing. Following behind me, the nurse kept saying, "Chris, you have to ride in the wheelchair. Please. Don't be that way."

Without a word, I walked down the hall until the nurse said, "Right here." I turned into the room. I didn't check the number, it didn't matter. It was a four-bed ward. I didn't have to be told what to do. I went to the empty bed, pulled down the covers and climbed in. The pressure of the tight sheets on my toes made me mad. No one said anything after the nurse left. They knew I wasn't in the mood.

Soon, a matron brought what things I had from the South Wing. The only extra baggage I had was the clothes I wore out on pass. I had planned to wear them when I was discharged. I put them in the bottom of my nightstand.

I stood up on the bed and jumped around stomping my feet. Then I got out of bed, loosened the sheets all round the bed, got back in bed, slapped my pillow around, laid back and closed my eyes. I'm sure the other patients were watching me but I didn't care.

I went through the rest of the day with a blank mind. It's hard to think when you can't get past the moment. I just went through the same routine: lunch, rest hour, bedpans, medications, supper, medications, lights out. However, that night I had to make up my mind about how I was going to spend the rest of my time in this bed and be happy. I did it before, now I must find a way to do it again. All those dreams of going home had to be disposed of some way.

My biggest worry was Mama and Daddy. Mama was so sick when I left her at the car. All during our vacation I could see it. She tried to cover it up but it was there in the sallowness of her skin, the haunting look of her eyes, the forced smile, trying to hide the pain. It was hard to think that was just yesterday! Now, it was like a dream. *Did it really happen?*

I tossed and turned half the night, wrestling with my thoughts. How could I tell Mama and Daddy I was not coming home? Should I just let it be? If I wrote to them, I could just see Mama reading it. She would cry. Coming to that, in my thoughts, I could not do it. I thought if I don't write, they would take it a day at a time like me.

But Mama's words haunted me. During the pass, she cried, "Sissie, I pray God will sent you back to us soon because I don't know what He has planned for me."

I tried to console her, "Mama, I'm on South Wing. It's just a matter of time and I will come home."

My "Aunt" didn't help matters, she said, "Sissie is so grown up and pretty. You will have to hang onto her when she gets out of the hospital. She's 18 now, you know."

I think Mama and Daddy felt me slipping away because Daddy said, "Tissie don't forget your Mama needs you."

I might be 18 now but I knew nothing else, I wanted nothing else. I was still that little girl and my dreams were of my Mama and Daddy and the mountains.

I was happy that the Good Lord gave us time together and I thought, *I got well once, I will get well again. Forget about yesterday, don't think about tomorrow, live for today.* Laying on my side, I felt the pressure of the firm pillow against my cheek.

The next morning the girls asked questions. "Where did you come from?"

"How old are you?"

"How long have you been here?"

The patient next to me, Debbie, was about 24 years old. She had light brown hair, almost blonde. She was pretty and gave me the feeling she knew her way around before coming here.

Straight across from me was Tina. She had dark brown hair, a round face with light skin and was pretty. She was 19 and came from Alaska.

Across and to the left was Leona. She was 26, had dark brown hair that looked like it needed washing. She was thin, pale and had a pained and very unhappy look.

When the breakfast trays came, the matrons wound up our beds but Leona didn't want to sit up. She laid on her side while eating.

Other than Leona, I knew I was in an upbeat room. While having breakfast, I tried to answer all the questions. I had to go through spending nearly two years on North Wing, getting well and moving to South Wing. But, when I got to the relapse, Leona burst into tears.

She pushed her tray away and began to moan, "Oh, I will

never go home. I will never get well. I'm going to die here. Oh God... oh God. What will I do?"

Man, it scared me. I never heard anyone cry like that since I'd been there. When I looked at the other girls, they just kept eating as if nothing was happening.

I learned later that Leona had five little boys and a husband at home. She could not bear to be away from them. She worried constantly about being sick, afraid she might die. She would lay flat on her back day after day and moan. The nurse asked her if she would like to sit up once in awhile but she refused. The doctor and nurses tried to talk to her, "It will take time, just be patient and you will get well." She would get so upset the nurse would have to give her a shot to calm her down.

After awhile it got on my nerves. I felt like saying a lot of things to her, like, *shut up! You're not the only one sick around here. In fact, you're making ME sick!* But, I held my tongue.

Even though I worked on my mind to accept the setback, I remained in a slump. I went through the morning, afternoon and evening routines I knew only too well. Without effort, my mind did not go beyond the happenings around me. I slept during rest hour. At night, I didn't toss and turn, I went right to sleep. It was as if my mind took a break. After asking all the questions, the girls left me alone knowing I had to have time to settle down.

A week had gone by when Debbie whispered to me during rest hour. "Hey, Chris. A guy by the name of Howard is calling for you. Do you want to talk to him?" She had been on the earphones.

I thought about it for a few minutes. "Okay, I'll talk to him."

I took my earphones off the bedstead. I listened for awhile then, I heard him call my name. "Howard, I'm here. Can you hear me?"

"Chris! Where have you been? I went to your room and you weren't there. Your roommates didn't know where you had gone."

"I'm sorry I didn't let you know but I'm back on North Wing. I had a setback. I'm back to square one."

"Are you handling it okay?"

"I don't plan on staying here forever. The day will come and I will go home. You know how it is."

"Can I still come and visit you?" I could hear the sadness in his voice.

"Sure. Nothing has changed but my address and a new hard mattress. Just let me know when you're coming so I can be at home." After that conversation, we went on as usual.

After I had been in the ward about two weeks, Debbie asked, "Chris, do you want to dance?" I thought maybe she was kidding.

She got off her bed, disappeared behind it and came up with a phonograph. She had it stored under the bed. She plugged it in and put on a 33 record. When the music began, I wanted to dance!

"Tina, you're on watch," Debbie said as she went to the middle of the room. It didn't take me long to join her.

I thought I could dance before but this was dancing! While Leona moaned in the background, we danced until we were out of breath. Then Debbie put on another record. It was Tina's turn while I watched by the door. If we saw someone coming we would jump in bed and act innocent. Sometimes, the nurse or matron would ask Debbie to turn down the music.

All the while, Leona groaned, "You girls will never get well. Please stay in bed. I can't stand to watch you."

When we got tired of dancing we would sit on one bed and talk. Debbie had the best stories. The stories both girls told were exciting. Of course, it was about the boyfriends they had when they went to school. I couldn't add anything but I sure learned a lot! It made me feel good when Debbie said, "You know Chris, when you first came and stomped on your bed, I knew I would like you".

It made me feel like adding something to this group! So, one afternoon, during rest hour, I asked the girls, "Would you girls like to go to the movies?"

Both of them sat up and looked at me with surprise.

"Are you kidding? Where do we go to the movies?" Debbie asked.

"I'll take you girls tonight if you're interested."

"Yeah, I'm ready to go at any time you say," Tina said.

"Okay, but we have to make plans first." I went on to tell them about going to the movies on South Wing. When I walked down the hallway to my new room, I noticed the North Wing had received a TV also. It was in the six-bed ward at the end of the hall the same as the South Wing. The girls spread the word that the movie came on at 10:00.

That night I turned on the TV and turned to the movie channel. Everyone settled back on their blankets and pillows as I looked around. Light from the TV screen sparkled in the eyes of the girls as they waited for the movie to come on. It made me proud.

The movie was a comedy and we made too much noise laughing. Suddenly, Debbie gave us the signal that someone was coming!

Every girl made a dash to their hiding place while I turned off the TV. I ran for the side of the door and pressed myself against the wall. When the nurse came in, she opened the door while I stood behind it.

You could hear a pin drop in that room while the nurse scolded the patients to be quiet. When she left, I could hear someone complaining, "You were laying on me."

"Damn, you stepped on my hand."

"Gawd, you were right in my face."

"You were laying on me I could hardly breathe."

After settling down, I turned on the TV and we finished watching the movie.

My whole attitude changed after that. I no longer stood at the window and dreamed. I no longer prayed to God to make me well. I no longer cried in the night from loneliness. Every now and then it would creep in and I would do something daring.

Every morning, Dr. Salli made his rounds about 10:00 with the head nurse following him. I would watch for when he started, then I would sneak to the ward ahead of him and hide behind the door, under the bed or behind a screen.

The times I hid under the bed, I would watch his feet as he stood and talked to the patient. The patients were full of smiles as he went from bed to bed. He must have thought they were happy to see him. I'm sure it made his day a few times.

This one evening I got bored and told the girls I was going visiting. "Visiting?" Debbie asked.

"Yeah. I would like to see who else lives on the North Wing, I'll see you later." I went to the door and looked up and down the hallway. It was clear. I could hear Leona moaning in the background as I made a dash to the next ward to my right. I planned to make my rounds starting there.

I would run into a room and slide towards the window and say "Hi" to the girls. They would laugh at me. I would tell them my name and ask theirs. If someone had a radio on, I would dance to the tune. The exciting part of my journey was getting past a nurse or matron without getting caught. When I was in a room and heard a matron or nurse coming, I would slip under a bed or I stand behind the door.

I found there were many patients from different tribes. They came from all over Montana, Washington, Idaho, Alaska, Nevada, Utah, Arizona and many other states. Most of the Navajo and Alaska Indians didn't speak English but they saw the humor in my visit.

There were some very sad cases. Some looked very sick, others were fat and happy. There were old and young, cute and ugly. Still, there were patients that had been there for years and others that were just starting to serve their time.

I made my way from room to room but it wasn't until I got to the last ward at the end of the hall, past the center desk, that broke my heart. There were four patients that looked like skeletons. I

THE WHEELCHAIR

couldn't believe my eyes. They laid on their backs, half covered, exposing their legs, arms and ribs. Their hair was so thin I could see their scalp. And, I could see hair that had rubbed off on the pillows.

1942 – Age 6
Mama always knew what to do if we got hurt or sick. I asked her, "Mama, how did you learn how to fix everything?"
She looked at me then lowered her eyes, "Sissie, years ago when I was going to school, I wanted to be a nurse. It didn't work out but I went on to help people when something happened to them."
Curious, I went on to ask, "Did you ever find something that you couldn't fix?"
She gave it some thought, as if it was too painful to remember. "One day a sickness began to spread all over. It was called the flu. Many people got really sick and many died."
I imagined what she saw, "Mama, it must have been awful to see the people die. What did you do or what could you say?"
She gave an answer that touched my heart, "When I knew death was near, I lit a candle to light the soul's way to heaven."

When I walked in, they smiled. The deep lines from the smile slowly faded as they struggled for the next breath. Their eyes looked like holes in their skulls. Their cheek bones stood out and dropped, leaving a hollowness that made their teeth look too big for their face. The knees, elbow joints and hands were large, leaving bones that looked like sticks that joined them. Their skin, moist from sweating, covered the bones that had no flesh. This ward was marked with death and an odor hung in the air I couldn't put a name to.

Immediately, I realized what was taking place in this ward. What it all meant. I held back the expression of surprise but said my usual, "Hi, my name is Chris. I came to dance for you." I then danced around each bed. When I finished, I told them I got bored and wanted to go visiting. My dancing was an added attraction. It made them smile.

When I went to the door to see if anyone was coming, so I could get back to my room, one of the patients asked, in a low, weak voice, "Are you coming back?" I nodded my head, she smiled.

It was really depressing to think of all the sick patients. It made me realize how lucky I was. I got well once and I knew I would again. I could not think of it any other way. But, there were patients out there like Gladys, who gave up thinking about ever going home.

There were evenings that I didn't feel like making my visits, but I did go to the ward at the end of the hall, past the center desk. I knew they waited for me to visit them.

This ward was for the hopeless. They were put together and kept out of sight of other patients. To see them, one would lose hope. It was the end of the line and, in a matter of time, they would meet their maker. I felt like I wanted to spend time with them, to let them know someone cared. Maybe my dancing made them forget, for a moment, their fate.

On one of my visits, the patient by the window pointed to her nightstand. Going to her bedside, I opened the drawer. She whispered in a weak voice, "Picture. The picture."

Looking in the drawer, I picked up the picture she mentioned and looked at it. It was of a beautiful woman, about 30 years old. It was a sunny day and she wore a white sleeveless summer dress with long black hair that hung passed her shoulders. She had a big smile that made her teeth shine white against her bronze skin.

I heard her whisper. I looked at her. She pointed at herself as I saw tears roll down the side of her face. My breath caught in my throat. I felt the tears coming in the back of my eyes. Putting the picture back in the drawer, I pushed it closed. To hide my tears, I started to dance. As I danced around each bed, their hollow eyes followed me. I went to the door, gave a quick tap dance and made my way down the hall to my room.

That night I prayed for them and counted my blessings. My visits made me realize we were all in the same boat. Our futures were uncertain and there was only one way we could live, one day at a time. However, for the ward at the end of the hall, the prayer was for the Good Lord to take away their last breath.

Two months had passed since I returned to North Wing. I was talking to Howard on the nightline and he asked me if I was going to be at home the next evening at visiting hour. I told him I would have to look at my schedule. He said he had a surprise for me.

The next day, I could hardly wait until visiting hour! I fixed my hair, borrowed some lipstick and put a touch on my cheeks. I wound up my bed, got in, straightened the sheets over my lap and waited.

When he came in, he looked so tall and handsome. The only thing that reminded me of where we were was the mask that he wore. He took a chair and sat it by my bed and asked Debbie if he could borrow her phonograph.

He sat it on my nightstand, plugged it in and put a record on it. "Do you know what song this is?"

"Our song." Looking up at him, I smiled.

"Do you know what it means?" he asked.

I couldn't say anything, I felt it was up to him to say.

When I didn't answer, he put it in words, "It means I love you and the time will come when we will be together."

It was all so romantic! He put the needle on the record and it started to play, *I'm In the Mood for Love*. Turning it down low, he took both of my hands, kissed them and said, "I have been discharged. I will be leaving here tomorrow."

My heart sank! Oh, my God, he's going to leave me. Then the feelings I had when I was given the news I was well came back. It was the one thing we all prayed for. How could I think about myself when I should be happy for him?

The mixed emotions brought tears to my eyes. "Oh, Howard, I'm so happy for you but I'll miss you. I hope you won't forget me."

"No, no. Remember, I asked you to marry me and you said yes. All there is now is for you to get well. I'll be out there waiting for you. Just remember that!"

Hearing him say that made me feel better.

Reaching in his robe pocket, he pulled out a small package that was beautifully wrapped. He handed it to me.

"This is my going away present to you. When you get lonesome, look at it and play our record. It will remind you that I love you and I will be waiting for you."

Anxiously, I unwrapped the package. It was a gold bracelet that had green jewels down the middle of it. It was the most beautiful thing I ever had!

Feeling the urge, I reached for him. Standing up, he came and held me to him for a long time. Being held and knowing someone cared made me cry.

"Tomorrow I will be flying over the hospital at 11:00 A.M. When the plane passes over I'll be looking down at the hospital. I will imagine you at the window. Will you be there?"

"Howard, you can bet I will be at the window." I felt the excitement of him being well and the fact he would be going home!

Giving me the last hug, he left. Laying back, I asked Debbie if I could listen to the song one more time.

Debbie and Tina had to look at the bracelet. As I closed my eyes and listened to the song and the words that cried out to me, I heard the oooh's and ahhh's over the bracelet.

"Boy, this guy really has it bad for you," Debbie said.

"You mean he asked you to marry him? How come you didn't tell us?" Tina asked.

"It's something I couldn't talk about."

"But, you said yes!" Debbie said.

"I know. I really care for him but he's in Alaska and I live here with my folks. He's well and I'm sick."

The next day, I could hardly wait until 11:00. When the time neared, I went to the window on our side and looked towards Seattle. I figured the plane would be seen coming from there. About five minutes to the hour, I saw it come into view. I watched until it disappeared behind the hospital. I ran across the hall to the other ward. Stretching my neck, I looked up and in a few seconds the plane came out from behind the building. I could picture him looking out the window at the hospital. Even though he couldn't see me, I waved. I watched until the plane grew smaller and smaller and faded into the blue sky. It brought a tear to my eye to see him go, knowing I would never see him again. He had made my life in this hospital a happy place.

Chapter 7

13 MILE CABIN

After rest hour when the medication and the regular routine was over, a matron came with a wheelchair. As she wheeled me down the hall, I wondered what Dr. Salli wanted to see me about. What did they want to do to me? Maybe they were going to give me a new medication or a new treatment.

When I got to the doctor's office, both doctors were there. Looking at the box on the wall with the light behind it, there was the same images of my chest x-ray with the red circles on it.

Dr. Salli was the first to greet me. "Dr. Kulla and I have reviewed your case and it's time to make the next step."

Dr. Kulla stepped forward to shake my hand. I hadn't seen him since my relapse. "Chris, since you are 18 years old now, you can make your own decisions. Therefore, we will not need the permission of your parents. After reviewing your case, we feel our next option is to give you an operation. In this operation, we will take out eight ribs on the right side. This will collapse the lung so it can heal."

Sitting behind his desk, Dr. Salli went on to explain; "However, this does not mean you can go home after the operation. You will remain in the hospital until all traces of the bug are gone. As you know, we cannot tell you how long it will take. In the meantime, you will be tested every three months, as before. There is also another option. We could remove the top infected lobe of the right lung. To do that, we would have to remove five ribs. Then, after you recover, you can go home."

Sitting there listening to the doctors, my expression did not change. Nothing they said surprised me. I had nothing to say, there was no question to ask. I somehow knew what I was going to do but I had to take time to give it some thought.

"Okay, Chris, it is all up to you. Let us know as soon as you make up your mind," Dr. Kulla said.

As the matron wheeled me back to my ward, I remembered a patient that showed me her operations. She had eight ribs taken out on one side and five on the other. She had been in the hospital 14 years. She had the operations during those years. It was sad to look at because it had deformed her so. It seemed like she only had a backbone which was curved. Later, at the point of release, she hemorrhaged and died. And there were others. I had seen a lot and I had heard stories. Now I was in the driver's seat.

That night I asked Debbie if she had a writing tablet and an envelope. I spent the rest of the evening writing to Mama and Daddy. I told them of the relapse and that the doctors wanted to operate on me. I told them I did not want the operation. *'Please, come and get me. I want you to know, I am not well but I would like to go home for two weeks. There is a hospital in Spokane called Edgecliff where I want to go so I can be close to home where you can visit me.'* In the letter, I stressed again and underlined it, *'I am not well.'*

The next morning, I asked if someone had a stamp. Tina gave me one and the letter was on its way. Now it was a matter of time.

Debbie and Tina were surprised when I told them I was going home.

"How come? Does the doctor know?" Debbie asked

"No."

Sitting up in bed, Tina said, "But you're still sick. You can't go home, you'll die!"

"I know that."

"But how can you get well at home?" Debbie asked.

"Okay you girls, let me tell you something so you won't worry. What I plan on doing is to visit home for two weeks then go to the sanatorium in Spokane. It's close to where I live and maybe Mama and Daddy can come and visit me."

With tears in her eyes, Tina begged, "Oh Chris, will you promise to go to the hospital, please?"

"I believe you will, Chris," Debbie said.

"Listen girls, if you ever get the notion in your head about leaving, take a trip down the hall to the ward past the center desk. It's on the right and faces the desk. You'll change your mind."

When the letter went out that day, I sat back and relaxed. I knew it would take time for Daddy to get my letter and some money before they could make the trip. One thing that worried me was I hoped they didn't think I was going home to stay. I made it clear but Daddy was a hardnosed old man and he wanted me home. To him, I looked well. I didn't cough and I had put on weight. He had said several times on our vacation, "Tissie, you sure look good." I knew how his mind worked but I felt like I could handle it when the time came.

It took six weeks before Mama and Daddy walked into my room. Even though I was expecting them, I was surprised. Jumping out of bed I ran and hugged Mama.

Hugging Daddy, I told him, "Oh Daddy, I'm so glad you guys could come so soon. I was afraid you couldn't get any money."

"Tissie, you got to thank your brother for this trip and for the vacation. He worked for the Tribe piling brush. He got enough money to buy an old car and money to come and get you. Yes, Manny made it all possible," Daddy said with that familiar grin I loved to see.

Mama was looking at me with tears in her eyes. "Hurry Sissie, change your clothes so we can leave. Daddy, let's go out in the hall so Sissie can get dressed."

When they stepped out and closed the door, I took out the sack from my bedside stand. It had the clothes they brought for our vacation. I got dressed and the girls sat up in bed watching me.

Debbie spoke up, "Chris, do you think you will come back?"

"No. Like I told you, I'm going to Edgecliff in Spokane."

"Promise us Chris, that you will go to the hospital," Tina said with tears in her eyes.

"I promise. Do you think I want to die?" After I was dressed, I stuffed all that I owned into the sack and waved to the girls, "Get well and do the last dance for me. I will miss you. Bye."

In the hallway, Mama and Daddy were anxiously waiting. With Daddy on one side of me and Mama on the other, we made the last walk down the hall to the doctor's office. They were not expecting us.

When we got to the office, both doctors were out. I had Mama and Daddy sit in the two chairs that were facing the desk. When the Head Nurse at the center desk saw us go into the office, she came in and asked Daddy who he wanted to see.

Not waiting for him to answer I spoke up, "We are here to see the doctors. I plan on leaving the hospital and want to tell them."

Glancing at me, her eyes went back to Daddy and then at Mama. "This is my mother and father. They came to get me," I said proudly.

She gave a look of concern as she asked us to wait. I heard the click of her heels as she rushed from the room. "Daddy, the doctor told me it was up to me to make the decision to have the operation or not because I was now 18 years old. Okay, I made the decision. So, when they come in, let me do the talking. When I get through you can say anything you want to."

We waited for about half an hour before the doctors came in. Dr. Salli rushed in and went behind the desk to face us. Dr. Kulla stood by the desk.

Dr. Salli was the first to speak. He looked straight at Daddy with piercing eyes, "I understand you folks came to take Chris out of the hospital."

Immediately, I spoke up, "Dr. Salli, you told me it was up to me to make decisions since I'm now 18. Well, since our last meeting on my case, I wrote to my folks and asked them to come and get me."

"Chris, do you know what you're doing? You're throwing away all the time you spent in the hospital. It will be just a matter of time and it could be too late. Don't do this, please!" He all but stomped his feet.

Dr. Kulla calmed Dr. Salli and took over the conversation.

"Mr. McDougal. Do you know what will happen to your daughter if she goes home before she's cured?" He asked with a gentle voice.

With a little grin, Daddy said, "My little girl knows what she is doing. Right now, she wants to go home and we're here to take her."

Dr. Kulla turned to me, "Chris, tell me, what is your plan?"

I told them of my plan and my reasons for it. Then added, "I've been in that ward," pointing to the ward just outside of the office where the four patients were taking their last breath, "I know what to expect if I do not go to a hospital."

He looked in the direction and knew what I meant. "You've been in there? When?"

"Doctor, I've visited them many times," with a little grin, "and I even danced for them."

Smiling, he came around the desk and shook hands with Mama and Daddy. When he took my hand, he said, "I want to wish you well, Chris. Don't give up."

"Thank you, Dr. Kulla and," looking around him, "Dr. Salli. I thank you for all you've done for me. I will go home for two weeks, then I will check myself in at Edgecliff in Spokane. I got well once and I will get well again, only without an operation, no matter how long it takes."

I had arrived at Cushman Hospital in November of 1951 and I'm finally leaving in October of 1953.

Winter 1952 – Mama and Daddy
The man was so cold that when he talked, his face hardly moved. He held the cup with both hands and slowly sipped the coffee. "It's been a couple days since I ate. Yeah, I could sure use some food."

"Well Mister, we don't have much but you're sure welcome to it. Go in the other room, the Missus has something you can change into while I get something for you to eat," *Daddy said, as he scraped the bottom of the frying pan and put a piece of fried bread aside for him. Whoever he was didn't matter, he needed food, a dry change of clothes and a place out of the weather.*

The man said his name was Joe, but he didn't give his last name. He came from Republic and was on his way to Spokane for a job opening. He had missed his ride and decided to hitchhike but there wasn't any traffic.

"Well Joe, from the looks of the weather, you might have to stay awhile."

"If you don't mind I would sure appreciate it," *he said between bites.*

As the days passed, Joe didn't have much to say. He never gave out any information on himself. He seemed to be a nice guy and helped Daddy chop wood for the cook stove and he shoveled the snow leading up to the spring so they could have fresh water. And, he was very respectful of Mama.

There were days they played cards to pass the time. Daddy said that, "You can usually tell about a man by how he plays his cards." *This man was mysterious. He may smile but his eyes didn't. Most of the time he avoided eye contact.*

When they ate with the use of the candle, he stayed back in the shadows and didn't have much to say. He never washed his hands or face and needed a bath. Daddy had a sweathouse down by the creek that he used. He told Joe he could use it any time but he refused.

The weather cleared up and it was now the first week of December and time for the per capita checks to be disbursed. The road to the highway had to be cleared out. Daddy and Joe took the shovels and began to shovel the snow. It took them all day by the time they got to the highway.

On the way back, Daddy told Joe, "It's time for us to go to Republic tomorrow to get some grub. You're welcome to come with us."

Thinking for a while, Joe said, "I'll let you know tomorrow. If the weather holds out, I might go on my way."

The next day, Daddy cleared the snow away from the truck and worked on getting it started. It had sat for several weeks and didn't want to start. It took until noon before it began to groan, promising with a little more work, it would take them up town.

By the time they were ready to leave, fog moved in and it began to snow. Daddy again asked Joe if he wanted to go with them since the weather didn't look good.

"I'll stay and keep the fire going. You guys can go ahead. I'll be alright."

"You're welcome to make yourself some coffee and find something to eat. There's not much but it will put something in your gut. We'll be back soon."

The old truck groaned as they pulled onto the highway. With the snow coming down, Daddy smiled. "Well, Mama, looks like we'll be eating good for the rest of the winter. It can't get better than that!"

Driving up the highway, Mama looked at the mountains, hoping to see a deer, "I wished I could still hunt. I would love to have some fresh meat."

"Maybe Manny will come to see us. I know he would go out and get us one," Daddy said.

"Daddy, it's per capita time. They won't have time for us."

"Now Mama, don't start feeling bad. I'll fry some bacon when we get back and make you some flapjacks. That reminds me, don't forget the syrup."

When they pulled into town they went to the post office and picked up the $50.00 check. Daddy didn't receive one. The Tribe said he wasn't a member, even though he was. It was in debate.

Then they went to the store. They made their way around the store picking all the things they needed. Daddy's eyes passed over the stacked shelves like a kid in a candy store. Mama saw a wash tub that was being sold for a dollar because it had a big dent on it. They decided to buy it and put their groceries in it for the ride home. The one they had leaked and the dent didn't matter.

The man at the store helped them load their groceries into the truck. He then gave them a sheet to cover the groceries, protecting them from the falling snow. After filling up with gas, they headed home.

It was getting dark by the time they got to the turnoff to the cabin. As the old truck rumbled up the hill on the bumpy road and came into view of the cabin, there wasn't any smoke coming out of the chimney.

"Looks like our house guest didn't put any wood in the stove," Daddy said.

Nearing the cabin, stretching her neck to see if there was any life, Mama thought he might have fallen asleep and didn't put any wood in the stove.

When Daddy stopped the truck, Mama got out and went to the cabin. If he was there, he could help carry in the groceries but the house was empty. It looked like Joe had left.

Going back to the truck Mama told Daddy Joe was gone. Looking around on the ground, Daddy saw his tracks that headed down the road. *"Well, I guess our guest decided to leave. Seems funny he didn't thank us or say goodbye. Oh well, let's get our groceries inside before they get too wet."*

Together, they carried in the tub of groceries. Having a small kitchen, they put it in the main room. Then Daddy brought in the sack of flour and potatoes.

Since it was dark, Mama asked Daddy to turn on the truck headlights so she could fill the kerosene lamp. Taking the lamp outside, she asked Daddy to get the kerosene. Looking around, he couldn't find it. Then Mama remembered that they forgot to buy some.

"We still have some money left. We better go back to town. If we wait until tomorrow, the way the snow is coming down, we may not be able to get out to the highway. Come on, let's go," Daddy said. Making sure the door to the cabin was closed, they left. By the time they got to the town, it had quit snowing.

When they got back to the house, Mama went in and brought out the lamp and filled it in front of the truck, using the headlights to see. Taking the lamp into the house, she sat it on the table and made fire in the cook stove while Daddy drained the truck radiator.

With the lamp lit, fire built and the truck drained, Daddy got out the hunting knife and began to sharpen it to cut the slab of bacon. Mama put on the tea kettle to heat for coffee.

With a big smile, Daddy said, "What do you say, when that stove gets hot, I start frying the bacon?"

"Yes, Daddy, I would like that," Mama said, going into the main room where the tub was.

A few minutes later, "Daddy, bring in the lamp. I can't find the tub."

Putting down the knife, he carried the lamp in to the room. The room was small and couldn't hide the tub. They both looked around the room. The tub was nowhere to be seen, in fact, all the groceries were gone!

They looked at each other. "He couldn't, Daddy, he couldn't do this to us!" Mama cried.

They hurried outside with the lamp and checked for car tracks. Sure enough, they could see where a car had turned around and *there were several footprints.*

Going back into the house, Mama sat down at the table and cried. Daddy hugged her, "Don't cry. Lord knows, he might have needed it more than us. Don't worry, we will get by. I guess Joe came back to thank us while we were gone." Putting away the hunting knife, he said, "Guess I won't be needing this."

The next morning, when Daddy brought Mama's coffee to her he said, "Joe left us something. A coat was lying over the sack of flour and he missed it. So, it looks like we won't starve, there will be lots of bread and pancakes. And I've been thinking, we still have gas in the truck. We can visit the dump, it has been pretty good to us."

The ride home was the happiest I'd ever been and the saddest. Daddy was so thin. The veins stood out on his neck when he coughed. However, the smile he gave me took my mind off what was ailing him.

Mama also lost weight. Her eyes looked hollow and sunken. Her skin looked sallow. All the way home she held me close and there was an odor about her. I had smelled it before but couldn't place it. She would lay her head on my shoulder and say, "Oh Sissie, we are so glad to have you home. You can't believe how we missed you." Then she would start crying.

Daddy would pat her on the knee and say, "Don't cry Mama, she's with us now and everything will be alright."

My heart broke to see the joy, the hope, the loneliness and the need these two little people had, knowing I had to leave again. I was sick too! I wanted to scream and tell them, *Mama, Daddy, I can't stay. You've got to understand, I'm sick. If I don't go back I will die!* How could I tell them? How could I make them understand? I told them in my letter but all they knew or wanted to know, 'I want to go home.'

Looking at me with teary eyes, Mama said, "Sissie, when we moved into the little log house, I remembered when you kids were little," again she began to cry.

I put my arms around her and held her close... *the odor... the odor. Oh, my God, the odor!* It was the same odor I smelled in that death ward! *Mama is dying!* I began to cry uncontrollably. "Mama, Mama, you can't leave me!"

Trying to calm me, Mama asked Daddy to stop somewhere off the road. It took him awhile before he turned off the highway onto a dirt road. At a distance were some trees and bushes. He drove to them and stopped.

Getting out of the car, Mama said, "Maybe you're hungry. Daddy get the grub box out of the back. Let's have something to eat."

Daddy brought the box and blanket. He spread the blanket on the ground and put what food they had on it. The food was so different but familiar. We ate dried deer meat, fried potatoes and biscuits.

The blanket was worn, the dishes were tin and the knife and forks were mismatched. When I looked at Mama and Daddy, their clothes were old and worn. *How come I didn't notice this before? Was it always like that? Who changed, them or me?* I looked down at the clothes I was wearing. Yes, they were the same clothes I had before. They were worn too. They had been washed but they were not clean. Maybe Daddy was doing the washing and he didn't do a good job.

Mama urged me, "Eat, Sissie, we want you to stay well. Let us know if you get tired. You can lean against me on the way home."

Daddy looked up at the sky, "We better hurry, it's a long way home. Looks like it will be way after midnight before we get there."

It seemed like we drove forever before we got to 13 Mile. When we turned off the highway to the cabin, we had to cross the creek. Daddy had made a bridge by placing four logs across, two for each tire track. While crossing, it seemed like we were suspended in the air. I held my breath hoping we wouldn't fall off.

From there, the dirt road had big boulders with the tops sticking out causing us to bump around in the car.

It had been years since I had been here. It was when I could first remember the little cabin being built. I was anxious as the car lights beamed ahead, shining on the trees and bushes, then the cabin came into view. It looked small and low to the ground. It seemed so dark and remote. As we got closer, there was a pile of split wood and a block with an ax stuck in it. Near the house, several blocks of wood were stacked up. Driving into the yard, wood chips shined white as the lights passed over them.

I could hardly wait to get out of the car. Daddy got out and came around and took Mama by the hand. I ran to the house, shouting, "Mama! Daddy! I'm home! I'm home!"

Opening the door brought tears to my eyes. *The bolt latch, Mama made it!* As I pushed the door in, it dragged on the floor. As I walked in, the floor boards squeaked. The smell of burning wood and charcoal met me and brought back memories.

Mama came in behind me and struck a match as she went to the table and lit the kerosene lamp. In the dim light, I saw the cook stove with the tea kettle on it. The same old stove I had cooked on so many times. The cupboard with the curtains that were made from flour sacks and strung up on bailing wire attached on each end with a nail that was bent over. It was pulled aside exposing the old tin dishes we had for so many years. They were tan in color and had a green fine line around the edge. The black spots were where the dish had been chipped.

The lamp lit up the table which was rectangle and covered with an oil table cloth with little flowers on it that were faded. The flowers were worn off on the corners and on the edges of the boards that made up the table. In the middle of the table were the familiar salt and pepper shakers and the old sugar bowl. A small Mason jar held three spoons. I had to fight the tears that blurred my vision. It was all still there like I remembered. This scene was played out in many different places in the mountains but it was always home.

Daddy came in with that same grin I missed so much. "Well Tissie. How does it feel to be home?"

"Oh, Daddy, how I missed being at home. Everything is like I pictured. I can't believe it!" I said, turning around and around in a circle with my arms up in the air. "Oh Daddy, I'm home!"

He started to make the fire. With his pocket knife, he made shavings from a stick of wood. After he got it started, he took sticks of wood out of the box Mama had made.

To make the box, she cut a square hole in the wall of the kitchen right by the stove. She attached a box on the outside that had a lid to keep the wood dry. The lid had hinges made out of leather. On the inside, she made a door that slid back and forth on a track with a handle made of wood. It really served them well. They didn't have to go outside to get wood and it also saved room since the kitchen was so small.

Looking around the kitchen, by the door was the wash basin with a nail above it and a towel hanging on it. On the opposite side of the door, four nails on the wall had coats hung on them. The window had a thin plastic covering that gave light but through it only blurry images could be seen.

Taking the lamp from the table, Mama asked me, "Sissie, come in the other room with me." I followed her to the far wall of the little room. "Look, I took the best blankets we had and put it on your bed."

"Oh, Mama. You didn't have to do that. Just being home is all that matters. Believe me, laying on the floor would be better than those hospital beds."

Looking at her holding the lamp, I saw mist in her eyes. "Oh, how we waited for this moment, the preparing, the waiting. Now you're here."

Looking around, the room seemed so small. When I first remembered this old log house, I was three. At that time, it seemed so big. Mama and Daddy's double bed sat in the corner on the right side of the room with the familiar crucifix that hung on the wall above it. That crucifix traveled around the mountains with us for as long as I can remember. The bed was the same one given to Mama and Daddy years ago.

By their bed sat the same old orange box that served as a nightstand. At the foot of their bed was a single cot. The boys used it when they came home. The one bed worked out because the boys seldom came home together.

By the only window in the room that faced the highway was Mama's old singer sewing machine with the peddle that ran it. At the foot of my bed, on the wall, was Mama's big antlers, "The Granddaddy of Them All". Mama's 30-30 Winchester rifle and the .22 lay across the tangs.

Daddy had drained the radiator of the truck and come in. By this time, Mama and I were back in the kitchen. "Well Tissie, how do you like 'er?"

"Oh Daddy. It's beautiful! It feels so cozy and warm. I'm so happy to be home. I can't wait until tomorrow so I can go outside!"

"Are you hungry, Sissie?" Mama asked, "I can fix something for you to eat."

"No. I can wait until morning."

"I'll cook you some sourdough pancakes in the morning," Daddy said. "The old sourdough is still a-going," he added.

To lay in my bed was like Heaven! The blankets were heavy compared to the hospital sheets and the smell of the house was comforting. It reminded me of the campfire. And, when Daddy blew out the lamp, slowly, the window came into view. Looking at it I wondered if I could ever leave again.

The next morning took too long in coming. I woke up several times during the night just waiting for daylight. I wanted to just look at Mama and Daddy and feel their closeness. I wanted to touch them, to know they were real, that this was home and I was not dreaming. I wanted to go outside and look at the mountains and listen to the wind blow in the tops of the trees. Maybe hear a woodpecker pecking on a tree in the distance.

I could hear Daddy snoring and Mama groaning now and then. I could hear an owl hoot near the cabin. I hadn't heard one for so long, I wondered what kind of weather he was predicting. Was his hoot high or low? I hoped it was high, so we would have nice weather for a few days.

Leaving the hospital wasn't like in my dreams. I didn't walk down the steps in that beautiful blue dress with the sun in my face. Mama and Daddy weren't waiting for me in the parking lot with smiles on their faces. Instead Mama wasn't well, her eyes showed constant pain. I wished I knew what was making her sick. Daddy's pain was different. He suffered too, but it was for her. It seemed like a part of him was dying a day at a time.

When I realized what it was doing to him, I was glad my illness was deep inside of me where he couldn't see. I looked healthy and didn't cough anymore. I didn't feel tired and had energy compared to when I left for the hospital. However, I knew it wouldn't last long. Looking and feeling like I did would go against me because Daddy would think I didn't need to go back to the hospital. This worried me. Somehow, I had to make them understand.

As I laid in my bed waiting for morning, the thoughts were like nightmares. I had a keen sense of everything around me, sounds, smells and feelings. What weighed heavy was everything felt so hopeless. *How long will it take for me to get well, six months, a year, two years, five or maybe ten years?* I thought of Gladys. *Could Mama wait for me? Could Daddy hold together until I came back?* The future seemed to float into nothing. I was floating in space without anything to hang onto. If I stayed, it was certain death. They would know then that I had to go back to the hospital. But, it would be too late and I would be sent to the ward at the end of the hall. *They need me... I've got to get well... I can't go back... I have to go back... how long will it take?... can they wait?* I buried my face in the pillow and cried. Exhausted, my body gave in and sleep took over.

Daddy's call woke me up, "Tissie, breakfast is ready. Come and get it before I feed it to the hogs!" He was in a great mood. "Your mama already had her coffee and maybe she will sit at the table now that you're back. She hasn't sat at the table since you left. Your mama said she wouldn't until you came home. Now is the time."

Mama was sitting on the bed when Daddy told me of her pledge, she started to cry. I jumped out of bed and ran to her. When Daddy heard her, he hurried from the kitchen.

"Mama, are you alright?" I asked, putting my arms around her.

"Your mama is feeling bad, Tissie." Daddy said, petting her head. "She cried every time we sat down to eat for the first year after you left. She vowed never to sit at the table until you came back."

"Mama, I'm here, please don't cry." I got down on my knees and laid my head in her lap. She began to pat my head.

"Sissie, I can't go to the table. Not yet. You will be leaving again. I will when you come back home to stay for good."

With my face buried in her lap, I cried. My sorrow came from deep in my heart, like I was being ripped apart. I pressed my face into her lap to muffle my screams, my anguish. "Oh, Mama..."

Daddy sat on the bed beside her and, in the Indian language, he said, <*Don't worry Mama, she will stay with us. We won't let the Whiteman Doctor take her away again.*>

Her answer, <*She is not well, we can't keep her. She knows it. She has seen and lived with death. Her eyes are wise. Now, she is crying for us. Let us hold her to our hearts until the time comes for her to go.*>

Not knowing that I understood what they were saying, it made me feel better. I knew Mama would let me go so the time I spent with them would be up to me. Drying my tears, we sat by Mama on the bed and ate our breakfast.

After I washed the dishes and cleaned up the kitchen I went to the bed where Mama and Daddy were having their morning cup of coffee and a cigarette. I kissed both of them and told them I wanted to go outside and look around. I told Daddy I heard the owl that morning and was sure we were going to have a good week.

It had been nearly fifteen years since we left the cabin. I tried to recognize things, the trees, the mountains, but everything had changed so much. The trees had grown up and the bushes looked thicker and I wasn't sure if they were all there before. But the tree that sheltered us those many years ago was still there.

I could still picture the campfire with the smoke trailing up and fading into the night sky. Trixie sitting by the three of us kids while we watched and listened to the music coming from the log cabin. Daddy playing the fiddle. People dancing. Everyone happy, laughing and talking.

I remember getting cold and crawling under the blankets and pulling the canvas over us. When it snowed on top of the canvas, it felt heavy and kept us warm. Trixie would lay on top of the canvas and stand guard.

Poor Trixie, she had passed away almost two years ago. I knew she would be in Doggy Heaven. She was more to us than a pet. She was our friend, our playmate and our protector. And, she always had a smile for us.

Tiny was killed about the same time. Manny accidentally backed the truck over her.

As the days passed, I spent time with Mama and Daddy talking about the past, when the cabin was built, the different places we moved to cutting wood. It was great. It made me feel like the past two years didn't happen.

But, in all the reminiscing, Daddy didn't want to talk about the hospital. Neither one asked how everything went for me. It was something they did not want to face. I knew from that day on, I had to find a way to convince Daddy how important it was for me to go back to the hospital, that I didn't have a choice. I decided to spend as much time as I could with them and enjoy it. When the time comes, I would make it happen. Looking up to the Heavens, I prayed, *Thank You Dear Lord for this time with Mama and Daddy. Let me know when the time is right.* Putting all my worries behind me, I set out to enjoy this time at home.

In the evenings, when it was dark, we would sit and visit. The only light came from the cracks around the door of the cook stove. The lamp was lit only when I cooked and we ate. It was important to save the kerosene.

I loved the sound of the wood crackling in the stove and the smell of the wood burning. I loved to listen to Daddy talking and hear him walking around with those big loggers he called shoes. I loved the smell of their cigarettes, the coffee and the potatoes frying in the deer grease.

I would watch Daddy take Mama to the outdoor toilet. Hand in hand, they walked slowly down the hill. Waiting for her, he would stand by the door, looking around at the trees and up at the sky, all the while, he's talking to her. I wanted these memories to be ingrained in my mind, to be stored for the future.

During those times, Daddy told me about the boys, their running around the reservation and drinking with their friends. They tried to stop them but the boys wouldn't listen. With Mama's illness and the lack of money for gas, they gave up the chase. Daddy said it was breaking Mama's heart.

However, Manny would come home once in awhile. He would go out and hunt for them, prepare the meat, get the wood they needed and leave.

Daddy told me about moving from Lynx Creek. Leaning back in his chair, Daddy looked around at the inside of the house, "Yeah, I think we done the right thing moving back to our old log cabin. Adding the kitchen really made it nice." Getting up, he poured a cup of coffee for himself and Mama. Adding sugar and milk in her cup, he stirred it. "But, the old cabin isn't warm enough and the roof needs fixing. All I can say is, when she don't rain, she don't leak."

A few days later I woke up in the morning and my pillow was wet. I looked up to see where it was coming from when a drop hit me on the forehead. Daddy was cooking breakfast and he had put several pots around the room, ping...pong...ping. Each pot, according to the size, gave a different sound. "Tissie, you better get up and start dodging the drops. And, if you change those pots around in the right place, we could have some music."

Laughing at Daddy's sense of humor, I went into the kitchen to get another pot. Looking around, Daddy said, "I think they're all used up. Use the wash basin."

Helping Mama out of bed, Daddy brought her into the kitchen and sat her by the cook stove. He put food on a plate and sat it on her lap. Daddy and I sat at the table while we ate.

"Daddy, I have an idea. When it stops raining can we go to the Republic dump and find something to patch the roof? And can we get some cardboard boxes for the walls? I would just love to fix the roof and nail the cardboard up!"

"Tissie, I don't know about the roof but fixing the walls would be okay."

"But Daddy, the roof isn't very steep. I can do it. Please," I begged.

"Well, let me think... it's ... Saturday. People use the dump on the weekends. If the rain stops we can go up there on Monday."

I was so happy I danced around the kitchen. "I get to do it, Daddy. I get to do it!"

Just like I prayed, on Monday the rain stopped and we were on our way to the dump!

When we got there, Mama found a stick so she could dig around while Daddy and I looked for roofing. We found several large pieces but all the cardboard boxes were wet.

Mama was on the far side of the dump, "Mama, hey, come on, let's go," Daddy called.

I couldn't see her, I could only see things flying up in the air as she dug with the stick. Then she called me to help her carry the food she found.

Mama had a big smile as I walked up to her. She was so proud of her find. Man, she had several carrots, cabbage, lettuce, potatoes and a slab of bacon! Oh my gawd, Daddy will be happy!

Daddy was standing by the truck waiting for us. When he saw the things we were carrying, he came to help. "Judging by the happy faces, you had a good day."

Hiding the slab of bacon behind me, "Daddy, you can't guess what Mama found."

"Hard telling what a man can find in this place," grinning at me.

Not being able to wait any longer, I pulled the slab of bacon out from behind me. "Look, Daddy, look. A whole slab of bacon, the very kind you like!" I handed it to him.

Looking at it, "Yeah, a little green but that can be cut away."

"Well, let's load 'er up and go to the store. Being late in the day, they might have some boxes for us," Daddy said as he helped Mama into the truck.

It wasn't long before the back of the truck was loaded with boxes, roofing and food as we headed down the road. Yes, it was a great day! I couldn't wait until I could start tacking up the cardboard on the wall.

Turning off the highway, the old truck bumped and swayed back and forth as we went over the big boulders in the road. Looking at the cabin from the distance I could see all the different colors of roofing. I was anxious to add another color or two on it.

It was getting late in the afternoon and I wanted to get started on the cardboard. "Daddy, can we unload the truck now so I can get started right away?"

"Tissie, if that will make you happy, we'll do it."

We unloaded the truck while Mama went into the house to start the fire in the cook stove. After, I began to cut the cardboard boxes apart. Daddy went into the house and began to peel the green off the bacon.

The tea kettle began to boil. "We'll have pancakes and bacon tonight after I get the coffee ready. Mama, you just sit there and watch Tissie and I work."

After moving a few things out of the way, I began to tack up the cardboard. Mama sat at the table and watched me. The smile she had let us know how happy she was. While Daddy cooked, he done his little tap dance back and forth in front of the stove. Just knowing Mama was happy made his day and the smell of the bacon frying, his favorite, made him smile. I wondered how long it had been since he danced. I wanted this evening to never end. It was a time I wanted to be frozen in my mind.

After supper, I lit the kerosene lamp and continued to tack up the cardboard. Mama and Daddy sat at the table and watched me while they had their coffee and cigarette. Looking back at them I said, "You know, one day I will be putting up wallpaper instead of cardboard in my house."

"Yes Tissie. Your mama and I know you will. And, when it rains it won't leak," Daddy said with a smile.

After I finished tacking up the cardboard Daddy stood back and looked it over, "Well Tissie, that looks pretty good. It should see us through the winter. Now we can get started on the roof."

"Daddy, you have to let me do it. I don't want you to get up on the roof," I said, knowing he would worry about me falling off.

Early the next morning, Daddy's call came, "I heard the old owl hoot last night and he tells me there's rain a-coming. You better get up Tissie, the roof's calling."

Not used to working, I ached all over but I didn't let Mama and Daddy know it. Mama was sitting up in bed with her coffee.

"How do you feel today?" she asked. She seemed to watch my every move.

Sitting up and swinging my feet onto the floor. "Oh Mama, I can hardly wait to fix the roof. I've been thinking about it. I plan on starting right above our beds and work towards the kitchen, in case we run out of roofing," I said ignoring my aches.

"Tissie, help your mama into the kitchen. Come and get'er while she's hot."

Easing Mama out of bed and holding on to her, we walked to the kitchen. "Mama, I'll set a chair outside so you can watch while Daddy and I work, okay?" Bending close to her ear, "I'll get Daddy a chair too."

After breakfast Mama told me, "Sissie, you go with your daddy and start work, I'll clean up the kitchen. I know you're anxious to get started."

With my pockets full of tacks, Daddy leaned up a couple of boards against the house for me to get up on the roof. Then he started handing the roofing to me.

Dragging it to the back, which was above our beds, I began to place the largest pieces. Suddenly, I heard a car coming. Watching it coming up the road, I realized it was Manny.

I was so happy. "Daddy, it's Manny!"

When he drove into the yard, smiling, Daddy said, "Hey, you got here just in time to help your sister."

Getting out of the car, Manny looked up at me with a big grin, "Hi Sis, need help?"

I was really glad to see him. "Yes, I need help, but first get two chairs from the house for Mama and Daddy to sit on so they can watch us."

It wasn't long before he threw more roofing on the roof and climbed up the board onto the house to help me. "You can put the pieces in place while I tack it down," I instructed him.

Mama and Daddy sat on the chairs and watched us. I could see how happy they were. This was the first time Manny and I worked together since Lynx Creek, making cedar posts. It brought a tear to my eye thinking about it.

We ran out of roofing before the job was done. "Well Sis, looks like we will have to make a trip to the dump to finish."

"We'll have to wait until next Monday because we took all there was."

"Why do we have to wait until Monday?"

"People work on their roofs and take the scraps to the dump on weekends. So, Monday is our day."

Seeing that the job was done for the day, Mama and Daddy went into the house. Manny and I sat down on the roof and talked.

"Sis, I put in for a job piling brush for the Tribe and I'm waiting for them to stake out the area. I think it will take about a month before I can start. I should be able to make a thousand bucks!" Manny said.

"Gee, a thousand bucks! That's a lot of money, Manny."

"Yeah. So, I came home to see if Mama and Daddy needed any wood and some meat."

"Can I go hunting with you? Remember, I wasn't able to get my deer before I went to the hospital?"

"Well Sis, let's get the wood this week, go to the dump next Monday, finish the roof, then go hunting. Okay?"

"Oh, Manny, I'm so glad you came. It's like a long time ago!" I said all excited.

That night at the supper table, Manny told Mama and Daddy about the job he was waiting for. Mama asked where he would be piling brush.

"It will be at 23 Mile. The job will take about a month. It depends on the size of the area."

That really made Mama happy. "We can go up there and set up camp and stay as long as it takes," she said.

I saw Daddy look over at Mama. He knew she loved to camp out and when he saw how happy she was with the idea, he looked away and smiled.

The next morning Daddy asked Manny to help him get the sweathouse ready for that night. "Your mama and I want to take a sweat tonight. We need fresh boughs for the sweat house and wood for the fire," he said as he cooked breakfast. "And Manny," looking at him with a twinkle in his eye, "I need you to help me. I want to wash clothes and need you to help me carry the water to heat."

"Sure, you guys work me to death!" he said. I knew he felt good knowing he was needed.

After breakfast, Manny started to carry water from the creek while I built a fire in the yard. I adjusted the large rocks around the fire for the tub. After Manny filled it, he went with Daddy to prepare the sweathouse.

While I waited for the water to heat, I went into the house to sort the clothes. First of all, I needed to clean Mama and Daddy's bedding because Mama spent so much time in bed. I sat a chair in the middle of the small room and helped Mama to get out of bed so I could wash the bedding.

"Oh Sissie, it is so good to have you home. You make our home come alive," she began to cry.

Hugging her, "Mama, you don't know how many times I dreamed about doing this for you and Daddy. In my dreams I washed the clothes, raked the yard, I cleaned the house, I cooked and sat at the table with you and Daddy. Mama, don't feel bad."

"Sissie, sit down and let me tell you what happened when you left."

I got a chair from the kitchen and sat it in front of her so I could face her while she talked to me.

"When your daddy and I went to the hospital to see you that evening, we knew where your room was, so we went on down the hallway. When we came to your room the bed was empty. Your daddy looked for a nurse. He asked where you went and the nurse said that you were taken to Tacoma by ambulance. When Daddy asked how long you would be gone, she said there's no telling. It could be a long time."

Leaning close to me, Mama went on to say, "Sissie, I passed out! Those were the last words I remembered. Daddy said I cried for days. My heart was broken. It wasn't until March before I came out of my 'sleep'. Daddy told me I had gone to the outhouse and when I returned to the house, a large hunk of snow fell off a tree and hit me on the head. Because my stomach hurt, I couldn't button my pants at the waist so I was holding them on. The snow fell into my pants and pulled them to the ground. It brought me back to my senses." She began to cry. "Oh Sissie, I lost you all over again!"

Standing before her, I held her head to my breast and pet her head. "Mama, don't cry. I know how you felt. Back then, I was lost too. I didn't know where they were taking me or for how long. All I ever wanted to do was come home. But, now I know." Lifting her chin, I looked into her tear-filled eyes. "Mama, I learned one thing in the hospital. Don't dwell on yesterday or worry about tomorrow, you have to live for today. God has given us this time together so be happy for the time we have." Petting her head, my tears rolled down my cheeks and as they fell onto her head, I brushed them into her hair. I knew I had to leave again and for how long, only God knew. I just prayed she could wait for me. I needed more time with her and Daddy.

Wiping her eyes on her sleeve, she said, "I better dry my eyes, your daddy feels bad when he sees me cry."

I took a chair outside and sat it where Mama could watch me while I worked. Helping her to the chair, "Now you just sit there and I want you to know, I'm enjoying myself!"

While I was gone, they had acquired a washing machine that was run by a little motor. After filling it with water, I spent some time trying to get it started. Manny heard me and came from the creek. After pouring some gas in, he primed it, stepped on the peddle a few times and putt...putt...putt... it went. As puffs of blue smoke shot out from the motor he flipped a switch and the water started to agitate. "Okay, put the clothes in. Now, I'll show you how to wring them out."

He took the wringer that had a handle on it, clamped it on the edge of the tub and tightened the screws. He dipped a dishrag in the water then demonstrated by putting it at the rollers and turning the handle. The rag went between the rollers squeezing the water out. I watched in awe!

"Sure better than the washboard, would you say?" Leaving me to my task, he went back down to the creek.

A washing machine! This was like Heaven. Gawd, Manny was right, this was a far cry from that washboard. Imagine, no blisters on my knuckles with this method.

Anxious to get started, I wanted to make Mama comfortable first. It seemed a bit chilly so I brought out a blanket for Mama's knees and a cup of coffee. The washing machine was so loud we couldn't talk. So, while the clothes washed, I cleaned out the house. I really enjoyed myself. I made believe the time at home would never end.

The sweathouse and creek couldn't be seen from the house but I could hear Manny and Daddy chopping wood. Late that afternoon I could see smoke coming up from the creek. Daddy had made the fire to heat the rocks for the sweat. Manny came back to the house and picked out the blankets to cover the sweathouse, making it ready for Mama and Daddy.

I was able to finish all the bedding for the beds that day, leaving the clothes for the next day. After hanging the bedding up to dry, I cooked supper and sat up a table outside so we could eat and enjoy the evening. Manny made several trips down to the sweathouse to put wood on the fire.

As night closed in, the glow from the fire showed reddish orange on the trees and bushes by the creek. Every now and then, sparks sprang up from the fire and disappeared into the night. It brought back memories of the many times we, as a family, sat around the campfire after a hard day's work and stared into the coals. I would have loved to turn back time.

Now, the "tree" was branching out. We were all going in different directions and it saddened me. I wasn't ready to leave, I needed more time at home.

Finishing their cup of coffee and cigarette, Daddy told Mama, "Well, I think it's time to take our sweat." He gathered up their change of clothes, took Mama by the hand and slowly they walked down to the creek.

Watching them made me think of the many times we moved and made up our camp through the years, Daddy had always built a sweathouse by the creek. It was used once a week, winter or summer. Never, in all the years, did Daddy bathe in the house. When it was winter, he broke a hole in the ice to bathe in.

The sweathouse was sacred, a place to worship. He built his sweathouse out of red willow bushes from along the creek. He would select branches that were about an inch in diameter and crisscrossed them in a curve with the ends tied down giving the height he wanted in the middle forming a dome-like structure. At the point each branch that crossed over the other, he tied it with a strip of bark from the willow. He cut another branch that formed the doorway. When it was completed, it measured about six feet wide and four feet high.

On the inside, a hole was dug to the left of the door which was about six inches deep. This was where the heated rocks were put. It was important in the selection of the rocks. They had to be the right kind that would not crack when heated and when cold water was poured on them, which gave the steam. On the floor, fir boughs were interwoven making a mat and covered with blankets.

At the time of the sweat, blankets covered the sweathouse, holding in the heat and steam. The door was made of canvas, which was attached to the doorway at the center. A stick was attached across the bottom of the canvas, keeping it spread out.

After they left, Manny and I sat at the table in the yard and stared at the trail long after Mama and Daddy had gone out of sight. I wondered what he was thinking. Did he see what I saw? Did he worry about Mama and Daddy? Was the pull to be with his friends too strong? Somehow, I think I knew the answer. He sat in the middle. Otherwise, he wouldn't make trips home as often to make sure they had meat and wood. Thinking about it eased my mind.

"Well, Sis. I'll help you bring things into the house. It's time for me to hit the rack."

He planned to sweat in the morning while the blankets were still on the sweathouse. "I'll do that while you finish washing the clothes, then we can go out and get some wood for the house. We might have to fall a couple dry trees first."

He went in to bed while I waited for Mama and Daddy. I went to the clothesline to get their bedding. As I gathered the blankets, I could hear them praying and singing songs of worship. A lump formed in my throat. The blankets were dry, taking them from the line, I made up their bed.

When I saw them coming up the trail, I lit the lamp and put wood in the cook stove to heat up the coffee for them. Mama's hair hung loosely to her waist. After pouring them a cup of coffee, I combed her hair. Parting it slightly off center, I braided it into two braids. She took the loose hair from the comb and wound it around the ends of the braids to keep it from coming undone. As the hair dried, soft waves formed around her face. When I was through, she smiled up at me.

My mother, who never wore make-up or tweezed her eyebrows, had a natural beauty that took my breath. Even in her illness, her sunken eyes, high cheek bones and high forehead brought out her delicate features. Even with the loss of weight, her bronze skin was void of wrinkles, except around her eyes and slight creases on her forehead.

The next day, Manny had his sweat while I washed the clothes and hung them up to dry. In the afternoon, we went out and fell two trees and spent the rest of the week cutting them up into blocks. We stacked the blocks by the house and chopped up several piles of stove wood to last for awhile.

Now, it was Monday, time to go to the dump for roofing. Mama and Daddy stayed home while Manny and I made the trip. It was a good day. We found several pieces of roofing to finish the job. After driving the last tack, the roof looked like a patchwork quilt!

Manny and I stood on the roof, looking at our work. "You know Sis, I kinda like the different colors. Gives it character."

I looked around at the roof. "Yeah, you're right. I like the red, black and green but we could have had more red."

"Well Sis, tomorrow, we hunt." Manny said as he ran down the board that leaned against the house.

Taking my time, I backed down the board, "What time will we go?"

"I have to help Daddy fill the holes in the road in the morning. So, we can go in the afternoon. We're not going very far because you shouldn't walk too much."

"Manny, you got to let me get the deer if we see one. I have never gotten a deer in my life and you have. So, give me the first chance, okay?"

"Okay, but I'm not going to wait long."

"You better let me or I'll never forgive you!" I scolded.

"Okay, okay. I'll give you a lot of time," he said with that grin that used to make me mad.

The next morning, Daddy's call came, "Get up you kids. Mush on the tab." A little time later, "Come and get it before I feed it to the hogs!"

Mama already had her coffee and cigarette. I was so tired from the day before, I slept through Daddy's little ritual with Mama.

"Daddy, why do we have to get up so early in the mornings? We don't have to go to work at any special time," I asked.

"Tissie, it's great to get up early in the mornings. You have the whole day to enjoy. And, you'll lay down a long time after you're dead."

During breakfast, Daddy asked, "You kids plan on going hunting?"

"Yeah, we'll leave after I help you fix the road," Manny said.

"In that case, I'll clean up the drying rack and get some brush wood. It will sure be good to have some dry meat," Daddy said with a smile.

"Go ahead, Daddy," Manny said. "If we don't get one today, we'll keep hunting until we do."

While Daddy and Manny worked on the road, I brought in the clothes from the clothesline and put them away while I visited with Mama.

"Oh Mama, it will be so good to dry some meat. It's been years and I can hardly wait!"

"Yes, Sissie. And, it's so good to have Manny home. He's been good to come home when we need wood and meat." Looking at her as she spoke, she looked down at her hands. I saw the sadness.

Nearing noon, I made lunch and gathered up shells and the rifles for us to take. Daddy cautioned Manny, "Remember, your sister has been in bed for a long time. Take it easy and don't go very far."

"Don't worry, Daddy, I'll let him know when I'm tired. And, he promised me, I get the first shot."

With the rifles over our shoulders, shells in our pockets and Manny in the lead, we headed up the mountain. He knew the area well and knew where to go.

Leaving the cabin, the ground was level for a time then we began to climb. The mountain was so steep, to the point I had to hang onto bushes and pull myself up. It wasn't long before I was begging Manny to stop and let me rest. I thought we'd never get to the top.

When we got to the top of the mountain we took a long rest. Looking around, I could see the tops of other mountains. It was beautiful! Ahead of us were bald mountains with trees in the gulches. It was like being in another world. Seeing how awestruck I was, Manny said, "Sis, one day I will take you up there to get one of those big bucks, you know, six to eight pointers."

"Oh Manny, why can't we go there now?" I asked. Just the thought excited me.

"First of all, it's too late in the day and those mountains look close but it would take over an hour to get there. Don't worry Sis, we have many more hunting days ahead of us."

Rested, we headed out. We hunted for about three hours, making a big circle that would take us back to the cabin. It was getting late so we started to come off the mountain.

It was getting dusk when we came onto a deer trail. After following it for awhile, Manny stopped short in front of me. Stepping off the trail, he pointed ahead of us, "There, along side of the trail, get him!"

Lifting my rifle into a shooting position, "Where is it?"

"Right there by the trail, get him!" he whispered.

I looked and looked but I couldn't see anything. "Where? I can't see it!" Taking too long, the deer was gone. Even when it moved I couldn't see it.

"Man, Sis, you have to be blind. That's it, if you want to get a deer you'll have to go hunting by yourself. If you go hunting with me I'm not giving you anymore chances."

"That's just fine. The day will come when I won't wait for you. So, you better keep in practice," I said with my chin up. We headed home.

Manny got up early the next morning and went hunting. He came home about one o'clock in the afternoon dragging a deer. I was happy for him. I could not have climbed the mountain again.

It was a happy day! While Daddy made the fire under the drying rack, I set up the table to cut the meat. Manny hung the deer, skinned it out and quartered it, making it ready to be cut up for drying.

After the fire was going good, Daddy stood by Manny, waiting for him to cut off the ribs. Taking the rib, he wove a sharp stick between the bones and stuck the stick in the ground, leaning a slight bit towards the fire. It didn't take long before the meat started to sizzle. With a big smile, Daddy watched the meat while it cooked. Every now and then he would turn it. The aroma soon filled the air making the rest of us smile and look at his cooking.

Starting with the front quarter, I began to cut up the meat for drying. When I finished the first one, Daddy began to lay the meat on the drying rack.

As I began to cut on the next one, Daddy stopped everything. His rib was cooked and it was time to share it.

Holding up the rib that was dripping juice, "Okay, you people. This is the best part of the hunt." He looked up at the sky then bowed his head, "I want to thank the Good Lord for bringing Manny home for this day." He made the Sign of The Cross while speaking the Indian language. Now, it was time to eat.

He began to cut pieces off and handed them out. It had been a long time since I tasted freshly cooked deer meat, I savored every bite. Oh, how I missed these times. I wanted it to be this way for the next hundred years!

We worked on drying the meat way into the night. Daddy had his long stick with a fork tied to the end to turn the pieces. He piled the pieces that were done at the end of the rack where the smoke drifted giving the dried meat its flavor. The meat was left on the rack for the night. It was important for the meat to get really dry before storing it.

With everything done, wood for the house, the roof fixed and a deer dried for Mama and Daddy, Manny told us he was leaving. It made me feel bad to see him go. Mama cried and begged him to be careful. "I'll let you know when the job starts up at 23 Mile," Manny said as he climbed into his car.

Standing in the yard, Daddy told him, "It would be nice if you came home before we go up there. I would like for you to get another deer, we'll need the meat."

"Okay, I'll do that." Starting the car, he looked at me standing by the house, "See you later, Sis."

I walked over and stood by Daddy. We watched as the dust trailed behind the car before going out of sight. I knew Daddy didn't want him to leave but there wasn't anything he could do.

Walking to the house, Daddy said, "Would you like to cook some of that tenderloin we saved? It would sure taste good."

The days spent with Mama and Daddy were great. With the weather being nice, I would set up the table outside to have our meals. It made Mama happy. To have Mama happy kept Daddy's spirit high.

The snow piled up around the little cabin. Daddy and I kept the trails open to the spring, outhouse, sweathouse and wood pile. The roof Manny and I repaired held up. Other days, we shoveled the snow to the highway but it was an endless job. When the boys came home, Daddy would put them to work on it. Then the winter '53 became the spring of '54.

I don't remember much about the trip to Spokane that May. I just laid my head back on the seat and closed my eyes. There were times I lifted my head and watched the country go by. I didn't want to think about where I was headed. A place filled with uncertainty, loneliness and where the only thing you have control of is your mind. In Cushman, I had learned ways to blank out thoughts that saddened me and bring in the present. I looked at the sky and thought about the clouds. I looked at the trees to see how many I could count. I counted the cars that went by.

Daddy and Ernie talked about different things but nothing about the hospital. Before we knew it, we were in Spokane. Somehow, they found the way to Edgecliff Sanatorium in the Spokane Valley. Ernie pulled into the parking lot, got out with his camera and waited for Daddy and me to get out of the car.

When we got out, Daddy reached in his back pocket for his wallet and gave me $2.00. In the meantime, Ernie took out a suitcase and sat it by me. I was surprised, I hadn't seen anyone packing it for me. I'm sure Mama had something to do with it. While Daddy gave me the money, Ernie took our picture.

They both hugged me, said goodbye and drove off. I stood there and watched as the car went out of sight. I waved but I knew they didn't look back. It was just a gesture. Something to do before turning around, as if a few seconds made a difference.

I looked at the two big doors that led into another world, took a deep breath, picked up the suitcase and walked up the steps. I pulled at the right door. It felt like lead, as if it didn't want me to go in.

13 MILE CABIN

Christine Cassano

Chapter 8

MAKE US PROUD
Age 19

Stopping at the foot of my bed, the doctor said, "Well Chris, I have good news for you today. All your tests and x-rays came back with good results. You can make plans on getting out of the hospital."

I sat there and looked at him with my mouth wide open. I could not believe what he was saying.

"You mean I'm well... I can go home... are you sure?"

"Yes, I'm sure. But there are a few things you have to do first."

He turned to the nurse and said something to her. Then he went on to say, "I will be sending a case worker in to see you about your future. We want to make sure you have some kind of training to support yourself when you get out."

What he was saying didn't make sense to me. All I could think of, *I'm going home! I can see Mama and Daddy!*

Seeing that I was in shock, the doctor leaned over and patted my foot. "It will be in a few days but the time is here." Saying that, he and the nurse left, leaving me staring at the door.

April 1954 – 6 months Home from Cushman Hospital
I got down on my knees by the bed and gently whispered,

"Mama, you've got to save me."

Without opening her eyes, tears began to run down the side of her face, "I knew this day was coming, Sweetheart. I know you have to go."

I was shaking as if I was cold. "Mama let me tell you how it was. Let me tell you how it was to live not knowing what tomorrow would bring. Let me tell you how I missed you and Daddy. Let me tell you what I fear. Please, I must explain it all to you," I begged.

Turning her head towards me, opening her eyes, "Sissie, I understand." When she saw me shaking, pulling herself into a sitting position, "Here, put this blanket over your shoulders, you're cold," she urged.

"No Mama, I'm just nervous I guess." My teeth began to chatter.

"Please, get under the blankets. You're cold. I don't want you to get sick."

"I swear Mama, I'm not cold. It's because I'm nervous and waited so long to talk to you about the hospital. And I know Daddy will get mad. It is all up to you to make him understand." Laying my head on the bed, I began to roll it back and forth. "Please, Mama."

I sat there for a few minutes thinking about what just happened. "Oh my gawd, I'm well. I'm well!" Looking around the room, "What will I do? Oh, my shoes." I jumped out of bed, put on my shoes and went to the door and started dancing. The tapping was faster and went on much longer. Then, I went down to the ward where the elderly ladies were and told them I was well. I would tap and spin around and tap again. They clapped their hands when I left. Oooh man, was I happy! It's like the losing team catching the ball in the last few seconds and runs all the way to a touchdown! I wanted to scream!

That night when the lights were put out, my mind started to work. *What did he mean, the case worker? Who was that?* "You *have to support yourself."* What does that mean? *I have to stay here for a few more days. Why?*

I had another worry, *how will I get home? I don't know where I am. I know I'm in Spokane, but where? How far away is home? Who will take me home?* I had been in Edgecliff for a year and I was sure Mama and Daddy were the only ones that still remembered me and where I was. I really began to feel lonely. I knew no one outside of the hospital. Suddenly, shrinking down in my bed, the world seemed so big and I felt so small.

That night was the longest of all. I must have turned over a hundred times. Finally, I thought, *getting home is the real problem. When I get out, I'll ask questions and walk home.* With the problem solved I turned over and fell asleep.

The next morning after breakfast, Mrs. Olney came to visit me. "I hear you're leaving us," she said with a big smile, pulling the chair up to the bed.

"Oh, Mrs. Olney. I'm well, I'm well! I can't believe it. I'm going home to Mama and Daddy!" I said clapping my hands.

July 1954 – 2 months at Edgecliff Sanatorium

After breakfast, there was a soft knock on my door. I didn't say anything, I just waited to see who would look around the door. Soon, this lady with reddish blonde hair slowly peeked at me from the door.

"May I come in?"

My bed was still wound up in a sitting position from just having breakfast. I nodded my head.

Mrs. Olney wore glasses and stood about five foot two, heavy set, square in build and her legs seemed far apart. They seemed like they were attached on each end of a square. When she walked, she rocked from side to side. But the most outstanding thing about her was her smile. This woman never knew a stranger! She began talking to me as if she knew me all her life and that smile never left her face.

Pulling up the chair, she sat close to the bed, "Okay, Christine... I mean Chris. I was told you liked to be called Chris. Could you tell me something about what schooling you've had? That will tell me where we can get started."

I wasn't quite sure how to answer her, I had to think about it. When she saw my hesitation. "Were you close to graduation when you became sick?" *she asked.*

"No. I'm not sure just what grade I'm in. But when I started school in Inchelium they put me in the 8th grade. You see, we had a hard time staying in school because we lived in the mountains and we always got snowed in."

Her smile almost left, then she brightened up, "I'll tell you what we'll do. I'll give you a couple of tests and find out where you stand. Don't worry about it. Now, I want to know more about you. Tell me about your family..."

There was something about Mrs. Olney, I ended up pouring my heart out to her. I talked and I cried and I talked... I found someone who really cared and who cried with me.

She became a friend that I would turn to many times for advice and someone to talk to in dark times. When I was lonely, she was there. When I cried, she lent me her shoulder. I no longer felt alone.

Mrs. Olney put up her hands to stop me from talking, "Chris, there is something I have to explain to you," she said with a serious look.

"Is there something wrong?"

"Chris, listen to me. You will need training in some kind of a career to support yourself when you get out in the world."

There goes that word, "support" with a new word, "career".

"Mrs. Olney, the doctor told me the same thing. I don't know what you're talking about."

She started to explain it all to me. The case worker worked for the Rehabilitation, which was a program that trained people in a career so I could work for money to pay for food and a place to live. But while I was being trained in a career, they would pay for my schooling, food and a place to live.

To get started, the case worker would give me a test to see where my interest was. When that was taking place, Mrs. Olney would help me find a place to live while I was going to school.

It all seemed so much to digest... a career... tests... a place to live... food.

"Mrs. Olney, can I ask one question? When can I go home to see Mama and Daddy?"

Dropping her eyes, "Chris, I don't know. You can't leave the hospital until this is all set up. When it is all done and you are in school, we can find a way for you to visit your folks."

"Visit my folks? You mean I can't go home and stay?" I began to feel sick.

"Chris... listen. You need to be able to support yourself. I'm sure your folks would want you to go to school. Please, give it some thought." Pushing the chair back, she got up to leave. "Chris, you are a smart girl. I know you will do the right thing."

After she left, I laid there with my arms behind my head, looking at the ceiling. Now I understood. *I will be going to school. I will have a career. I will be able to support myself. I wonder what my career will be? Hmmm.* After all that was said, I still didn't quite know what "career" meant.

When the nurse came to close my door for the night, I asked her, "Can I ask you a question?"

"Yes, Chris. What is it you would like to know?"

"Did you have to have a career to be a nurse?"

She smiled at me and looked a little bit surprised, "Being a nurse is my career." Closing the door, "Good night."

I stared at the door after she left. *There's a whole new world out there waiting for me.*

The next morning, looking out the window, was the most

beautiful day on earth! The words came to me, "Lemlmts (thank you), dear Jesus, for taking me through another year and giving me a new chance to live. Amen." This gave me the full meaning of what Mama and Daddy felt when each spring came.

This was spring and I would grow with the grass, the flowers and those baby birds that are being hatched right now. My wings would begin to grow and I would soon fly on my own. Yes, it was a good sign.

I was well and I was getting out of the hospital! The breakfast that morning looked good, tasted good but I couldn't remember what I ate! I had to tell everyone that came into my room, the nurse, the cooks and yes, even the janitor.

When the nurse came in to change my bedding, I put on my shoes and danced to the door, I continued down the hallway to the ladies in the last ward. When I got to their door I danced vigorously. They all stopped what they were doing and looked at me. I purposely waited for someone to ask me why I was so happy.

"Boy, Chris, that is some dancing. We know that you're going home but why are you so extra happy?"

I stepped into the room and twirled around and around, tapping my feet, "I'm not only well but I'm going to have a career. I'm going to go to school! Can you believe that?"

One little lady said in a sad voice, "Oh Chris, we will miss you and your dancing."

Another lady said, "Please stay well. We will miss you and we will pray for you." It made me feel good that someone would miss me.

The next day Mrs. Olney came to see me. She told me I would be given an "aptitude test" to see where my skills were. The word "test" scared me.

"Oh, don't worry you can handle it. All you have to do is answer the questions and she will bring a board game that has different shaped holes in it." She made it sound so easy.

"When will she come? I want to get on with the tests so I can get out of here." Things were not happening fast enough for me.

"Now now, Chris. All this will take time. Please be patient."

"Mrs. Olney, you can't understand how long I've waited for this day. I still can't believe I'm getting out!"

"Yes, I can only imagine but I have a surprise for you," she said acting coy.

"Tell me. Hurry, tell me!" I begged, knowing it was going to make me happy.

"I'm taking you out on a pass tomorrow. I'm taking you to lunch and then to a movie. Would you like that?" she asked with a smile.

Sitting straight up, "Oh... Mrs. Olney, I don't have anything to wear! The only thing I have is what I wore when I came to the hospital. I think the nurse has the sack it's in."

Getting up to leave, she said, "Don't worry I will bring it when I come to take you out. That's tomorrow! Be ready right after breakfast."

"Mrs. Olney, I still have some money from my monthly check. I didn't have anything to buy so I kept the money. Maybe you can help me buy something else to wear, okay?"

"It will be fun to shop."

March 1954 – 5 Months Home from Cushman Hospital
One day, I could hear them sawing and chopping wood at a distance from the house as I made my way to the outdoor toilet. Sitting there, I looked at an old J.C. Penny's catalog, our "toilet paper". I turned to the dresses. It reminded me of when I was in the hospital. My eyes lit up! The dress! I began to turn the pages. There it was! I tore the page out and hurried back to the house.

"Mama, look at this dress. This is the dress I wanted so bad when I was in the hospital. Just look at it, isn't it beautiful?"

Mama looked at it and smiled. "Yes, you would look really pretty in it."

"Do you think there is a way I could get it? I've never had a new dress," I said looking sad.

"You worked real hard with the boys. Maybe there will be enough money to get it for you. We'll see."

I could hardly wait for the boys to get back from work. Thinking about it while I waited, I didn't know where I would wear it, but right now it didn't matter, I wanted that dress! My eyebrows drew together, "They better get it for me! If they don't I'll never forgive them."

Soon as the boys walked in the door, "Guess what?" I asked, looking both of them in the eye. "I'm going with you when you turn in the slip to get the money."

Surprised, Manny asked, "Why are you going with us?"

I showed him the picture of the dress. "I helped you guys piling brush so I'm buying this dress with what is owed to me." He smiled. "And a pair of shoes to go with it." I added.

He didn't fool me, I knew it was pennies compared to what he would be getting. But it didn't matter to me, I wanted the dress and it meant a lot to me.

Lifting my chin, "And, don't forget Mama and Daddy. They spent time and gave a place for you to sleep and food to eat."

"Okay, okay." Manny said. "But, why do you have to go with us to get the money?"

Glaring at him, "Because I'm not too sure you guys will come back. I'm just protecting my interest."

The following Monday the boys and I headed for the Tribal Agency in Nespelem to turn in the slip. While I waited for the boys to collect the money, I asked the lady at the desk where there was a J.C. Penny's store. She told me there was one in Omak.

Getting back in the car, I told Manny, "Let's go to Omak. There's a J.C. Penny's store there."

"Why do we have to go there?" he asked, aggravated.

"Manny, the dress! That's where it is."

Heading for Omak, the boys looked annoyed. "You boys better straighten up. I don't ask for much and I've never had anything new. Now, you're going to ruin it for me," I scolded.

Breaking the mood, Manny said, "Okay Sis, I can't wait to see you in that dress."

When we got to Omak, not trusting the boys, I told them they had to come in with me and wait. Walking in the door of the store, grouching, Ernie asked, "How long do we have to wait?"

"I know exactly what I want so it won't take long," I said heading for the dresses. I showed the lady that was straightening up clothes on the rack the picture of the dress I wanted.

She looked at me, up and down. "I think you're about a size 5 or 6." Then she began to pull back the hangers that held the dresses. "What color are you interested in?"

Smiling, as my eyes passed over the dresses, "I would like to have a blue one."

Checking the sizes, she pulled out a blue dress. There it was! She held up the dress for my inspection. It was sheer and pale blue with little pink flowers on it. It had a matching underskirt and lining on the bodice with narrow straps. It was fitted to the waist, had a narrow belt, from there it flared out. It had small cap sleeves and a Peter Pan collar. Yes, this was the one!

"Would you like to try it on?" she asked.

My heart skipped a beat. 'Oh my gawd!'

Seeing my expression, she smiled, then led me to the dressing room. She hung the dress on a hook and stepped aside for me to enter. It was like I stepped into Wonderland.

After she closed the door, I felt the dress. It was crisp to the touch and the little flowers were fuzzy. Imagine, no one else has ever worn this dress before and it's all mine. I quickly undressed and stepped into the dress. I zipped it up, which was on the side, and turned to look at myself in the mirror. Oooh, just as I expected! Not used to seeing myself in something that fit my body, it made me blush. I looked at myself this way and that way. I twirled around to make the skirt flare out. It made me feel like a real girl. Maybe the word dainty fits! After all, it was a far cry *from Levi's and a boys' shirt that I wore all the time.*

All too soon, the lady knocked on the door. "How does the dress fit?" she asked.

"It fits good. I'll take it. I'm changing right now," I said as I took one last look in the mirror.

When I came out, I handed the dress to the lady. "Where can I buy a pair of shoes to go with it?"

That Friday was one of the most wonderful days of my life! When Mrs. Olney brought my sack and suitcase, I opened the sack and took out the clothes I wore when I came into the hospital. The biggest surprise came when I opened the suitcase. I hadn't opened it in the year that I was there. It held my little blue dress and white shoes! "My dress, my dress!" I buried my face into the dress, "Oh Mama, Mama you knew it. You knew I would wear it someday!" It took a minute to get control of myself. "My my, what a beautiful dress," Mrs. Olney said with a smile.

"Yes, my brothers and I worked piling brush and I bought this with my money."

"Okay Chris, we have to leave soon before the day gets away from us. Save the dress for special occasions and wear the skirt and blouse."

Driving into the city was the greatest feeling. I was going somewhere! We went into the different stores and with Mrs. Olney's guidance, I bought some underclothes, a nightgown, lipstick, a new comb and some candy. Man, it was like Christmas! But, it was strange, I never saw any Indians. All I saw were white people. Afraid to get lost, I stayed close to Mrs. Olney.

We went to lunch then to the movie *Duel in The Sun*. That movie left me breathless. The Indian girl fell in love with the cowboy! He treated her awful. I loved and hated him at the same time. I was glad when she shot him. But then he shot her! Oooh, then they crawled to each other and died in each other's arms. That made it right and so romantic! To top it off, a rose grew in the desert each year where they died. Now, that was real love!

When we got back to the hospital, I was really tired. My skin felt dirty. The dirt felt like it was caked on my skin. I took a shower and crawled into bed. When the lights were turned off, my fears began to grow. I dreamed this day would come, I had prayed to God to get me well. Now, I was afraid to leave. *How can I live out there? I don't know anybody. How will I know where to go? What if they find out I've been sick? I just know they will turn me away. They will be scared of me. I have to find a way home to the mountains. That's where I belong. That's where I want to go. It's where I can feel safe.*

Deep in the night I peeked out from under the covers and looked out the window. Fear gripped me and my heart began to beat fast. I was afraid to leave this room, this bed! Crying into my pillow, exhausted, I fell asleep.

The next morning when the breakfast tray came, I asked the nurse to send word to Mrs. Olney. I needed to talk to her. About an hour after breakfast, Mrs. Olney came. Trying to catch her breath, "I was told that you needed to talk to me. Is there something wrong? It sounded serious."

Before I started to talk, I began to cry, "Mrs. Olney, I'm afraid to leave the hospital. I'm not used to people and they might not like me if they find out I've been sick."

Coming around the bed, she patted me on the back, "Now, now Chris. You can't start talking and feeling like that. You'll do fine."

"I've been thinking, maybe I should go home. Mama's sick and I know they need me to help them," I said wiping my eyes on the sheet.

"Chris, now you listen to me! You need a career to help yourself. You have a chance now! Your schooling will be paid for. You will be given an allowance each month to buy food and pay your rent. The time will come when your parents won't be here and I'm sure they will want you to go to school!"

When she got through talking, her face was red!

She got up and went to the door. Turning back to me, "I want you to stop feeling sorry for yourself. Mrs. Fry will be seeing you this afternoon. She will be giving you the tests I told you about." I knew she was very upset when she left.

That afternoon, the lady came in with a "board game" and papers for me to fill out. "My name is Mrs. Fry. I was sent by your case worker to give the aptitude test and," handing me the papers, "I would like for you to answer as many questions as you can."

I filled out my name, address (Republic?) and started to answer the questions, skipping the ones I didn't understand, like "education" and "occupation" and other strange words. When I was finished, she took the papers and looked at the answers. A little frown appeared. I knew it was the questions I skipped. Then she began to ask me those questions. When she asked me in a different way, I could answer them.

Then out came the board with the different holes. Setting it before me, she explained, "Each peg has a different shape and the board has a matching hole. I want you to place each peg into the right shape. You will be timed to complete the task."

Taking them out, she scrambled the pegs and told me to start. She started the clock and I put them all back. It was easy and I wondered what this was all about.

When we were through, she gathered up the papers and board with the pegs. "Thank you, Chris. The caseworker will see you in a couple days."

The next morning Mrs. Olney came to visit me. "Chris, I'm so pleased. You passed the test with flying colors! Now, you will have to decide what type of a career will interest you."

"Mrs. Olney, I know nothing about careers." She handed me a slip of paper with a list. It was like trying to read Greek. Secretary, telephone operator, librarian, beautician... my eyes stopped and went back to "telephone operator". *I know what that is, it deals with phones.*

Pointing to the big name, "I'll do that. I'll be a telephone operator." I felt proud to be making such a big decision.

"Yes, I'm sure you could do that and be good at it but I want you to think about this one," she pointed at "beautician".

I looked at the word, it didn't mean anything to me. "Telephone operator" told me what it was. I looked at the other words, librarian... secretary... the list went on.

Feeling a little disappointed, I leaned back on my bed. "What does a beautician do?"

"It has to do with fixing hair. You would be giving haircuts, permanent waves and coloring people's hair. I think you would be good at it because your tests show you have good hand control and you are quick with your mind and learn fast."

It was hard for me to understand how those tests told them so much about me and what I could do. I wondered how Mrs. Olney came up with "beautician".

The room fell silent while I looked at the word and thought about it. *Cut hair... permanent waves... hmmm. People will always have hair, it will grow and it will have to be cut again. When they have a permanent wave, it grows out and it will be cut off and they will have to permanent wave it again. That means my career will never end. That sounds good to me.*

"Okay, I can do that. When do I start?"

With a sigh of relief, she said, "Soon Chris, soon. First we have to find a place for you to live and pick a school for your training."

I just couldn't believe everything that was happening to me. Laying back in my bed, "Mrs. Olney, I am sooo happy!"

"Yes Chris, I can imagine how it was for you. Now, you will have to see your case worker and fill out the necessary paperwork." Getting up to leave she had tears in her eyes.

I quickly sat up, "Mrs. Olney, I don't know what I would do without you. Please, don't ever leave me."

"Chris, remember, there is always someone that would help

you, all you have to do is ask. One day, you will be helping someone. Right now, I will walk you through each step to get you settled."

After she left, I thought about what she said, *"Someday, you will be helping someone."* I couldn't imagine that I could help anyone. I knew nothing!

When my dinner came, I was so excited, I didn't taste anything. Halfway through the meal I just had to dance. I got out of bed, put on my shoes, danced to the door and down the hall to the little ladies' ward. While dancing I told them I was going to be a beautician. They clapped their hands, keeping time with my dance.

After wearing myself out, I went back to my room. I got back in bed and started to imagine fixing someone's hair. But, I couldn't get passed cutting the hair off... *how would I cut it?* I could imagine rolling the hair up on a rod. A girl at school did mine once. When she took the rods off, it was curly. *Hmmm... maybe I should look at some books to get an idea.*

At 9:30 the next morning Mrs. Olney came and told me I had an appointment with the case worker at 10:00 to fill out papers for financial aid. She waited while I put on my robe and shoes.

Walking down the hall with Mrs. Olney made me smile because now we were making progress! We went to the basement and entered the office of Mrs. Smith, the case worker. Mrs. Olney introduced us and left.

1945 – Age 9
Ernie came into the house. He held this long stick in one hand and stroked it with the other. Looking at it from one end to the other as in sizing it up, he asked me, "Do you know what this is for?"

"No."

Tilting his head to one side, he smiled, "I'm going to measure you so I will know how big to make your coffin because I'm going to kill you." Knowing he had said fighting words he jumped back and put up his dukes, ready to fight. We were in the house so he couldn't get away from me. We started to fistfight. We beat on each other until he gave up. The cook stove was in the middle of the room and the door was closed. I chased him around and around the stove. He started to holler for Manny to open the door for him. Trying to keep out of the way, Manny opened the door.

Making the last round, Ernie had to make a quick turn to go out the door. Doing so, his foot slipped. When he went down, I dove on top of him and started punching him in the back and head. I quit when I saw blood on his head.

Jumping up, he ran out into the yard, holding his head. When he took his hand down, he saw blood and started to scream, "I'm bleeding, I'm bleeding!"

I stood at the door and watched as Manny ran out to examine the cut and see how badly he was hurt. I figured he wouldn't die so I told them they couldn't come back into the house until Mama and Daddy came back. They were both barefooted and it didn't take long before they started begging to come back into the house.

I let them stay outside until they got good and cold. Before I would let them in, I made them promise me that they had to help clean the house, finish the dishes, bring in wood for the stove, and not to call me names.

"I hear you want to become a beautician" she said, looking at the papers I filled out before.

Feeling a little scared, I said, "Yes. I think I would like that."

Somehow, I didn't like this woman's attitude. She acted like she was so important and she was doing me a big favor. She began asking me questions and writing down the answers. This went on for about 10 minutes. All the while, she didn't look up at me. When I didn't answer the question quick enough, she would look annoyed.

My heart began to beat faster, I could feel anger coming on. I didn't like the way I was being treated. I began to feel like the animal backed up in its cage and she's poking a stick at me. I was ready to fight!

Finished with the questions, Mrs. Smith pushed the paper across the desk for me to sign. Glad it was over, I took the pen she handed me and looked for the line to sign.

By this time, she got up from her chair, walked around the desk and watched me sign the papers. Then she walked back around the desk, stood behind her chair and folded her arms in front of her. Giving me a firm look, she said, "Now, I want to point out one thing to you. I would like to hope when you get started in school that you plan on finishing the course. Not like so many other Indians I have worked with that start school and quit."

After signing the paper, I looked up at her. Digesting what she just said to me, my blood began to boil! I stood up leaned over the desk and looked her straight in the eye, "How dare you talk to me that way. Who the hell do you think you are? Don't you ever, ever compare me to anyone else, I don't give a damn who they are. I am ME!" pointing to my chest.

I was so angry, I pushed the paper back across the desk, glared at her and headed for the door then stopped. Looking back at her, I added, "I don't want to ever see you again. Before I talk about school again it better be with someone else!" With that I walked out and slammed the door behind me.

The next week Mrs. Olney came to see me. "I met your new case worker, Mr. Abey. He's a very nice man and I just know you will like him. He's anxious to meet you."

"Did you tell him about my other case worker and what happened?" I asked because I wanted him to know so he wouldn't do the same thing.

"Oh yes. It made him want to meet you," she said with a smile.

After lunch, we headed out to meet Mr. Abey. We parked on

the side street and Mrs. Olney pointed to a big building. "That is the Hutton Building. In the future, if you must see him you'll have to know where it is. His office is on the second floor."

When we went up the stairs, the inside looked a little old. The stairs sort of squeaked. Mrs. Olney had to rest a couple of times going up. At the top, we went down a hallway and she knocked on a door. A man called out, "Come in."

When we entered, a short man stood up behind his desk and gave a big smile, "Mrs. Olney, it's good to see you. I see you brought my new client, Chris. Good. Sit down and let's get acquainted."

When I looked at this man I knew I would like him. He was short and fat. His hair was white and balding. His smile, his personality, his manner was genuine. Yes, I knew I didn't have to put up my guard.

Coming around the desk, he put out his hand to shake mine. "I was looking forward to meeting you. Mrs. Olney told me all about you and I'm sure we will get along just fine."

With the tone of his voice and a twinkle in his eye as he spoke, like Mrs. Olney, I knew I had met a friend.

He told me that he had arranged for me to live at the Isabella Club, an apartment house for girls and that I would be attending the Morse Beauty School in downtown Spokane. Two school uniforms would be delivered to me.

During our conversation he let me know, "I feel that a person's race has nothing to do with their ability to succeed."

When our visit was over, Mr. Abey handed me his card. "Put this in your pocket, it has my name and phone number. Anytime you need anything, have a problem, don't fight the battle, call me. I will be checking in on you from time to time. Good luck."

On the way back to the hospital, Mrs. Olney asked me, "Did you like Mr. Abey?"

"Oh yes. I liked him very much. He is a kind man and I know he will treat me right."

She smiled and looked a little relieved.

It was the last week of May 1955 when the doctor, a nurse and Mrs. Olney came into my room right after breakfast with papers in hand. This was the last time I would rest in this bed! This was the day I dreamed of for so long and was afraid to hope for. It was time to go!

The doctor handed me the papers and asked me to sign on the X. "I'm happy to say, Chris, the papers you are signing are your release," he said with a smile.

I got out of bed and got dressed in the same skirt and black t-shirt I wore when I entered the hospital a little over a year ago. A lump started to grow deep in my throat.

Mrs. Olney picked up my suitcase and asked me if I was ready. We went to the door, I looked back to see if I left anything. Looking around the small room made me feel sad. This bed I laid in many days and nights eased my pain and the pillow muffled the sound as I cried of loneliness and fear. This room kept me warm while I watched the snow come down and the trees bend in the wind. Now that I'm well, it's time to go.

Walking down the hall, the only sound was my shoes clicking on the shiny clean floor. I stopped and did a little dance. The sound of my shoes echoed down the long hallway.

As we drove away, I looked back at the hospital as tears ran down my cheeks. It was bittersweet.

Sitting beside Mrs. Olney as we drove to the Isabella Club, my heart began to beat fast and I could hear the pulse in my ears. I had let go of security and now I was stepping into the unknown. The thought of her leaving me, the only person I had real contact with from the outside world, made me want to scream, *please, don't leave me when we get there!* But I was able, barely, to hold it in.

When we pulled up in front of the Isabella Club, it felt like the blood was draining out of my body. I began to feel light headed and tears blurred my vision. My knees felt weak as I followed Mrs. Olney up to the entrance.

She knocked and Ms. Barness opened the door. We stepped in and the two ladies began to talk. I was fighting a war within myself and didn't hear what they were saying.

Standing by Mrs. Olney, I couldn't hold the tears back anymore. I began to cry. Startled, both women looked at me. Quickly, Mrs. Olney put her arm around my shoulders, "Chris, what is the matter? Is something wrong? Are you sick?"

The more she tried to comfort me the more I cried, until she excused us and walked me to the living room where the fireplace was. Patting me on the back, she waited until I slowed down the sobs, "Good Heavens, Chris, what happened? Is there something I can do?"

When I could finally talk, I told her of my fears, "I'm afraid when you leave. I know no one. I'm afraid I won't know what to do. I'm scared of being alone." Looking at her with pleading eyes, "Please tell me what to do."

Her worried look broke into a smile, pulling me to her, she hugged me and said, "Oh Chris, is that all? My my, you'll do just fine. Before I leave I will make sure you still have my phone number, like I told you before. If you need me, call and I can be here in half an hour. Or if you just need to talk, call. Now, don't be scared I'm just a phone call away."

I felt relieved but the fear was still there. She dug around in her purse and pulled out a Kleenex, "Here, dry your eyes now and we will go up to your room and get you settled in. I will explain to Ms. Barness to let you call me any time you need to. I'm sure she will understand so don't worry your little head about anything. I will take care of it."

Wiping my eyes, I took a deep breath. Okay, I was ready to meet the day. Ms. Barness stood at the foot of the stairway waiting for us.

Walking up to her, Mrs. Olney told her, "Okay, we are ready

to show Chris her room. Afterwards I would like to have the written rules of the house so she will know what is expected of her."

"Yes, that will be no problem. It is important that my girls adhere to the rules. I try my best to keep things nice for them." I noticed her voice had softened.

It made me feel better because I felt that Mrs. Olney had control of the situation. Before, Ms. Barness had an air about her that made me feel uncomfortable.

As we walked up the stairs, I looked back at the front door. I wondered if it was locked from the outside. *If I wanted to, could I leave? Maybe one night I will test it to make sure.*

When we got to the top of the stairway, Ms. Barness explained where the laundry room was and the bathroom. The rules were posted for everyone to follow.

Standing at the entrance of the bedroom, she told me that I was sharing the room with another girl by the name of Kathy. The room was neat and clean. My bed had a plain light gray bedspread on it which was tucked under the pillow and did not have a wrinkle on it.

Stepping aside, leaving space for us to enter, she said in a firm voice, "See how this room looks. It is neat and clean. That is the way I expect you girls to keep it! Put all your things where they belong. The beds are to be made each morning before you leave for the day. There are to be no visitors in the bedrooms. The visitors are to remain in the living room at all times. If you go by the rules of the house there will be no problems." The way she spoke her words, I knew she had said them many times and enjoyed it.

When she finished her ritual, with her chin up, she walked to my bed. She removed the pillow and began to turn down the bedspread, laying it in neat folds, about a foot wide, until the last fold sat at the foot of the bed.

Finished, she stood up and faced me. "See how I folded the

bedspread? Before you retire for the night I want you to do as I did. Please do not sit on the bed before first folding down the spread. This is how we keep things nice for those who will follow, after you leave."

Then she went to the dresser. She opened the top drawer, "This is where you will keep your clothes. Please keep your things off the floor and if you have things to set on top of it, keep it neat and dusted." Turning around, she asked, "Are there any questions?"

Mrs. Olney and I stood there watching her go through the ritual. She had to ask twice before we realized she was asking a question.

"Oh, no, there are no problems with the rules. I'm sure Chris will be able to follow them without any problems."

"I'll get a copy of the rules for the both of you," she said as we left the room.

With the rules in our hands, I followed Mrs. Olney to the car. "I will pick you up in the morning at 7:30 for your first day of school," she said with a smile. She took my suitcase and sack out of the trunk "Chris, I'm so happy for you! Please don't worry."

It made me feel good to know she was coming back. "Before you leave, can I ask you a question that worries me?"

"Now now, what is it that worries you?" She asked in a teasing way.

Looking back at the house, "Does that door lock from the outside?"

The question made her laugh, "Heavens no. It just locks from the inside to keep people out. It is against the law to lock the door from the outside, in case of fire." Putting the car in gear, "Okay, I will see you in the morning."

Fire?

I felt sad and alone as she drove away. It was late in the afternoon and I wondered what I would do to pass the time. I walked up to the door and wondered if it was locked. When I turned the knob, it opened. When I stepped in and looked around, the house seemed big and hollow and I didn't know where Ms. Barness went. My footsteps echoed throughout the room. The stairs squeaked with every step as I made my way up to my room.

I sat my suitcase and sack by the dresser. I opened the second drawer and started to put my things in: Two white uniforms, two pairs of nylons, one garter belt, two panties, two bras, and two white underslips. In the top drawer, I put in my toothbrush, comb, hairbrush, and two bath towels with matching washcloths. When I closed the drawers, they sounded empty.

I went to the small closet to hang my blue dress. It was filled with Kathy's clothes. To make room, I pushed them aside and hung my dress. When I let go, her clothes flipped back swallowing up my only dress. On the floor, I sat the white shoes along side of Kathy's pretty shoes of many colors and styles. Closing the door, I thought, *gee, I never knew one person could have so many clothes and shoes, she must be rich.*

Standing back, I looked at the two dressers. Kathy had several pictures of her family and pretty bottles of perfume. Looking at mine, *all I have to do is dust it, I guess.*

Later in the day, I heard the front door open. The person ran up the stairs and in came a tall, slender girl. "Hi. You must be my new roommate. My name's Kathy. What's yours?"

Standing there, not knowing what to do with myself, "My name is Chris."

She was so pretty. She had shoulder length dark brown hair that had soft curls that bounced as she pranced around in the room, changing her clothes. Her skin looked so pale and smooth. It made me feel dark and drab. I wished I had on my blue dress.

The black t-shirt and gray checked skirt I wore came from the church rummage sale some years ago. It was hard telling how old they were. The skirt cost 15 cents and the t-shirt was 10 cents. I felt awful! I wanted to crawl under the bed but she didn't seem to notice what I was wearing.

I don't know how long I sat there in awe, watching her. Then she turned to me and said, "Well, it's time to go down to supper. Remember, we can't be late. Ms. Barness gets so upset. Come on, let's go," as she headed for the door.

I was glad she was there or I would have missed supper. I remembered I was told not to be late unless I gave notice. I hurried down the stairs behind her.

When we got to the dining room Ms. Barness stood at the head of the long table. There were six places at the table. Kathy went to the empty chair on the other side of the table. It left one across from her. I figured it was for me so I took my place behind it.

Ms. Barness gave us a stern look. Then she put her hands together, closed her eyes and said grace. When she finished, she sat down. This gave all the girls permission to sit down. We waited as she served herself and passed the food down the line.

When we began to eat, Ms. Barness spoke to the girls, "I would like you to meet our new tenant, Chris. She will be sharing a room with Kathy." She asked the girls to give their names.

Then she gave me some instructions. "Chris, every evening we have a dinner, except on weekends. I would like for you to be properly dressed and it is important that you be on time. The dinner is formal and using the right utensils goes along with it. In other words, do not eat your peas with a spoon. If you are not sure what to use, follow my example.

"You can have seconds on everything except coffee, tea and milk. I would like to add, do not take more food then you can eat. And, please do not leave the table until everyone is through with their meal. That will be all for now."

From the side, I watched everything she did. When she picked up her fork I picked up mine. Whatever she stuck it into, I done the same. I was so nervous, I didn't taste a thing! Everyone ate without saying a word.

When Ms. Barness was through eating, she stood up and pushed her chair back to the table. All the girls did the same. Still standing behind her chair, she put her hands together, closed her eyes and gave the prayer. Then we were excused.

Man, I was so glad when the meal was over I felt like throwing up! I ate too much because I took a bite every time Ms. Barness took one. I'm sure I staggered up the stairs to my room.

Not having anything else to do, I carefully folded down the bedspread. Thinking the day would never end, I laid my poor, tired body down. I couldn't wait until Kathy put the lights out.

I thought back to that morning when I left the hospital. It seemed so long ago. I missed my room, I missed the nurses, I missed the smell, the sounds of the hospital. I missed the protection I felt there. I didn't like this new world I was in.

I thought of tomorrow. *How can I face those strange new people? How will I find my way back here? How will I wake up in time for breakfast? Will Kathy be there so I can follow what she does? If I can just get through one more meal, maybe I will be able to do the right thing after that.* Drifting off to sleep, my last thought, *just one more meal...*

I'm sure I was the first one to wake up that morning. Everything was real quiet on the second floor. Downstairs I could hear doors open and close and noise from pots and pans. I figured the cook was getting breakfast ready.

Laying there I thought about the hospital. It made me feel lonesome. I didn't have to worry about tomorrow and meeting new people. I wished I could have just went home to Mama and Daddy. Thinking about it made my stomach turn over. It would be alright if it was just Mrs. Olney and Mr. Abey.

I wondered what time it was. Laying there with the blanket up to my chin, I looked around the room wondering if Kathy had a clock. I looked at the top of her dresser with all the things on it and saw a little clock. It was ten minutes to six. I wondered what time she usually got up. Ten minutes took forever to pass, then it rang.

Kathy sprang out of bed, looking over at me she said, "You

better get up now if you want to shower before the others get there. Hurry, get in line behind me." She grabbed her robe and ran out the door.

I didn't have a robe so I grabbed my uniform and underclothes and ran down the hall as Kathy was closing the door. I got there just as another girl came out of her room. Now she had to wait for me to take my shower.

That was my first lesson. Run like hell and get ahead of the next man. Don't be nice. No one cares if you are late. It's all about me and the hell with you!

Wow! That was not the way I was raised. When we had company, they were served first and we ate whatever was left. And the elders always came first in everything. However, Mama always waited until everyone was fed before she ate. Now, I was in a new world and I had better learn fast or be left out.

After I took my shower, I realized I forgot my towel to dry off. Man! I looked around and decided to use my nightgown. When I got back to the room Kathy was already dressed and putting on her makeup.

"You better hurry up or we'll be late for breakfast," she said while she looked in a small mirror and put on her lipstick.

Since I didn't wear makeup, I dressed and ran a comb through my hair. By this time, Kathy was going out the door. I was at her heels by the time she got to the bottom of the stairs. I was so close to her, I hoped she wouldn't stop too quick. Instead of going to the dining room, she went to the living room.

"Breakfast isn't ready yet. We can wait here, we don't want to upset Ms. Barness," she said with a smile.

As we sat and waited, she told me she worked as a secretary and took ballet lessons. I never heard of ballet lessons and felt stupid to ask. I just let it go by, smiled and said, "That's nice."

Then she asked, "Where do you work?"

I had to think awhile before I answered, "I'm starting school to be a beautician. Today is my first day and my friend, Mrs.

Olney, will be picking me up at 7:30." I held my breath, hoping she wouldn't ask me where I came from.

While we talked, I could hear the girls running back and forth upstairs. I don't know how they done it but by 7:00 they were all standing behind their chairs!

Like the night before, Ms. Barness stood behind her chair with her hands together, she looked around at us girls, making sure everyone was ready, then bowed her head. Everyone done the same. However, with my head bowed, I looked sideways at her and the others. When she said, "Amen", I quickly closed my eyes and slowly raised my head before opening my eyes, as I knew everyone else would do.

The prayer she said before and after the meal was different from what I was used to. And, she didn't make the Sign of The Cross. "Amen" was my cue.

After we were excused, I stood at the living room window and waited for Mrs. Olney. I watched the girls leave one at a time. Some took the city bus and others had cars. Not sure of myself, I planned to ask Mrs. Olney again to explain to me where the bus stopped for me, coming and going.

It made me happy when she pulled up in front of the house. When I got in the car, she was excited about school and could hardly wait to sign me in. It may have excited her but it scared me.

When we pulled away from the house I asked her, "Could you drive on the streets that the bus will take so I will know if I'm going the right way? And, show me where the bus will stop when I get off."

She was quick to answer that she had the bus schedule. "I have it marked. It will show you where and when the bus will stop. The bus will come by every 15 minutes during the time you will need it." She smiled and added, "Soon you will be an old hand at it."

"Mrs. Olney, I need a robe. Maybe we can go to a rummage sale and get me one. What do you think?"

She laughed and said, "Mr. Abey gave me permission to get

the things you will need. We can go shopping after school. Don't worry, as time goes by there are other things you will need and we can get them for you."

"It worries me. Who will pay for them? It makes me feel bad."

"I can understand how you feel but Rehab allows so much for each student while they are in school. You will receive $165.00 per month that will pay your rent, bus fare and lunches. However, you will be getting more in the first month to get you started."

Feeling like a beggar, "All this money that is being spent on me makes me feel awful."

"All you have to do is go to school and finish the course. When you graduate and go to work, there will be taxes you will have to pay. Those taxes will start paying back the money.

"Like I said, the Rehabilitation Program is meant to rehabilitate people like you. You have been sick and now you need schooling which will prepare you so you can support yourself. You will not get very much money each month so you will have to stretch every dollar. Your check will come each month on the same day. And, a warning, the first thing you must do is pay your rent. That means you will have a place to stay. Now don't forget!"

By this time, we were going down Riverside Ave. She pointed to the Zukor Building, "That's where we want. The school is on the fourth floor. I know things look different from this direction. The bus you will take back to the house is across the street."

After she found a parking place on the side of the street we headed for the school. When we got to the elevator, the lady in the cage waited while people wedged themselves in beside us. When it was full, the lady shifted the gears, the elevator jerked a few times and started to go up. By the time we got to the fourth floor, I began to get nervous.

May 1954 – First Day at Edgecliff Sanatorium
Standing inside, I heard the door click shut behind me. I looked around. The reception area was small and looked more like

a living room compared to Cushman Hospital. A nurse was sitting behind a desk in a small sectioned off room at the far end.

"May I help you, Miss? Are you looking for someone?"

I had to think for a moment, not knowing what to say, "Oh, is this the Edgecliff Hospital?"

Getting up, she came to the window. "Yes, it is. Is there someone you want to see?"

"No. I'm sick and I need to be in a hospital. I heard about this hospital and my daddy brought me here and left." Suddenly, fear gripped me. What if she turns me away? A lump began to grow in my throat, "Please, my mama is sick and I have to hurry and get well so I can go home."

Realizing I was about to cry, she quickly came out of the room and took me by the hand, steering me to a chair in the reception area. "My name is Ann. Would you like to have some tea?" she asked, trying to make me feel better.

Looking up at her through my tears, I nodded. Handing me a tissue, she hurried down the hall.

When she came back she had a cup of tea and some cookies. "Here, drink this and tell me about what brought you here."

The doors going into the school were open. The waiting room was empty as the client appointments didn't start until 9:00. Mrs. Olney and I went straight to Mrs. Cady's office. When we walked in she was sitting behind her desk. She quickly stood up.

"Chris, I'm glad to see you. I was told you got sick. I hope you feel better now. Please, if you have any problems with your health let me know."

Mrs. Cady looked to be about 35 years old. She was really pretty and slender. She wore a white uniform and shoes. In a small pocket on the left side of her uniform, near the collar, was a perfectly folded handkerchief that served as a brooch. Her hair was dark brown with a white streak on the left side of the bang area and was swept over to the right, forming a soft wave which blended into the dark hair. She wore black rimmed glasses. Her hair, uniform and make-up looked perfect.

There were class pictures of the students on the wall. It was clear to me because they had the white uniforms on. Her desk had a glass that completely covered the top. Under the glass were pictures of several students. Thinking to myself, *one day my picture will be under that glass.*

Mrs. Olney informed her that I had a few worries and to be patient with me. Smiling at me, Mrs. Cady said, "Chris, if there is anything that worries you just come to my office and I will explain whatever it is." Then she went on to say, "I had a long talk with Mr. Abey about your case and I understand why it will be different for you here. He informed me that you will go to school just four hours a day, from 8 to 12. If there is anything you need for school, let me know and I will call him. You let me worry about that part of it."

Looking down at the papers on her desk, she read the school rules to me then she picked up a small school kit. She opened it up and took out the items that were in it - two hair brushes, four black combs, four rattail combs, one shampoo cape and a box of black bobby pins. Then she handed me the cosmetology book. "You will need this to get started. We may have to get more things as time goes by." Looking over at Mrs. Olney, "She will need a three-ringed notebook, paper and pencils."

Standing up, Mrs. Cady asked, "Are there any other questions? I would like to introduce Chris before theory class starts."

Mrs. Olney reminded me that she was going to pick me up after school. Feeling proud and happy to see me start school, she left and Mrs. Cady took me to meet the class. Following her, I felt like my shoes were filled with lead.

Meeting the students was the last thing I wanted to do. It's hard to explain how it made me feel. Bashful is a nice cute word and it does not come close to the feeling I had that gripped me at the pit of my stomach. If someone looked at me I wanted to sink into the floor. I felt ugly and dumb. All I wanted to do was close the door to the world.

When we entered the classroom, everyone turned and looked at me. Mrs. Cady put her arm around my shoulders and introduced me. "I want you to meet Christine McDougal. She will be joining us starting today. I am sure you will make her welcome."

The students sat facing each other at the long table. Others sat on the couch and chairs. Mrs. Cady began to give their names. At the end of the table sat Nelly, one of the instructors. Giving me the once-over, the class said "Hi" at the same time. Losing my voice, I smiled.

After class I stood around watching the students cut hair, wrap permanent waves, set and comb-out hairstyles. I watched Nelly give instructions to students on hair tinting. I watched other students give manicures. It was all so interesting. I was fascinated! I thought, *I can do that... yeah, I can do that!*

The morning just flew by before I knew it, Mrs. Olney came to pick me up right at noon. I didn't want to leave.

"Now now Chris, remember, the doctor wants you to be at school for only four hours a day," she cautioned. "This is only your second day out of the hospital and your health is very important."

When we got in the car she asked me how I liked school. I was so excited. "Mrs. Olney, I just love it! I wanted to do some work myself but all I done was watch the other students. Mrs. Cady said I could start tomorrow. Oh, I can hardly wait, but she has to show me how first."

While we had lunch, she listened to me chatter about all that I saw that morning. When we shopped for the things I needed, I followed behind her and went on talking about the school.

When she dropped me off at the Isabella Club, she said, "I know you will be good at whatever you do and I know you will make me proud."

When I got to my room I folded down the bedspread and laid

down. I stared at the ceiling, not seeing it. With a smile, I lived through the whole morning in my mind. When I got through, I started over again. I pictured myself doing the work.

That evening at supper time, I no longer suffered the small stuff. I went through it without a problem. I just wanted to get it over with so I could go back to my bedroom and dream again. I couldn't wait until tomorrow!

After the "Amen", I hurried upstairs. I pulled off the tags from the things that we bought and put them in my drawer. I laid out everything I would need for morning, crawled into bed, found the place on the ceiling and went into my dream world.

I was the first to take my shower, dress and sat in the living room to wait for breakfast. I still needed to follow Kathy's lead during the meal. I didn't want to make Ms. Barness mad. I noticed she looked at me and at my plate several times during the meal. I didn't ask for seconds nor did I want to. However, I stretched out the meal to get through when the rest of the girls were finishing.

Going out the door to make sure, I asked Kathy where the bus stopped to take me downtown to Riverside. She pointed to a small sign that read, "BUS" and waved goodbye. Making sure I had the 10 cents in hand, I waited.

By the time the bus came, several people waited with me. Taking a seat near the front, I watched the buildings go by making sure I was going the right way. I noticed people would pull a lever and the bus would stop for them to get off. Still worried I might miss where I had to get off, I kept close watch. Then as I recognized the buildings on Riverside, my heart beat slowed down. I noticed people would go to the front of the bus and hold on to the pole before it stopped.

Looking up the street I saw the Zukor Building. I quickly went to the front of the bus and hung onto the pole. When the bus stopped, it made me smile only to find out it was the wrong stop. I felt foolish so I pretended like it was the right stop and got off the bus.

Afraid I would be late for school I ran up the street, crossing the intersections at full speed. A car tooted its horn and a man hollered at me, "Hey lady, do you want to get killed?" I kept running.

When I got to the entrance of the Zukor Building I looked back and realized I ran through a red light because the people were waiting for it to change. As I waited for the elevator, I thought, *Man, I've got to check this town out. It's kinda dangerous.*

Getting there early, I found a place back in the corner, pulled up a chair and watched as the students slowly drifted in. When the theory class started, it sounded like they were talking Greek.

It was when the second half of the class started that Mrs. Cady used one of the students, Sylvia, as her model. She took her to the shampoo bowl and demonstrated giving a shampoo, my interest kicked into high gear.

After giving the shampoo, she took her back to the classroom and began to comb her hair. I watched as she parted the hair and began to fingerwave. When she got half of the head waved, she began to lay pincurls into the second half. Then she put Sylvia under the hair dryer. An hour later she combed the style out. It was beautiful! I couldn't wait until I could do that!

But, I was disappointed. All Mrs. Cady had me do for the rest of the morning was shampoo customers for the students. Then, I would watch as they set the hair and combed them out.

The morning went by before I knew it. Mrs. Cady came and told me it was time for me to go home. I felt like I didn't do anything and now I had to leave. She saw my disappointment and asked me to come to her office.

Reaching in her desk drawer she took out a text book. Leafing through it she came to the chapter they were on that morning.

"I want you to read the chapter when you get home. It will get you caught up with the rest of the class. There will be a test on this subject next Friday."

She went on to explain that a test was given at the end of each chapter and how important it was because at the end of the full course I would be given a written and practical exam by the State Board. In order to receive a license to work, I had to pass both the written and the practical exam.

Boy, suddenly I felt sick. I looked at the thick book she held and wondered how I could learn all that! Sitting up straight in the chair, I asked, "How long do I have to learn all this?"

"Well, it usually takes a year, depending on how many hours a student attends class. Every day or hour a student misses class must be made up. In your case, since the doctor will only let you go to school 4 hours a day, it will take you twice as long. Don't get disappointed when students that start now graduate before you."

It took a little while for all she said to come together in my mind. Two years is a long time, my mind drifted back to the hospital, at least I know there is an end to it. I must remember, take it one day at a time and live it. I thought of those customers out there... *yeah, I can do it!*

Mrs. Cady broke into my thoughts, "Chris, are there any questions?"

Getting up to leave, "Yeah, could you show me where to catch the bus back to the apartment?"

Standing at the bus stop, I thought of all that took place since I left the hospital. *Man, it seems like months ago and I've only been in school two days, I mean, half days. I have so much to remember- the bus stops, reading the chapter in my book, fixing my bed cover, getting to the meal on time.* Thinking it over, the one thing that bothered me the most, *when do I use my spoon and when do I use the fork or the knife?*

When I got back to my room I felt tired. I folded down the bedspread, laid down and fell asleep. It wasn't until Kathy got back that I woke up. I guess the doctor was right about going to school for only four hours.

By the third day a pattern was set. I had to get up early, take my shower, wait for breakfast, keep my eye on Ms. Barness, wait for the "Amen", catch the bus, get off the bus at the right stop, go to the classroom, take my place in the corner and keep my eye on the book hoping no one would look at me.

The worst times were the breaks. I would go to the hair cutting room, if someone came in I would leave. Then, I would go to the tint room. If someone came in, again I would leave. I tried to find a place where there wouldn't be any students. The only time I felt better was when I had something to do. It kept my mind on what I was doing and I didn't have to worry if someone was looking at me. I tried hard to be invisible.

The third day in class, Mrs. Cady did a demonstration on Sylvia. She went through the hairstyle, the parting of the hair, fingerwaving and placing the pincurls to finish the style. She dried her hair and combed it out. I watched everything she did. It seemed like magic. I was in love with the art of hair!

As Sylvia stood and turned around, showing off the hairstyle, Mrs. Cady asked, "Now, who would like to repeat this hairstyle on Sylvia?"

There was silence in the room. Then someone said, "Have the new girl do it."

All eyes turned and looked at me! I could have sunk into the floor. It felt like my blood was draining down to my shoes. Sweat seemed to push out of my skin!

Mrs. Cady turned to me and said, "Okay, Chris, give it a try," handing me the comb.

I stood there dumbfounded. One of the students took Sylvia to the shampoo bowl and shampooed out the style. By this time, I pulled myself together and my breathing became regular.

When Sylvia sat down, my hands shook. I began to comb her hair. I parted her hair as I saw Mrs. Cady do. Then I began to put in the fingerwaves... the pincurls...

Students that were not working on clients stood around me

and watched my every move. As I worked, students asked, "Have you done this before?" ... "Where did you go to school?"

My answer, "No, I watched what Mrs. Cady done."

When I was through setting the hair, one of the students put her under the hair dryer. While she was drying, some students sat back and looked at me. Others questioned me, "You haven't done hair before?" ... "Are you sure you didn't go to school before?"

I was real uncomfortable with all the attention on me. The hour Sylvia sat under the dryer seemed like it would never end. Finally, she walked in and sat down to be combed out. It didn't take long before the students crowded around me.

I took the hair brush and began to brush out the set. I took the comb and put the waves back in. Then I arranged the pincurls into the fluff around her head. It amazed me how everything went into place! I couldn't believe I did it.

The students watching couldn't believe it either. One of the students went to Mrs. Cady's office and asked her to come and see what I did.

When she came in and looked at the style, she said, "Chris, you did a beautiful job!" She was so pleased she asked Sylvia to go with her. Several students followed them out the door. They left me wondering where they were going. She wanted to show off the style at the professional beauty salon down the hall, on the same floor.

When they came back Mrs. Cady told me, "Chris, Mr. Denny told me you had a job when you graduate. He was really impressed. He couldn't believe it was your third day in school and your first hairstyle."

That night, I laid in bed and went over and over the style. I couldn't get it out of my head. I wanted to go back to school and do it again! I didn't want school to ever end.

As the days went by, I began to add more and more hours to my day. Mrs. Cady would come to me and say. "Chris, the four hours are up. You have to go home now."

I would answer, "I'll go in just a minute, I have to finish what I'm doing."

It may be a manicure, a hairstyle, a permanent wave. Since students worked together on a client, I couldn't leave at just any time. I just had to finish the job.

When I would leave, I had to write down the hours I spent in school. They soon worked into full days. I think Mrs. Cady gave up on trying to make me leave school. However, at the end of the day, I would crawl into bed thinking I would die during the night, I was so tired. Yet, when morning came I couldn't wait to get back to school. My love for working with hair and the clients was growing!

The first month, I ran out of the extra money and didn't have any for lunch. Hungry, I would look at the clock and see how many hours I had to wait until supper time. It was a long stretch! Customers usually tipped 5 or 10 cents or nothing at all. When I ended up with 10 cents and didn't have another customer, I would buy a bottle of Coke from the machine. That soon came to an end. With an empty stomach, the Coke gave me such a bellyache I had to quit.

So instead, I would pretend like I was going to lunch and I would walk around the block. When I got back to the school, all that was missing was a toothpick between my teeth. I knew if Mrs. Cady found out, she would tell Mr. Abey. I didn't want him to think I couldn't handle my money

Try, as I could, there was no way I could make the $165.00 stretch the whole month after paying my rent. Something had to go. So, I decided to walk to school and save the 10 cents for lunch. Even that wasn't enough so I walked to school AND went without lunch. Boy, I could hardly wait until supper time and the "Amen" so I could eat and didn't mind asking for seconds.

Then one evening, after starving all day, I had an idea. At the evening meal, when someone asked for the bread the second time around, I held onto mine. When supper was over and we stood up for the prayer, I waited until everyone closed their eyes then I quickly stuffed the bun in the top of my uniform. It would make its way down to my waist. The uniform bloused out at the waist band so it couldn't be seen or fall out.

On my way to school I took it out and put it in my purse. At lunch time, I took a walk around the block. When I took the bun out of my purse it was hard and dry. I just chewed it longer, savoring every bite. In my pocket was 15 cents, I checked it to make sure it was still there. Tomorrow Mrs. Jones was coming in. She always wanted me to do her hair. When I would finish, smiling, she would hand me 10 cents. Yes, tomorrow I would have a hotdog at Newberry's for 21 cents and save the 4 cents for another day!

As time flew by, school became an obsession. Every pincurl, permanent wave wrap and shampoo had to be done perfect for me. However, when students worked on the customers, one would give the shampoo, another would set the style and still another would do the comb-out. That did not sit well with me.

When I set the customer's hair, I could feel that it was not shampooed good enough. Then, I would get upset when another student combed out my style. When I wrapped a permanent wave with help, I constantly checked the other side to make sure the wraps were done well. It drove me crazy! It was time to take the problem to the boss.

I went to Mrs. Cady's office and tapped on the door which was open. Looking at me from behind the desk, she saw that I was a bit upset. "Come in. My my, you look worried. What is the matter, maybe I can help?"

Sitting up straight in the chair and swallowing the lump in my throat, "Mrs. Cady, I have this big problem. When I work on a customer, I want to do it all, from shampoo, setting her hair and to the comb-out. When I do a permanent wave, I want to do all the work myself. The students all work different and I think they should do their own customer. If they want to share with someone, that's fine but I don't like it." It was a mouth full but I got it all out.

Mrs. Cady leaned back in her chair and laughed. "Chris, you sure know what you want and know how to tell it!"

"I'm sorry Mrs. Cady, but I get too upset and I worry every day about it."

"Okay, I will see what I can do. I know how you feel and don't want you worrying about it anymore."

After that conversation, all went well. When I was given a customer, no one was assigned to help me. However, I was slow. It seemed like one appointment lasted hours. After all, each pincurl had to be perfect! Each permanent wave wrap had to be checked and rechecked. The rods had to be in a perfect line and straight. Yet, the time didn't bother me, I was too busy concentrating on my work.

My days at school got longer and longer. There were times I was the last one to leave. The lady in the cage would say, "Well, I see we're late again."

On those days, I barely made it in time to sit down for the evening supper. Ms. Barness would glare at me, close her eyes with her hands together and wait for awhile before saying the prayer. She was trying to send me a message. I was too tired to care. I couldn't wait until the "Amen" so I could go upstairs and lay down.

My obsession with my work and going without lunch, which was most of the time, began to wear on me.

This one evening after taking the last ride of the day with the lady in the cage, I waited for the bus. Checking in my pockets I found that I didn't have the 10 cents to ride the bus back to the house and no way to make a phone call. I knew I was in trouble. I took a deep breath and started to walk back.

After the long walk in the heat of the evening, I was thirsty and hungry. When I walked in, everyone was eating. I hurried to my place, bowed my head, said the prayer and sat down. I avoided looking at Ms. Barness.

The dishes of food were passed to me, I took large amounts and ended up asking for seconds of milk. Every now and then, I noticed the girls would look at me and quickly look down at their plates. Hungry as I was, I used my spoon to eat the peas. I didn't want to waste my time chasing them around in my dish with a fork.

Before I could eat all the food on my dish, I began to feel sick. My stomach was not used to the weight of it. Feeling like I would barf, I backed up my chair and stood up, said the prayer, excused myself and went to my room. All the while, the girls just looked at me, knowing the rule. I really didn't care. I would play the game another time but tonight I had to lay down.

Going up the stairs took all my strength. When I got to my bed, I just fell on it and threw the bedspread over me. I was so tired I couldn't think or sleep. After I laid there about an hour, I heard footsteps coming to the door. When the door opened, Ms. Barness walked in and came straight to my bed. She was fuming!

With her hands on her hips, "How dare you come home and interrupt dinner like you did. How dare you eat like a pig and not follow the rules of the house! Then, asking for seconds on servings such as milk and leaving food on your dish! And eating your peas with a spoon like some low life that doesn't know any better!"

Laying there, tired to the bone, I just listened.

"Get up and look at me when I'm talking to you! Get up!" Then she noticed I was laying with the bedspread over me. "Get up this very second! How dare you use that bedspread like that. I gave you strict rules of how to fold it down before sitting on it. I'm ordering you to get up. Now!"

I had heard enough. I slowly sat up and looked at her. "Ms. Barness, I'm tired and I'm not in the mood to play games. Please. I'll do better tomorrow."

Raising her voice, she said, "I'm just trying to take the place of your mother and I will not tolerate you breaking the rules! Now, get up off that bed and do as you were told!"

When I heard, "I'm trying to take the place of your mother..." Suddenly, I was angry!

I slowly stood up. She was standing close to my bed and we were face to face. She began to back up. As she backed up, I walked forward, "How dare you even try to take the place of my mother! Don't you ever say that to me again. You will never, never take the place of my mother! And I'm sick of your little rules. My room and meals are paid for and it does not include mothering me or teaching me how to eat with the right tool."

By this time, we're getting close to the door. Her eyes are big and I see fear in them. "You call me low life? If it means not being phony like you, then that's what I am! Now get the hell out of my room!" As she backed out of the room I slammed the door in her face.

Walking back to my bed I heard her running down the stairs. I yanked the bed spread off the bed, laid down and went to sleep.

I woke to a soft knock on the door. I waited for awhile, thinking I was dreaming. The knock came again. I bristled, ready for a fight. I went to the door and waited for another knock.

"Chris, this is Mr. Abey. May I come in?"

Ms. Barness didn't take long to call him and she was nowhere to be seen.

Feeling a bit rested, I opened the door and asked Mr. Abey to come in. "Well that didn't take long. Please sit down." I closed the door and moved the chair close to my bed.

He sat on the chair and had this little grin, "Now tell me, what is this all about? She told me you threw her out of the room. Was it all that bad?"

I told him all about the rules and I was too tired to play the games. There were times, which was most of the time, I was not in the mood. I just wanted to eat and go to bed.

"I talked to Mrs. Cady just before I came and she told me you are working long hours and long after the school is closed." This time he wasn't smiling.

"Mr. Abey, it's hard to leave when you are in the middle of an appointment. If I'm combing the customer's hair, I have to finish it and it seems like everyone has left by then."

He was really concerned, "You know Chris, if you keep this up, you may end up back in the hospital. Now, I'm sure you wouldn't like that."

The hospital didn't cross my mind. It was something I had filed away. It was another life of someone I knew in the past. I looked down at my hands and thought for a moment. *Gosh, it seems so long ago. But, here I am. and I must keep well.*

I looked up at Mr. Abey. "Yes, I understand. I will try to do better. I promise." Yet wondering if I really could.

The smile was back. "I'll tell you what, I want you to take two weeks off and go home. I know you worry about your father and mother. You need the rest and it would make you and your parents very happy." Getting up from the chair, "Now, you go back to bed and rest. I will inform Ms. Barness and Mrs. Cady. I will see you when you get back. Have a good visit."

I was shocked! I never dreamed I would be able to go home. I fell into bed and cried!

That night I thought about going home. *Mama and Daddy will be surprised that I am well and going to school. Now the question, how will I find my way home? There has to be a way.*

Waking up in the morning, I looked at the ceiling with a smile, *thank you dear Lord. You planned it this way and thank you Mr. Abey, I'm going home! How long has it been? A year and a half? I'm not sure. I wonder how Mama and Daddy are getting along. They think I'm still in the hospital. Everything, getting set up in school, the apartment, learning how to live in the outside world, made time go by fast.*

I sort of felt guilty for not going home right away. But, with the persistence of Mrs. Olney to get me set up for school, she gave me no choice. Maybe she felt that if I went home I would not return. She might have been right. But, I couldn't worry about that, I had to find a way to get home.

At the breakfast, there were strained looks on the faces around the table. Ms. Barness kept her eyes on her plate. The silence in the room spoke loud. Just the clink of the utensils broke in now and then. I knew everyone had heard or wondered what happened. I held my head up and followed the rules like a good girl. After all, I was going home!

Knowing I had a long way to go, during breakfast I stuffed two rolls in my blouse. When we were excused, I informed Ms. Barness that I would be going home for the next two weeks. I almost heard her sigh with relief.

I wasn't sure how long it would take to get home or when I would get back. It all depended on getting a ride. But I didn't tell her that, it would be wasting my time. She wouldn't understand what it's like to be a low life.

Early that afternoon, I walked downtown on the same route the bus took so I wouldn't get lost. When I got to the corner by the school, I stood there wondering what to do. *Where do I go from here?* Then an idea came to me. *I'll wait until someone comes by that looks like an Indian and I'll ask them where I could find a ride to the Colville Indian Reservation.* After waiting for a half hour or so, no one came by that looked like an Indian. I began to feel stupid standing there.

Man, I had to do something, this was getting me nowhere. *Maybe I should ask a man.* I waited for the right one, he had to look like an ordinary man, no suit and tie, maybe like someone from the country.

Finally, a guy came up the street and waited for the light to change before crossing the street. Getting up enough nerve, I walked up to him. "Mister, could you tell me where I could find someone from the reservation?" I asked in a weak voice.

Looking at me with a smirk, "You mean an Indian?"

I nodded.

Pointing down the street, the direction he was facing, "Go down to the next street. That's Main Street. Then take a right and keep going. There's two taverns across from each other, it's called Indian Crossing, that's where they hang out."

The light changed and, laughing, he crossed the street. I stood there and wondered why he laughed like that. It gave me an ill feeling in the pit of my stomach.

Trying to shake the feeling, I crossed at the next light change. Following his directions, I came to the two taverns. It didn't take long before I knew I was in Indian country. I stood on the street and watched as Indian people walked back and forth. I wondered where they all went, now I knew.

I worked at getting up enough nerve again to walk into the tavern. Knowing I had to, I went in. Everyone in the tavern was happy. They were talking, laughing and hugging each other.

Two guys near the door looked at me, one of them said, "Hey, what do we have here? Hey, sweetheart, come here and have a drink with me. Man, you sure are pretty, you can have anything you want."

The other guy pushed him on the shoulder and said, "Hey man, she don't want anything to do with you, you're too ugly. Come honey, sit with me."

Ignoring them, I went and wedged myself between two guys sitting at the bar. With all the noise going on, I waited for the bartender to get within earshot and asked him, "Is there anyone here that will be going to Keller or Republic today? I need a ride."

He couldn't hear me and asked me to repeat. Shouting, I asked him again. "Hey... quiet!" he shouted, as he pounded the bar with his fist. The noise quieted down and everyone looked towards the bar. "This little lady would like a ride to Keller or Republic. Anyone going in that direction today?" Then all the eyes turned to me.

Some guy staggered up to me and said, as he leaned against me, "Little lady, I'll take you anywhere you want to go." He wasn't getting fresh, he just needed a little support for the moment.

Someone by the name of Jim, who was sitting with a lady in a booth, said they were going in that direction in about an hour and would be glad to give me a ride. He motioned for me to join them while I waited. They were really nice and made me feel comfortable. They asked if I would like to have a beer. I refused and waited until they were ready to go. When I told them who I was, they were surprised. They thought I had died. They knew Ernie and Manny.

Looking around the tavern and seeing all the Indians, I noticed there were a few white people too. Somehow, I felt safe and I knew I would always have a way home.

I told them my mother was sick and I hadn't seen them for a year and a half. I was anxious to go home. Jim said not to worry, "We'll take you all the way home."

The tavern was smoky and dark, I was glad to leave.

On the way, Jim talked about Manny and Ernie and how much fun they had partying and hunting. They took me right to the turn off at 13 Mile. They wanted to take me to the house but I told them I wanted to walk in. I thanked them and Jim told me any time I needed a ride, I was welcome.

I stood on the highway and watched as they drove up to the little campground and turned around. I waved as they passed by me, thinking they were such kind people. I had met friends. As they went out of sight, I turned and walked down the road to the house.

The setting sun shined bright and there wasn't a cloud in the sky. My shadow went ahead of me as if to show me the way. The old dirt road hadn't changed. The big boulders stuck out of the road and I could see dark areas where Daddy filled the holes with dirt when it had been washed away from the winter thaw. The road didn't look like it had been used very much. I even wondered if any one was home.

When the little log house came into view, I didn't see any

smoke coming out of the chimney. *Maybe, they ate already.* As I approached the house, I noticed it looked smaller due to the brush growing up around it. A feeling of loneliness crept over me. My heart ached. *Why did I wait so long to come home? Now, will I have the heart to leave again?* When I got to the cabin, I stopped and listened. There wasn't any sound. *Where are they? Am I too late?* I couldn't imagine where they would go.

Slowly, I walked around to the front of the house. The door stood open. I was afraid to go in. I stood there for awhile but there wasn't a sound. Then I called out, "Mama... Daddy. Is anybody home?"

I heard a noise, someone putting their foot down hard on the floor. "Hey, come in." The voice sounded different but it was Daddy! I must have sounded different to him also because he didn't call my name.

When I walked in, he was sitting in a chair by the kitchen table. He looked like he had been sleeping. "Tissie, am I glad to see you!" as he eased himself from the chair.

I ran up and hugged him. "Oh, Daddy I missed you so much. How are you and Mama? I worried about you guys. Where is Mama?"

"Your mama isn't doing so good. Go in there and see her. She's been talking about you and wondering if you would ever get well. Hurry, go see her."

The little house was so hot inside and everything looked dark. Daddy had hung a blanket over the window to keep it cool.

When I walked in, the scene tore at my heart. Mama sat on the bed with her arms wrapped around her knees, holding them tight to her chest. Her head rested on her knees and she rocked back and forth, moaning. She didn't know I was there.

Slowly, I walked up to her, trying not to startle her. "Mama, it's me, Sissie." I reached over and pet her head. "Mama..."

Slowly, she raised her head and looked at me. Her eyes were hollow and filled with pain. She had lost more weight and her skin looked pale and had a yellow cast to it.

Before a word was said, her eyes filled with tears that ran down her cheeks. My heart broke into a thousand pieces. "Oh Mama, Mama, I missed you so much." I gently put my arms around her. We hugged each other for a long time, rocking back and forth.

In a frail voice, "Sissie, are you well? How did you get here? I was so worried. It has been so long. I wondered if you would ever come home." The questions sounded like they took all her strength to ask.

I stood back and stretched out my arms, "Look at me, Mama, I'm well and going to school."

From the kitchen Daddy called out, "Wait, I'll get something to eat. We'll sit down and you can tell us all about what happened."

"Okay Daddy. Call me if you need help."

"Sissie, I can't get out of bed. When supper is ready we'll eat by the bed. Now, you go and help your daddy. He would like that."

Looking at Mama in her suffering, I fell to my knees and laid my head on the bed. Crying, I said to her, "Mama, you saved my life when you let me go back to the hospital, I wish I could do something for you. Mama, tell me, what can I do, please tell me."

Petting my head, "Sissie, your mama is beyond help. Right now, it's you that's important. You're well. That will ease my pain. We'll talk about it. Now go and help your daddy. When did you eat? I bet you're hungry," she said as she wiped her tears on the blanket.

When I went into the kitchen, Daddy was putting the coffee on. "Well, we don't have much but we can fill your belly." He had that grin that I remembered so well. He was happy and his actions showed it. His step was quick and his eyes flashed as he put things together.

"So, it was you that kept me awake last night. It was breaking daylight before I dozed off. I felt like I was waiting for someone or something," he said as he stirred the potatoes. He was frying them in deer grease and it smelled good.

It wasn't long before I heard the deer steaks hit the frying pan. This was home! This was where I wanted to spend the rest of my life, home with Mama and Daddy!

I carried two chairs into the other room and sat them by Mama's bed. I put two pillows behind her back so she could lean back while we ate.

Daddy brought in the food on plates to make it easier. When we sat down, Mama said she would try to eat but instead of the food we ate, she had some soup Daddy made from deer broth.

"Your mama hasn't been able to eat very much so I make soup. Sometimes I grind up the meat for her." Daddy said as he spoon-fed her. "She can't wear her teeth, they hurt her too much," he added. Every now and then a drip of soup would run down her chin, he would wipe it with the dish cloth.

After we finished eating, I gathered up everything. Then we sat and I told them all about my stay in the hospital, about the school and where I was staying. I told them about the Rehabilitation Program and how it worked. They were paying for everything!

I told them they were training me so I could support myself when I finished school. I explained what I was doing in school. The permanent waves, the hair cutting, hair coloring and setting people's hair and how excited I was about it. It took me awhile before I realized what I was saying, I would be leaving again!

Sitting there on the chair, smoking the cigarette that he had rolled, Daddy asked, "How long will you be staying?"

"My caseworker, Mr. Abey, gave me two weeks off to come home. But, now that I'm here it might be better if I stayed because Mama is so sick," I said lowering my head.

Mama said, "No, no. You go to school and finish. You need an education. It's your only chance to do something with your life. There is nothing here for you. When we are gone, you need to take care of yourself. I would never, never forgive myself if you quit now." Sweat rolled down her brow and cheeks. She leaned forward and closed her eyes, wrapping her arms around her knees, she began to rock back and forth, moaning.

I felt so helpless. What could I do to ease her pain?

I got up and wiped her brow with the blanket and asked if she wanted to lay down. Pulling the pillows from under her back, I put them so she could lay to one side, facing the wall. I covered her and waited until she quieted down. She seemed to be resting. Then Daddy and I went outside.

Daddy pointed to a block of wood and asked me to sit down, he would be back in a little while. He went down the hill towards the creek where the sweathouse was. He wasn't gone very long. When he came back, he sat down on the block next to me. I could smell whisky on his breath.

"I had to take some of my medicine. It helps me through the day," he said wiping his mouth on his sleeve.

I didn't like it but I knew what he was going through. *He is my daddy and if that's what it takes, so be it.*

Daddy was so against the hospital and didn't want me to go back, I was surprised when he said, "Your mama is right. You need an education. But try to come home as often as you can. I don't think your mama will be with us very long. There is nothing you or I can do for her now but to do as she asks."

We talked for a long time after dark about how things were for them. He and I wept for Mama. When the tears dried up, he said, "Well, it's time for me to take your mama to the toilet. You can help me."

When we went into the house, he pointed to something that was covered with a blanket in the corner of the room. Under it was an old mattress with a lot of the stuffing pulled out.

"I use that for padding on the bed under your mama. You can change the padding from the mattress while I take her to the toilet." Easing Mama out of the bed, Daddy held her up and slowly walked her out the door.

After they left, I went to her bed. I couldn't believe what I saw. There was blood and matter where she lay. The odor was of decay and death. The same smell as was in the death ward at Cushman Hospital, only worse. I knew Mama was slowly dying.

Crying, I began to roll up the used padding. I pulled off wads of cotton padding from the mattress and laid them out on the bed making sure there were no lumps. I covered it with an old sheet torn in half. When I finished changing the bed, I sat down and cried and cried. *Poor Daddy, he has done this day after day. What is he going to do when Mama can't get up?*

The two weeks at home tore my heart to shreds. I wondered how I could leave but when the time came, Mama would not hear of it.

"Sissie, we already went over this. You have to go to school but come home as often as you can. It makes me happy to know you are alright. Your daddy and I will be waiting for you. Go to school Sissie. Make us proud."

It was a tearful goodbye when, early in the morning, I headed for the highway, hoping to catch a ride to Spokane.

I didn't walk very far when a car stopped. A man and his wife were in the car. "Where are you heading?" he asked.

"I'm going to Spokane."

"That's where we're going. Hop in, we'd like the company." They were very nice people. They took me right to the house.

I continued going to school with a heavy heart. Every time the phone rang I wondered if it was for me. I knew the time was drawing near, but when?

Winter would soon be setting in and it was getting cold. To save money, I walked to school every day. Living at the Isabella Club put a strain on me so I decided to make a move. One of the girls, Penny, who lived at the house long before I came, felt the same way. Together, we looked for an apartment. We gave notice and moved to an old furnished house on the lower part of the South Hill.

With the help of Penny's family and the Goodwill, we gathered up blankets, pots and pans and set up housekeeping. The new place gave me a feeling of freedom and independence and the walk to school was shorter.

Penny worked as a secretary and loved Rock Hudson. She would go to his movies every night as long as it was in town. I wondered how she could see the same movie every night! It was a bit weird. However, we didn't see each other very much. She done her thing and I done mine.

The snow began to fall and it was cold outside. But no matter what the weather promised, every Saturday I headed for the "Indian Crossing" and sat in the tavern waiting for someone to give me a ride home.

Each time it was the same at home. The suffering and the loneliness of the two little people that hung onto each other through it all. Every night there, thinking of Mama's suffering, I cried myself to sleep. I worried about Daddy. How could he live day after day with the promise of death and still go on?

Make Us Proud

Christine Cassano

Manny

Chapter 9

THE CANDLE
Age 20

The phone rang. The student at the desk put it down and went into the office. When she came out, Mrs. Cady followed behind her. Both of them looked across the room at me. I knew it was time for me to go home.

Mrs. Cady came to me, "Chris, the phone call is for you. Go on, I'll get another student to take over your client."

I went into the office and picked up the phone, "Hello, Daddy is that you?"

"Tissie, you have to come home now. Your mother is calling for you. Hurry, there isn't much time left." Those words and the sound of his voice, I knew it was serious.

"Okay Daddy. I'll call Ernie and we will leave soon as we can. Tell Mama that we will be there soon as we catch a ride."

Mrs. Cady was standing by me while I answered the phone. When I put it down, she hugged me. "I'm sorry Chris. Don't worry about school, I'll take care of things."

"Daddy wants me to come home right away. Please call Mr. Abey and tell him I don't know when I'll be back. I have to call the Community College and tell Ernie to meet me. Could you find the number for me?"

When she found the number, it took a while before he got to

the phone. "Ernie, we have to go home right away. Mama is really sick and she is calling for us. Meet me at the tavern, I'll be there waiting for you. Hurry."

I arrived at the tavern first and asked around if anyone was going to Keller, Republic or Inchelium. It didn't matter, just as long as we got as close to the cabin, we could walk the rest of the way.

It was late in the day when the bartender called me. He introduced me to a man that lived in Keller. Sitting by him at the bar, I explained to him how important it was for Ernie and me to get home soon as we could.

"Where is your brother? We can leave right now and I'll take you all the way home." I'm sure the man was God sent.

I was glad we would leave right away, it didn't give Ernie time to drink. I didn't want him to have liquor on his breath, especially at a time like this.

When we arrived at the cabin, Mama's friend from Canada, Ellen, met us at the door. I was glad she was there. It meant that Daddy wasn't alone. And she was such a clean freak, everything in the house was clean and neat.

In a soft voice she said, "Your mama has been waiting for you. Go in and see her," motioning to the other room.

Mama was sitting in the same way I last saw her, holding her knees to her chest with her head down, rocking.

"Mama, I'm here. Mama...." She raised her head and looked at me. It took an instant before she realized who I was.

"Oh, Sissie, I've been waiting for you. I'm so glad you're here. Come, let me hold you," she said reaching for me.

1939 – Age 4

"Mama, are you going to tell us kids about the deer you got?" Ernie asked.

"Soon as we get settled by the fire," Mama said as she folded the diapers, making them ready for Manny. Ernie and I took turns

THE CANDLE

changing him while they were gone.

The campfire was going good and Daddy handed Mama her cup of coffee and started to cook breakfast. With blankets around our shoulders, we were anxious to listen to Mama's story.

She got to the top of the mountain by the time the sun came up, as planned. She checked out the trails the deer were using and hunted most of the day. Just as evening was approaching, she saw a big buck across a ravine. It was standing in an opening of trees looking in her direction. He had a rack of horns, the biggest she had ever seen.

Looking down the mountain into the ravine, sizing up the distance, she decided to go for it. She got on a deer trail which made it easier. However, now and then she would fall off the tracks and sink into the deep snow. It was hard for her to get back on the tracks. The trail led her to the bottom of the ravine and up the other side. Before getting to the top, night overcame her and it was too dark for her to continue. Excited about the size of the buck, she didn't think about the time of day before going down the mountain. At this point, she decided to spend the night. It made her feel bad knowing Daddy would worry about her.

Making a place to sleep, she piled up the snow around her to check the wind and to hold in her body heat. Making a small fire at the opening, she spent the night.

When morning came and it began to get light enough to see, she started up the mountain making her way to the spot where she first saw the big buck.

Reaching the top, she looked around until she found his tracks. There was no question when she found them. Standing there, she looked across the mountain and saw where she stood when she first saw him. Yes, this was his tracks!

She followed them most of the morning. The tracks led her up and over another mountain. Then she began to worry that he was going too far away and if she got him, it would be too hard to get him out. She decided to give it up. She cleared the snow off a nearby log and sat down.

Looking at the countryside, she rolled herself a cigarette. When she put out the cigarette and was about to leave, she saw him. He had made a big loop and was making his way back.

Excited, Mama edged her way through the snow, getting as close to him as she could to get a good shot. Adjusting her footing, she aimed and just as she pulled the trigger, he turned and with three big leaps, he went out of sight. She was not sure if she hit him. He didn't act like it but that didn't mean anything, she had to see if there was any blood where he stood. Due to the deep snow, it took her about half an hour to get to the place.

When she finally got there and saw his tracks, there was blood on the snow. But, according to the color, it looked as if it was a flesh wound. What worried her was, with a flesh wound, he could travel a long way. In that case, she would take her time following him because, depending how badly he was wounded, he might lie down. Best of all, he was heading back to where she first saw him the day before which was closer to the cabin.

After following his tracks for about an hour, she saw him again. He had crossed the ravine where she had spent the night. He stood near the top and was looking at her. It was kind of a long shot but Mama decided to take a chance. Balancing herself in the frozen deer tracks, she aimed and pulled the trigger. The buck turned and disappeared over the mountain.

Trying to see where he went, she fell off the deer tracks and sunk to her waist in the deep snow. Struggling, she got back on the trail. Now, she had to cross the ravine. She began to go down the mountain trying hard to stay in the frozen deer tracks. She said it was like walking on a tight rope.

Reaching the bottom, she began fighting her way up the other side. Watching her step and trying not to fall off the tracks, she happened to look up and saw the buck coming down the hill at full speed with his neck bowed. He was heading straight for her! Startled, she fell off the deer tracks and went to her waist in the snow. Knowing she could not get up, she twisted herself into a position to shoot. She aimed and pulled the trigger. The buck slid to a stop, turned around and headed back up the hill. At this point, she got mad, 'Damn, I'll get you yet,' she said to herself.

Determined, she got back on the deer tracks and made her way up the hill. When she got to the top, she found his tracks and followed them. He went down a little gully which was full of brush and trees. On the other side was a ridge that stood out bare of trees. At the end of that ridge, the mountain dropped off in an old landslide of shale rocks. Her big buck was laying down on the edge.

Mama said her heart was beating so fast she had to take a few minutes to catch her breath. She told us his horns looked like an uprooted tree and his body looked like a log laying there. Only when he turned his head and looked in her direction was she sure it was really him!

This time she wasn't taking any chances. She braced herself against a tree, took careful aim and pulled the trigger. From a laying position, the buck bounced up and went over the edge. She was sure she did not miss him this time. She slowly made her way to the spot where he had laid. His tracks where he had made two big jumps went over the hill. Going to the edge, Mama looked down the landslide. She saw where he fell and slid down about half way and was laying on his back, wedged next to a log that stopped him from going all the way down.

Mama stood there and watched him for awhile. He didn't move. Now she had to find a way to get close to him and make sure he was dead. She noticed that when he jumped down the hill and landed on his side and slid, there was ice under the snow. In the last few days, the snow had melted, froze and fresh snow had covered the ice. She had to figure out a way to get close enough to him without sliding all the way down the mountain. There was a tree about ten feet to the right of the buck. If she sat down and eased her way down the hill, the tree would stop her.

Sitting down, using the butt of the gun to guide her, she slid down to the tree. Holding on to it, she got up. Looking at the buck from behind the tree, she checked to see if he was breathing. After studying him for awhile, she noticed his eyes were closed and his nostrils were flared but he wasn't breathing.

When a deer is dead, his eyes are open and his tongue hangs out the side of his mouth. This was not the case but she had to make sure. Mama picked up some snow to make a snowball and threw it at him. When the snowball hit him, he bounced straight up in the air and hit the ground facing her. Digging in, he went straight for her and started hooking the tree. He would slip down the hill, find footing, and make his way back to the tree and start hooking it again, trying to get at her. Mama said there were times he would fall on his front knees and his horns would hook onto the tree which kept him from sliding back down the hill. He kept trying to get around the tree but couldn't keep his footing. At one point, his body was wrapped around the tree and trying to hook her from the other side. Mama took advantage of it, holding onto the tree, she took off the safety on the rifle, pointed the gun at him and pulled the trigger.

The buck fell and started to roll down the hill. Nearing the bottom, he slid and stopped against a tree. She sat down and held her gun above her head and slid down the hill coming to a stop near the buck. The cabin was at the bottom of the mountain within hearing distance. She whistled for Daddy to come. When he answered, she sat down to rest.

Smiling, she took out her Prince Albert can of tobacco and started to roll a cigarette. While she was putting the tobacco on the paper, she looked at his horns. She counted twelve points on one side and eleven on the other. The thing that took her breath was the tangs were sort of flat and sharp! The vision of him coming down the mountain at full speed and being stuck in the snow up to her waist, she knew he would have ripped her to pieces. She began to shake so much she tore the cigarette paper apart. Trying to roll

THE CANDLE

another, she did it again. She gave it up.

When my mama hunted, it was not her way to hunt for a trophy buck. It was our source of food but this hunt took her by surprise. This buck was the biggest she had ever seen. As she followed his tracks through the mountains, there were other deer tracks and she saw other deer but she let them go and focused on the "Granddaddy of Them All". For those two days and a night, there was only Mama and her buck in those mountains. He had threatened her life and she took his.

As time went by, many times we asked Mama to tell us the story about the big buck and how he attacked her. Looking at her while she told the story, we felt so proud of her. We just knew our mama wasn't afraid of being alone in the mountains. She was fearless.

She held me as if I was a little girl, rocking me back and forth. She petted my head and cooed like she had done so many times in my life. I felt the deepest love. It took me back to the times when she was well. She was so strong, kind and gentle. She always put herself last. Now she was suffering and there wasn't anything I could do.

Ernie was standing behind me, waiting. I told Mama that Ernie came with me. I stepped back and with tears in her eyes, she reached for him. As Mama hugged him I went into the kitchen.

Daddy and Manny were sitting at the kitchen table having a cup of coffee. They had been down at the creek getting the sweathouse ready for the night when we came. Ellen was preparing something to eat.

I went to Daddy and gave him a hug. "Tissie, I'm so glad you came. She has been calling for you." Bowing his head, "Tissie, your mama is really, really sick...." He couldn't finish.

Manny motioned for me to come to him. In a whisper he said, "The priest from Republic came here and told us that Mama has only one month to live. He told us to get everything in order." He began to cry.

"Manny I'm so glad you're here. I thought you had to go back to the Marines."

Wiping his eyes, "Yeah, I asked for extra time."

Daddy got up and went out the door.

Ellen stood at the stove, cooking. Every now and then she would wipe her eyes. "Are you kids hungry?" she asked.

Somehow, I couldn't cry. I felt detached. It was as if I was high above the cabin looking down on the family in their suffering. This feeling stayed with me all the while I was at home.

"Yes, Ellen. Ernie and I haven't had anything since this morning."

She was frying deer meat and potatoes. She also made biscuits. I was so hungry I could hardly wait. Standing by the stove watching her, I felt like she wanted to say something. She hadn't said anything since we came. I went and stood by her.

"Sissie, I've been here two weeks and your mama has only had about a cup of broth. We can't get her to eat. I think she is starving herself to death. Sissie, what can we do?"

Staring at the meat frying, I thought about the patients at the end of the hall. They were skin and bones and suffering. There was only one way out... death. They knew it and were waiting. At the end, all they wanted was for someone to hold their hand. Mama knows it and is waiting.

"Ellen, don't worry about Mama eating. Her time is near and she is waiting. Her pain is so bad we can't imagine. Sit with her and hold her hand. Love her. That is all we can do." With that, I left her with the cooking and went to sit with Mama.

We took our turns sitting by Mama. When it was my turn, I tried to have her lean against me hoping it would give her some relief. I pressed her against my breast and pet her head. I talked about old times, about the hunting trips we went on, the things us kids done when we were little. At times, she would smile.

I told her how many times I longed to be home just to hold her like this. Even though I was gone, there wasn't a day I didn't think about her and Daddy.

"Mama, when they took me away, I left my heart with you and Daddy."

She looked up at me, "Sissie, you took mine. When we went to the hospital that day and you were gone, I died inside. Your daddy and I have been lost ever since."

"I'm here now. We're all together, the five of us."

Several days passed and one morning Mama asked me to come and sit with her. "Sissie, I want you to do something for me. I want you to have the boys start a fire in the front yard. There are things I want you to burn. While they get the fire started, I want you to get out all my clothes and put them on the floor so I can see what there is."

I went into the kitchen and told Manny to go outside and start a fire in the middle of the front yard. He looked at me, puzzled. "Go out there and build the fire! I'll explain it to you in a little while."

I began to gather her clothes and put them on the floor. She didn't have much but I cleared them all out. She looked at the clothes. It had been a long time since she wore them. "Now, I want you to burn all of them."

I didn't ask any questions but done as she asked. I carried them all out to the front yard and began to put them on the fire, one at a time as not to smother the fire. With a long stick, I moved the clothes around on the fire.

As the clothes disappeared, Mama told me to make sure everything was gone. I looked around, her pants, shirts, belts, shoes, nothing was left but what she was wearing.

"When I leave, burn what I am wearing and burn all of my bedding. I don't want anything left," she said looking at me. She knew I would do as she asked. Both of us were dry eyed.

I went out and worked the fire until every speck of clothing was gone. Sitting on a block of wood by the fire, I prayed for the end. I wanted Mama's pain to end.

The life she led, the lives she saved, the babies she brought into the world, she gave everything and asked for nothing. God had a special place for her. She was waiting. We were waiting. God was waiting. A smile crept to the corner of my mouth. My eyes misted as I watched the dying coals burn out, leaving gray forms of what was.

The days passed as we went about the house in our own thoughts, waiting, as the glue that held us together was melting.

Ellen went about cleaning, washing clothes, and cooking. Manny and I spent our time cleaning up the yard and cutting down overgrown bushes around the cabin.

Daddy sat in his usual place by the kitchen table, glassy eyed. He would take a sip of coffee every now and then and when the light in his eyes began to dim, he would go out the door to take a shot of his "medicine". Ernie sat watching, hoping Daddy would ask him if he needed a shot.

We took turns sitting by Mama. It hurt me to see her sit there, rocking day and night and never laying down. I wondered if she ever slept.

One afternoon when I went in to sit with her, she pointed at her leg, "Look at this," as she pushed her finger into her leg at the ankle. Her legs and feet looked as if she weighed 200 pounds! When she pushed her finger into her leg, it made a hole about an inch deep. When she took her finger out, the hole stayed there. I saw other places where she had been poking her legs. It scared me. I asked her if it hurt and she said it didn't. I knew she was filling up with fluid.

The next day, Mama told Daddy to send each one of us kids to her bedside, one at a time. When he came to the kitchen table, he told Ernie that Mama wanted to talk to him.

He got up from the table and went into the other room. After about ten minutes he came out crying. Then Daddy told Manny to

THE CANDLE

go see his mother. When he came out, he left the house fighting tears.

Then Daddy looked at me and motioned with his head to go to Mama. When I went to her bedside, she looked at me dry eyed and gave me a soft smile. "Sissie, come, sit down," patting the bed beside her.

When I sat down, she reached for my hands, "Sissie, when a baby is born, a candle is lit in Heaven. And, of all my children, your candle shines the brightest. Please, don't turn your back on your brothers. Try to be understanding. I know it will be hard but they have a weakness. I know you will take care of everything for me."

Then pointing at her 30-30 rifle that was laying across the tangs of the big buck, "You know what my old pal means to me. I'm giving it to you because I know your brothers will only trade it in for money. Keep it. It has fed us through the years and I want it to do the same for you." I promised her I would do as she wished.

On the morning of the 6th of June 1956, I woke up and looked over at Mama to see how she was feeling. She was laying on her side as if she fell over in a sitting position.

I jumped up and ran to see what happened to her. "Mama, what is the matter, are you alright?" Kneeling on the bed, I put my hand on her shoulder.

She turned her head and looked at me. One eye and half of her face had dropped. She tried to talk but only a whisper came out. I could not understand her.

I leaned over close to her so I could hear what she was saying. She tried hard to talk. I knew I had to do something. Now! "Mama, lay still. I'll go and get help," I said as I pet her head and brushed the strands of hair out of her face. "It will take me awhile but I will be back soon as I can." I got down from the bed and started to get dressed.

While putting on my coat, I ran through the kitchen, "Ellen,

I'm going down to the lodge and call for an ambulance. Go and take care of Mama. Clean her up and the bedding and put some clean clothes on her, she's going to the hospital. Hurry!"

I ran to the highway and hoped someone would come by and give me a ride. As it turned out, I sprinted the two miles to the Westfork lodge.

When the owners Bud and Jean saw me, they knew something was wrong. They let me make the phone call to the hospital in Republic. The nurse at the hospital told me that an ambulance would be on the way. I almost shouted in the phone, "Please, bring something to kill her pain!"

Bud gave me a ride back home.

Ellen had Mama all cleaned up and the clothes she wore were Daddy's. With Manny's help, the bedding was changed.

Mama no longer sat up. She was laying on her back but the expression on the right side of her face showed the pain she was in. She could no longer talk to be understood, all that came out was in a whisper. Ellen told me it was called a stroke.

Within the hour, the ambulance pulled up in the yard and turned around. I ran outside and asked the man if he had something for Mama's pain. He took out a bag and came into the house with me.

I led him into the other room. He took out a little bottle and a hypodermic syringe, filled it and injected it into Mama's arm. It didn't take long before the expression of pain faded from her face. It brought tears to my eyes. Oh Mama, from here on you will never feel pain again.

I asked him if he had a pillow she could sit on and if she could ride in the front seat. I told him that Ernie and I were going with her. He didn't object.

I looked for Daddy and saw him hobbling down the trail to the creek. He couldn't stand to see her leave. Ellen was standing by the door watching everything that was taking place. Manny sat on a block of wood by the wood pile. He had a stick and was making

THE CANDLE

circles with it in the dirt. I went up to him, "Manny, after we leave, make a fire and burn all of Mama's bedding and the clothes she wore. Burn everything."

The man picked up Mama and carried her to the ambulance. He sat her in the front seat on the pillow. Ernie and I sat in the back. I sat right behind Mama and held her by the shoulders so she wouldn't fall to the sides.

On the way to Republic, Mama sat and looked at the hillside as we drove. She had done this so many times before, hoping to see a deer. Sitting there, she looked so petite. Her head looked round and her braids hung down to her waist. I looked at the soft wave in her hair. I looked at her all the way to the hospital, knowing it would be the last trip and I wanted to remember her beauty. Even though I knew she would not be returning home, my heart sang to know she would not be in pain again.

When we got to the hospital, Mama was put to bed. The nurse brought Ernie and me chairs so we could sit by the bed. I sat on her right and Ernie on the left, holding her hands. The vigil began.

Whenever I saw Mama's forehead wrinkle, I knew she was feeling pain and I would call the nurse to give her another shot.

Late in the night a nurse came and asked Ernie and I if we would like to lay down and get some rest. We were grateful. She told us we could sleep in the apartment in the basement of the hospital. She promised us that if there were any changes, she would call us.

Each night we took advantage of the apartment. Each morning we would check up on Mama. She seemed to be sleeping all the time.

On the 8th, the third day in the hospital, we came up from the apartment, stopped by the door of the ward, and the nurses were tending to her. Her back was to the door, the sheets were off and the nurse was painting something that was blue on her back.

To my horror, I saw a place on her back that was about eight inches long and three inches wide where the skin and flesh were gone. I could see the vertebrae of her backbone which appeared white. Higher up was another place where the skin and flesh was worn off.

I couldn't look any longer. I felt sick. Oh, how Mama had suffered through the years. The pain had to be beyond my imagination!

I don't know if Ernie saw it but I had to leave. "Come on, let's go and have something to eat while they take care of Mama. Let's hurry," I said as I ran out the door.

When we got back from breakfast, Mama was laying on her back and seemed to be looking for something. She kept lifting the sheets and looking under them. She would look at me and try to say something. Try as I could, I couldn't understand her. This went on several times. Each time I asked her what she wanted but she only looked at me, pleading.

Around 11:00, Daddy and Manny came in. Mama didn't show any expression of recognizing them but kept looking through the sheets and whispering.

1933 – Mama and Daddy

"Ned, she is a nice-looking woman. She is single and has a little baby. I think you would like her," he said. "She's my cousin."

Daddy was not ready to meet anyone and told Albert but he would not give up. Each day he came to work, he would tell Daddy about the woman.

"She seems sad. She cooks the meals for the family but never eats at the table. She stays upstairs and only comes down to cook and clean the house and goes back upstairs. She doesn't talk to anyone or go anywhere. Ned, maybe you can talk to her," Albert urged.

As the days passed, Albert kept on talking about her. Daddy's curiosity got the best of him and he accepted the invitation to supper one night.

Albert told Daddy that he had to come before meal time, while

THE CANDLE

she was still in the kitchen, so he could at least see her and make up his mind if he wanted to meet her. As soon as everyone would sit down to eat, she would go back upstairs.

That evening after work, he went home with Albert for supper. Mama was cooking in the kitchen and where Daddy sat, he could see her going back and forth.

When everyone was called to the table, Mama went upstairs. After about twenty minutes, she came down and poured coffee for everyone and left again. When the meal was finished and everyone left the table, Mama came down and cleaned up everything and went back upstairs.

When Daddy saw Mama and watched her work, he noticed she never looked at anyone but kept her eyes on what she was doing, as if she was in another world. Her actions seemed automatic.

That night Daddy could not sleep. He couldn't get Mama out of his mind. He felt her pain, her loneliness, her heartbreak. He wanted to know more about her. He asked questions but the family knew little of why Albert's father brought her home from Oroville.

Daddy asked Albert to find a way for him to meet Isabel. Albert suggested Daddy come to supper again. Then, when supper was over and Mama was cleaning up the kitchen, they could go back for more coffee. At that time, Albert would introduce them.

So, they met. Nothing much was said, but Daddy was careful not to ask questions about her past. He kept the conservation light. He asked about her baby and wanted to see him. Feeling a bit reluctant but pleased because of his interest, she went upstairs and brought the baby down. Daddy couldn't believe how small little Ernie was and Mama was proud to display him.

Days passed and Daddy came to visit without an invitation. He would go straight to the kitchen and talk to Mama while she cooked. He finally got up enough nerve to ask Mama to take a walk with him. At first, she wouldn't go. But after a time, she felt comfortable with Daddy. With the baby in her arms, they went for walks. Mama began to look forward to seeing him.

Daddy kept up the visits. Then one day he came and Mama was upstairs. Without asking, he made his way upstairs. He had bought two bolts of fabric. One bolt was for little Ernie's diapers and the other one was for Mama to make herself something to wear. He also bought some groceries for her alone. He noticed she never ate with the family and he worried about her.

It was the first time he had gone upstairs where she spent most of her time. It was then that he asked if she would come with him. He told her he had nothing, no home, no household goods, nothing but the love he had for her and the baby in her arms. That together, they could find their way.

"I found an old log house that has been abandoned for years. We can start there. It is summer now and by fall, I will fix it up for winter."

Daddy made his way to the side of the bed and took off his hat, turning it around in his hands. Looking at it for a moment, he looked at her and said, "Hi, ole girl, how ya doin'? Been missing you." He bowed his head for a minute, "I asked the priest to come and bless us, I know you would like that."

Just then the priest came in. He acknowledged us with a bow of his head. He went to the side of the bed between Mama and Daddy. He blessed them with the Sign of The Cross, speaking in Latin.

Then, in English, "There is no time for me to marry the two of you but with the life you led together, your love for each other, raising your family in hard times and being faithful to each other, if you are not married then no one is married. I bless you, in the name of the Father, the Son and the Holy Spirit. Amen."

During this time, Mama did not respond to what was taking place. She just kept on searching through the sheets, looking at me and whispering.

After the priest left, Daddy worked his way closer to Mama and gave her a kiss on the forehead. He backed up and made the

THE CANDLE

Sign of The Cross and closed his eyes. The rest of us followed his lead.

I looked down at Mama and, to my surprise, she looked up at Daddy and made the Sign of The Cross with us and closed her eyes. Daddy went on to say the Lord's Prayer, the Hail Mary and the Act of Contrition. Making the Sign of The Cross ended the prayer. We followed, including Mama. Then she went back to searching through the sheets. Somehow, she was with us during the prayer. Closing my eyes, I thanked God. I knew He intervened at a time we needed Him.

Getting ready to leave, Daddy bid Mama goodbye. "Well ole girl, we had a good life together. I'm really going to miss you. I will soon be with you." Bending down, he kissed her on the forehead. Again, this time in the Indian language, he said goodbye. Putting on his hat, he slowly turned around and made his way to the door. Manny went to Mama, kissed her goodbye and with tears in his eyes, he left.

Mama kept searching for something under, on top and through the sheet and blanket. With her eyes, she kept begging me to find whatever it was. I felt helpless. I wished I knew what she wanted.

It was late afternoon when Ernie and I took time to eat. Sitting in the restaurant listening to the songs on the jukebox, we talked about Mama and what she wanted. "Maybe, she wants a rosary. We should see if we can find one in town," I said.

"Yeah, you might be right. Hurry, let's go and look for one," Ernie said, getting excited.

We walked down the street and looked in the store windows. We went into a store that had a lot of trinkets in the window. There were so many things, we didn't know where to start. The man behind the counter asked us if he could help.

"We're looking for a rosary. Do you have one?" I asked.

"Yes, we do." He walked down to the end of the counter and there, under the glass case, were several in different colors.

We looked them over. There was one that had brown beads

that almost looked like wood. I asked Ernie, "What do you think? Do you like the brown one?"

"Yeah, I think Mama would like that," he said with his nose close to the glass top, getting a close look. "Yeah, that's the one."

I thought for a while. "You know, Ernie, Mama likes blue. Let's find something to get her that's blue."

The man behind the counter said, "How about a hankie?" Since we didn't have much money, we thought it was a good idea. We walked down the street with the rosary and a small thin blue hankie.

Excited, we thought we had solved the problem but when we gave them to Mama, she ran her fingers over the beads, took the hankie, gathered up the beads inside and tied the corners. Putting it aside, she began to search again.

We looked at each other. Ernie gave out a sigh, "Sis, untie it and give it to her again. Maybe she doesn't know what it is."

I done as he asked. I untied the hankie and put the rosary in her hands first. Not looking at it, she ran her finger over the beads. I waited for awhile, then handed the hankie to her. She again gathered up the beads, tied the corners and put them aside, continuing the search. Feeling defeated, we sat by her and watched. Ernie laid his head on the bed, feeling the stress.

I looked over at Ernie, "Hey, I think I know what Mama is looking for." He gave me a puzzled look.

I went to the desk and asked the nurse if she could get me a candle. "Please, if you can, get a long one that the church uses."

It didn't take long before she came back with a long white church candle and a holder from the chapel. Thanking her, I ran back to the room.

I sat it on the dresser that was against the wall at the foot of the bed. I took out a book of matches from my pocket, tore off a match and struck it across the bottom of the book. It popped and a spark flew across the room towards Mama. At that very moment, she sat straight up and with both eyes wide open, she stared at the match in my hand. Ernie, quickly grabbed her by the shoulders. "Mama, it's alright. Mama..." She was stiff. He couldn't make her lay back down.

I put the match to the wick and it slowly took hold. I blew out the match. I walked over to Mama and took hold of her by the shoulders. Ernie let go and sat down, stunned.

She stared at the candle as it glowed and flickered now and then. As I held her by the shoulders I could feel her began to relax. I gently eased her back down. I fixed the pillow under her head. I pulled up the sheet and blanket, covering her. She closed her eyes as I placed her hands on top of the covers and gently brushed the strands of hair from her face. She was at peace.

I sat back down and looked at Ernie. He was crying. "Sissie, oh Sissie."

"Ernie, don't cry. Mama is going to Heaven. Wait and see. This is what she wanted. Now we know how much time we have left to be with her. Don't cry. Be happy for her."

It was late in the night when I saw a wrinkle in Mama's brow. I called the nurse and asked her to give Mama a shot. When I saw her brow relax, I told Ernie, "Let's go and get some sleep. We have to be back early in the morning."

As we walked out of the room, Ernie looked at the candle, "Sis, do you think the candle will burn out in the night?"

I looked at the candle. I figured it would burn out close to noon the next day. "No. It will last until tomorrow."

We woke up at 7:30 in the morning and rushed upstairs to see how Mama was. The nurse attending her said she had given her a shot just before we came. "I kept a close watch on her all night. When I saw that she needed a shot, I gave it to her."

It made us feel better knowing how much the nurses cared. We sat with Mama until about 8:30. The nurse came and told us to go and have breakfast. Before leaving I looked at the candle, it had less than two inches left.

Walking up to the restaurant I told Ernie, "We have to hurry. We don't have much time left."

Hanging his head, "I wished you didn't light that candle. It scares me."

"Ernie, it was her wish. Can't you see it was the right thing to do?"

We got back to the hospital about 9:30. Mama's breathing was slow and spaced. When I looked at the candle, it was trying to go out. I hurried to the nurse's desk. "Please, call the priest, now!"

I hurried back to the room. Soon, the priest came in. He prepared to give Mama the Last Sacraments. Ernie sat on the right side and I sat on the left side of the bed. We held her hands. Two nurses stood by.

The priest began the ritual. The words were in Latin. He blessed her, applied the oils to her forehead and he prayed.

I looked over at the candle, the flame would stretch up and drop down, almost going out then it would light up again. I looked at Mama, her breathing came out slow and the space lasted longer before she took in a slow breath. I looked at her hand and saw her vein pulse. She took in the next breath. It didn't come out.

At that very moment, I looked over at the candle, the flame dropped down and went out. A slim line of smoke moved up and went into a curl then faded out on the last pulse of her vein.

The two nurses standing at the foot of the bed had tears in their eyes. Ernie broke down and cried. I sat there and just looked at Mama.

I wasn't aware when everybody left. My mind was blank. Slowly I got up and straightened up the sheet and blanket making sure there wasn't a wrinkle in them. I folded down the top edge and placed her hands on her chest. I gently brushed back the strands of hair off her face and took her braids and laid them on top of the sheet.

I walked around the bed and stood there, looking at her. She looked at peace. I looked at her face noticing the white pillow brought out her olive skin. The lines from suffering had faded. Her fine features, high forehead and high cheek bones were framed by her dark brown hair that had a slight wave.

"Oh Mama, you are so beautiful and how I loved you. This picture will stay etched in my mind for the rest of time."

I didn't want to leave. I felt like I was leaving her alone.

When I finally left, the nurse was waiting for me. "Let us know what funeral home you want your mother taken to."

"Have them take her to Oroville. But first I have to go outside and see my brother and we have to get some clothes for her."

When I got outside Ernie was standing by the railing, a few steps from the entrance. He was crying.

I went over and stood by him. Resting on the rail, I looked up at the sky. It was the 9th of June 1956, a beautiful sunny day. Two little puffs of clouds floated overhead.

"Ernie, this is the most beautiful day we could wish for. Mama isn't suffering anymore and it's a great day to go to Heaven! Don't cry. How could you want Mama to live and suffer like she has for so many years? Say a prayer for her, she would like that."

As I turned my face to the sun, I closed my eyes, took a deep breath and smiled.

Chapter 10

I WAS THERE
Age 21

It was good to get back in school. It kept my mind off my problems and gave me an anchor. Mrs. Cady and Mrs. Olney guided and encouraged me both outside and in school. Beyond them, I was afraid to trust anyone.

Mrs. Cady announced to the students that there was to be a hairstyling contest. It would be at the Davenport Hotel. Students and professionals from the whole state would be competing.

Without waiting, four students raised their hands wanting to enter. Happy with the enthusiasm of the students, she went on to explain that the student had to pick a model for the contest. The model could be a friend, relative or a customer of the school. However, there would be a charge to enter the contest. She wanted the entry fee two weeks before the date of the contest. Also, the students were responsible for any extra cost.

She said that as soon as they found a model, they could start practicing. They could make up their own hairstyle and type of clothes their model would wear for the contest. I stood back and watched the students that planned to enter the contest. They called their friends and asked customers that came into the school if they would be their models. The student would take the potential model into Mrs. Cady's office for her advice.

After lunch, Mrs. Cady called me into her office. After closing the door, she asked me, "Chris, are you interested in entering the contest? I'm surprised you didn't raise your hand. Is there some reason?"

"Mrs. Cady, I don't know what to do. I don't know anyone or how to get started. I would love to enter but I don't have any money." My voice faded by the time I finished explaining my reason.

Smiling she said, "Chris, I already called Mr. Abey and he said he would take care of it. The contest is part of your training so don't worry about it. I also found a model for you. She is really a sweet girl and I know you will like her."

I practically jumped off the chair! "You mean I already have a model?"

"Yes. Her name is Donna. I will have her come so you can start practicing next week."

On that day, Mrs. Cady opened a door to me that would forever change my life, the strive for perfection! All I knew and worked at was to make my work the best it could be.

Donna was beautiful! She stood about 5' 5", was slender and had beautiful skin, large blue eyes with thick dark eye lashes. Her hair was a light ash blonde and there was lots of it. She had a pleasing personality and smiled easily. I just knew we would get along fine. I could hardly wait to get started.

Mrs. Cady gave us a schedule for each day to practice on our models. The schedule was not enough for me so when I had a customer, I put the practice to use. I could hardly wait until the next one came in. At the end of each day I went back to my apartment and relived the day's work.

Up until the week before the show, the school buzzed with students working on customers and trying to get in as much practice on the models as we could. During the last week we colored the hair, practiced and decided on the clothes the models would wear.

The contest was to start Sunday at 1:00. Mrs. Cady told me to meet her at the front entrance of the school at 12:30. Donna had gone ahead of us to take her place. With everything I needed in my little kit, we headed down the street. I was so nervous I could hardly stand it!

When we walked in the big room I about crawled up Mrs. Cady's back! I never saw so many people in one place. I wanted to turn around and run. Sensing this, Mrs. Cady grabbed me by the hand and pulled me with her through the crowd.

The room where the contest was held had a platform that made an "X" in the middle. White sheets covered the tables and dozens of mirrors sat in the middle with a chair sitting before them. People sat in rows and rows of chairs all around the platform. It was standing room only!

On the stage, which was at the same level as the platform, the announcer stood waiting to start the show. First was to be the student competition, then the professionals.

The announcer called for all student contestants to take their places for the setting of the hairstyles. We were allowed an hour. When the students began to take their places, I couldn't believe how many there were. This was beyond my wildest dreams!

After the sets were done, the models were ushered to the different salons to dry the hair. Students were not allowed to go with them.

While our models were drying their hair, we watched the professionals set their models. "Chris, just think, next year you will be competing with the professionals," Mrs. Cady said with pride.

I looked up at the platform and saw the rows and rows of professionals and a cold chill ran down my back. I closed my eyes, *why does she expect so much of me?*

To top it off, Mrs. Cady knew so many people and she kept introducing me as her "Prize Student." Each time I would say a little prayer. *Please, let me win so I won't disappoint her.*

All of our models were brought back to the platform and when

I heard the announcer call the students to the platform for the comb-out, I practically flew up there. I laid out everything and stood back and waited. Soon, we were asked to remove the clippies from the hair and we had 45 minutes for the comb-out. Time was called and the bell rang.

Putting all my worries aside, I began the comb-out. I imagined I'm in the school practicing and everything is going into place as I planned. Donna moved her head in the direction I needed as I combed. We were like a pair of dancers gliding across the floor, one leading and the other following, as if we were one. The minutes passed which I didn't want to end. I was in my glory. Winning did not enter my mind.

"Students, you have one minute left. When the bell rings, step back." I began to gather my things up and put them in my kit as the bell rang.

Donna went into her pose. Before leaving, I looked up at her. She looked beautiful! She sat up straight and held her head high. I stepped down from the platform.

The three judges were introduced and began to go down the rows of models with their pads and pens in hand. There were trophies for the top six places. I thought to myself, *wow, it gives me more of a chance to win something!*

The judging seemed like it would never end. There were so many students, I had to be patient. I wondered if Donna could keep her pose.

After an hour, the judges handed in their pads. The models were asked to leave the platform and it was time for the professionals to do their comb-out.

Since Mrs. Cady said I would be competing in the professional contest the next year, I took special interest in their comb-out. I made my way through the crowd around the platform watching how they combed and placed the hair. I looked at the different styles, hair colors and models. I looked at the dresses they wore. Wow, I had a lot to think about! Before I knew it, the comb-out was over.

Finally, the announcer had the results. The room fell silent. He started out with the student contest. He began to call out the numbers. "For sixth place, model number 42." A scream and clapping came from across the room. "For fifth place, model number 29." Another cheer from somewhere. As each number was called out, my heart would almost stop. The applause grew louder for each place called.

Then the awaited 1st place trophy was held up. "Model number 13, please stand up!" People started to clap at a high pitch, it got louder and louder. I could hear whistles. It all confused me. The next thing I knew, Mrs. Cady was pushing me through the crowd. "Chris, you won... you won! Get up there, you won!"

Everything was happening so fast. Before I knew it, I was standing by the man at the microphone. He asked for my name, "My name is Chris."

"What school do you attend?"

I couldn't talk, I just pointed at Mrs. Cady who was standing by the platform. Knowing I was speechless, he asked Mrs. Cady to come up and give the information. Everything seemed to pass in a blur.

Standing there with weak knees, she put her arm around my shoulder and I leaned against her. She was talking but I could barely hear anything she said. "Chris is my student at Morse Beauty School here in Spokane. We are so proud of her!"

The announcer took back the microphone. "Chris has received a perfect score by the judges!" The applause rings in my ears.

December 1953 – 2 Months Home from Cushman Hospital

Since my gun was a single shot, I had to dig in my pocket for the shells. Loading the gun, I had to look at what I was doing, hoping it wouldn't run away. When I looked up, it was still there! I aimed and shot. I missed. Damn! I was just too excited. Before I could get another shell, it ran over the hill.

Slowly, I made my way up the mountain to where the deer had stood. When I got there, I looked at the tracks and saw that it made a loop and headed down the hill towards the highway. Standing there, trying to get my breath, I watched the area where the tracks led.

After about a minute, I thought, 'Mannn, I missed my chance. Damn!' Then I saw movement down the hill by some small fir trees. I waited to make sure it was my deer. I watched while I dug in my pockets for a shell. Then I saw it come out from behind the trees. Quickly, I put the shell in the gun, aimed and shot. It fell to the ground! I was so excited, I fell down several times going down the hill. Each time I would be covered with snow. I said out loud, "Tell me I can't hunt, Manny. I'll show you!"

I was feeling very proud when I got to my deer. After looking it over, I stuck the stock of my gun in the snow, took out my hunting knife from my belt and began to bleed out the deer. After cleaning my deer out like I saw Mama do so many times in my life, I looked to see how I would get it down the hill to the highway.

Thinking for the moment, I could ride the deer all the way down the hill instead trying to walk through the deep snow. The hillside seemed clear most of the way down except for a few little fir trees. However, the thick trees at the bottom of the hill along the highway might be a problem.

I tested the snow, it had a hard crust on the top. Yeah, it would hold the deer up. Making up my mind, I turned the deer around so its head was downhill making the hair lay back so it would slide better. I took my gun in my right hand, straddled the deer, sat down and pulled its head up between my legs. Holding my gun in the air, I pulled my feet out of the snow, held them up and leaned back. All that was missing in this picture was a cowboy hat and spurs. Man, I just flew down the hill! When I saw a tree coming at me, I would lean to the right or left to miss it.

As I went down the hill, I picked up speed. I was going so fast it was hard to guide the deer and miss the trees. Half way down, I was heading for a tree and tried to miss it. The legs hit the tree and spun me around like a top! As I was spinning around, I was going down the hill at full speed. Just before I got to the bottom, another tree hit the legs and spun me in the opposite direction. It was like a cowboy riding a bull. My gun was knocked out of my hand and I flew in the air and went head first into the snow!

When I got out of the snow and shook myself off, I looked around to see where my deer went. I could see it had slid down the hill and stopped against the trees at the bottom.

Now, I had to look for my gun. The snow was smooth so it was easy to find. When I flew off the deer, my gun went to the right and I went to the left. I brushed the snow off my gun and looked up the hill where my ride took place. All I saw was sky. Somehow, when I looked down the hill it didn't look that steep! I shook my head, "Oh man, that was one fast ride. I must remember never to do that again!"

Mama was standing in the yard as I came up the road dragging my deer. "Sissie, I knew you could do it. And, It's a young one, I'm glad! It means you will have good luck hunting all your life. But remember, you can't eat any of it. We will have to give it away since it's your first one."

There was blood on my clothes and my hands. I didn't change or wash, I wanted the boys to see it!

When they drove up, I went out to meet them. When I saw Manny, with a smug look I said, "I hope your first deer was a young one and I hope you gave it away. I will and my future looks great! So, if you want to get a deer you'll have to go by yourself!" Snapping my eyes at him, with my chin up, I walked away.

My days at school were busy, if I wasn't working on a customer Mrs. Cady had me help other students that needed guidance. I turned out to be part time teacher and part time student. I loved it. It didn't give me much time to think.

Two weeks after the contest I got a call at school.

"Hello?"

"Chris, this is Mr. Abey. How are you doing? I would like to have you come to my office when you get out of school. How about 4:30?"

I could hardly wait for 4:30. Excited, I ran up the stairs of the Hutton Building to his office. When I walked in he was full of smiles. "Chris, I have to go to the State Seminar and I would like to use your story as my example of how we can help people. You are truly what we are all about. Is that a deal?"

I was stunned! "Me? What did I do?"

Leaning forward in his chair, "The way I look at it, you came out of that hospital fighting. Your attendance is beyond what we expected, you've excelled in your training and you're almost finished with school. You are a credit to your race. When you graduate, I can only imagine what you will accomplish."

He made me feel a little bit embarrassed. "Yeah, it sounds good but I'm not doing any more than the other students."

He leaned back in his chair and looked at me, thinking for a moment, "Chris, one day you will understand why I'm excited about you and what you've accomplished to this point. Now, I'm planning on making an appointment to have your picture taken with me to bring to the seminar. Would that be alright with you?"

"Yes, it's okay with me but you'll have to call Mrs. Cady."

"Bring your trophy. It will give that added touch!"

When I left his office I practically danced all the way home! My cheeks got tired from smiling.

I had to prepare for the State Board Examination. It was held every two months. Mrs. Cady warned all the students that were taking the board to study hard.

When the time came, we got ready, packed the things we needed and went to the school where it was held. We took the written exam and the practical exam. I walked away glad it was over.

Wanting to keep busy, I kept going to school even though I had all my hours to graduate. I knew no one outside of school and it was where I felt safe.

One day, Mrs. Cady received a call from a salon that wanted to hire me as a "shampoo girl." Oh, she was so angry! If I had been asked, I probably would have accepted it not knowing what it meant. To me it was a job.

The day I received my license I couldn't wait until morning so I could go to school and tell Mrs. Cady!

"Chris, there is a salon down the street called The Western Hair Salon. I heard there is an opening for a stylist."

Excited, "Should I go now?"

"Yes, go right now before they hire someone else."

I stood back so she could see all of me, "Do I look all right?"

"Yes, yes. Hurry, go down there!" Mrs. Cady was as excited as I was.

I ran to the cage and waited for the lady to come up from the street. I wrung my hands. The cables of the cage clanked as she shifted gears and started to come up. *Mannn... this is the day I waited for!*

Following Mrs. Cady's directions, I went down the street and watched for the sign on the building. There it was, The Western Hair Salon. It sure sounded good. *I hope I'm the stylist they are looking for. Oh man, I will just die if they don't hire me.*

I took a deep breath, squared my shoulders and walked in. I walked up to the reception desk and stood there waiting for the manager to come to the desk.

Soon this tall, slender, beautiful woman came from the back of the salon. She had beautiful hair and large eyes. She looked like the models in the Vogue Magazine I saw in school. I didn't know they were real! "May I help you?" she asked.

I just stood there and looked at her.

"Do you want to make an appointment?"

"Oh no, I just graduated from school and I'm looking for a

job."

"I see. What school did you attend and what is your name?"

"I graduated from the Morse Beauty School. Mrs. Cady owns the school. I just got my license yesterday. She told me to come here. My name is Christine McDougal." By this time, I began to shake.

"My name is Maybelle. Please have a seat, I'll be right back."

I sat on the couch and prayed, *Our Father who art in Heaven... Hail Mary full of grace... Oh God, please tell her to give me a job.*

Then, I heard her footsteps. I opened my eyes and held my breath. She was smiling, "When would you like to start?"

Maybelle became more than my manager, she became my friend. After I worked awhile, she called me aside and told me to change my uniform from all white, as was the dress code for the salon, to a black skirt with a white, short uniform top. She wanted me to comb my hair into a French roll.

I didn't question her but done as she asked. I didn't understand why I should look different than the others. I did feel that it made me stand out from the other 30 hairdressers of the salon. It made me feel special!

She advertised for the salon by contacting the different ladies' groups. She would select three hairdressers of the salon to do hairstyle comb-outs during their bridge card games. She also had three hairdressers do comb-outs on a local TV channel each month.

I was not aware of it at the time, but Maybelle had singled me out to perform with two other stylists each time. It kept me busy working on a style and picking the right customer for each event.

I enjoyed my work. I went to work early and came home late. Every now and then, one of the girls at the salon asked if I would like to go out dancing. The thought of it scared me.

"Chris, you don't go anywhere. You should come with us.

Think about it."

They kept it up. "We go to a place in Idaho, it's called the State Line Gardens. You don't have to go with any guy. There's so many people on the dance floor, all you have to do is go out there and dance."

"Yeah, but I don't drink."

"You don't have to, just drink a Coke."

March 1954 – 5 months home from Cushman Hospital

On Saturday afternoon, the boys began to get ready to leave. Manny said there was a dance in Nespelem and they planned to go.

A dance! Oh, I could go with them and wear my blue dress! I questioned them- how much did it cost, when did it start, when did it end, and if I could go. Ernie said I had to ask Mama and Daddy. I noticed they didn't ask if they could go. Things really changed since I was home. The boys came and went as they pleased.

Mama and Daddy were sitting on the front porch. I went to them and asked if I could go to the dance with the boys. They looked at each other with a question. I knew there was a problem so I went into the house to give them time. It took them a long time to think about it. My nerves were on edge while I waited for them to decide.

Finally, Daddy spoke up, "Tissie, we would love to see you go but it's not the place for you to be."

"But Daddy, I will stay in the dance hall and not go outside with anyone. Please."

"Sissie, there is a lot of drinking at those dances and we would worry about you," Mama said feeling bad.

"Mama, you know I wouldn't drink and I won't dance with anyone that is drinking. I promise. Please let me go," I begged. At this point I began to cry. "I have never been to a dance before. Oh Mama, please let me go!"

"Tissie," Daddy said, "We love you and don't want anything

to happen to you. The boys will get to drinking and you may not have a way home. We can't take a chance."

"But Daddy, I'm 18 and I'm old enough. I know better. I will stay in the dance hall. I promise I will stay inside."

By this time, the boys were getting into the car, my last chance was slipping away. I looked at them sitting in the car then I looked back at Mama, she had tears in her eyes. My heart broke. As the car pulled away, I fell to my knees in front of Mama and laid my head in her lap and cried as she petted my head.

Later on that evening, I was so hurt I wanted to make myself sick. I went down to the creek and got some cold water. I put my head in it for as long as I could stand it. I kept it up several times. It only gave me a headache for the rest of the night.

When I went into the room to go to bed, I took the blue dress and put it into a sack and stuffed the shoes in with it. I didn't want to ever see them again. I made up my mind to never ask to go anywhere again. The dress, the shoes, the dance, none of it mattered anymore.

Finally, one weekend I decided to go with Jan and Vicky. I gave them my address so they could pick me up.

"Okay, we will be at your place at 8:00 sharp. We will be riding with Bill and Dan. They're a couple of nice guys. We went with them before. We're not 'going with them', they're just friends. Okay, see you at 8:00."

When I got home, I worried that maybe I shouldn't go. I'd never gone out dancing before. I wondered if I could dance like they would. It scared me to think there would be a lot of people. I wished I didn't agree to go.

Then I realized that I could finally wear my little blue dress. I decided to wear it with a crinoline underskirt. It had been so long since I bought it, I thought I would to try it on, just to see how it looked. I put the dress on and slipped my feet into the little white shoes. Then I twirled around in the apartment and saw how the skirt flared out. I thought it would look good. I took it off and laid it on the bed. I put the shoes on the floor, stood back and looked at them, "Yeah, I like that."

I took a long shower and put lotion on my face and made sure every little stray hair was plucked from my eyebrows. I put lipstick on and touched my fingers to my lips and smudged my cheeks. It reminded me of the times I had Martha fix my face when I expected Ernie or Howard to visit me.

I combed my hair and put it back into a French roll. I stuck a hatpin in the roll that had a slight bit of a sparkle. Not to ruin my polish, I got dressed then I polished my fingernails. I was ready!

It was 7:30, I hoped I looked alright. I kept going back and forth looking in the mirror. At last I heard a horn toot. I picked up my purse and went out.

A beautiful black limousine waited for me. It looked like it was brand new. The side of the car picked up the lights of the city and sparkled. I couldn't hear the motor. Walking up to it, I could hear my heels click on the pavement, I felt like royalty! A gentleman got out from the driver's seat and opened the backdoor for me. When I got in, the dashboard lit up like stars in the sky. There were green, red and white lights. Soft music filled the car's interior. The seats were leather and smelled new. I never dreamed a car could be so beautiful. When the car pulled away, it floated down the street! The man at the wheel had to be rich!

Both men were dressed nice. The man driving wore a black jacket with light colored slacks. He wore a white shirt and a multi-colored tie. Everything about him was perfect. The guy next to him was younger and wore a light brown jacket and dark slacks. His shirt was open. I was impressed!

The girls looked beautiful. They wore dresses and more make-up than when they worked at the salon. I wondered if I was good enough to be going along with these people.

The girls and the two men talked about everything I knew nothing about. I just sat back and listened but really didn't understand what they were talking about. It was like walking into a room and coming into the middle of a conversation. It all means nothing.

When we arrived at the State Line Gardens, the parking lot was full. I never saw so many cars in one place before. After finding a parking place, the gentleman at the wheel got out and opened the door and the three of us girls got out.

Walking to the door, I felt like I was alone. Somehow, I didn't fit in. I followed them to an empty table and we sat down. Bill, the driver, ordered a round of drinks. I told him I just wanted a Coke.

It wasn't long before the four of them were out dancing. I sat back and watched. No one came up and asked me to dance. I felt weird and just wanted to go home. This just wasn't the place for me. Unless I was with someone, I would never do this again! I couldn't wait until it was time to go.

At last the top lights went on that lit up the room and it was time to leave. Thank Heavens! We made our way to the shiny black limousine. Without any effort, we made it out to the highway and floated back to Spokane. The whole experience left me flat and disappointed. Everyone talked about the night while I sat and felt as if I didn't exist.

Bill dropped Dan off at his apartment. Then he took Jan to her home. When it was my turn to be dropped off, he went past my apartment to take Vicky home. I wondered why he didn't stop to let me off.

When she got out at her home and said goodnight, he answered her and asked me to sit in the front seat. When I got seated, I heard the door click. He drove to Division and made a turn to the right and headed north.

"Bill, why are you going this way? I live down on Monroe by the bridge." He didn't answer. He looked straight ahead and kept driving.

"Bill, did you hear me? You're going the wrong way. Please take me home."

He didn't answer. I knew then that I was in trouble! Fear gripped my insides! I understood why I caught him looking at me now and then throughout the night.

Sitting there beside him, I looked for a way to get out of this alive. Maybe I could jump out when he stopped for a streetlight. I found out that the doors were locked! Then I saw that the street lights going up Division just blinked on yellow which meant he didn't have to stop.

Not once did he look at me. He seemed cold and stared straight ahead. I knew crying or begging wouldn't change his mind. *Mannn... there has to be a way out!* I tried to think of a way to get away from him when we stopped.

He drove out of town on Division and headed towards Mead. All I could see was fields and a few trees against the sky that was just beginning to show light along the hills. I could feel the blood rushing through my veins. I was sure my heart would jump out of my chest, it was beating so fast.

He drove for about ten minutes and turned off onto a dirt road. We went through some trees and came to a clearing. He stopped the car and turned off the motor.

He leaned back in the seat and looked at me. "I want you to look around. Go ahead, look. If you scream, no one will hear you. If you run, I will catch you. Nothing you can do will change the outcome."

A new surge of fear gripped me! I felt the blood drain out of me. I began to feel dizzy, like I was going to faint. He made a gesture towards me like he was going to hit me. I ducked and screamed. He laughed. He toyed with me knowing I was scared.

He slowly took off his jacket and carefully folded it and laid it over the seat with care. All the while, he grinned. Suddenly, he grabbed my left wrist and turned it outwards to a point I thought it would break. He pushed a button and the doors clicked. He told me to open the door. He stiff armed me and backed me right out the door. When he stood up, he towered over me. My head came to his chin. As the pain shot up my arm, it felt like my elbow was breaking and my shoulder was coming out of the joint. I knew the fight was lost!

With one hand, he began to unbuckle his slacks and dropped them to the ground. Still twisting my arm, he bent down and picked them up. With his every move, I thought my arm would break. He carefully laid his slacks over the jacket.

This was fear like I had never experienced before. Through it all I was thinking, *just give me a chance you son-of-a-bitch and I will kill you!*

I was sure my arm was coming out of the socket and the pain went right to my heart. If he let go I couldn't have used it.

With one leg, he kicked my legs out from under me. I fell backwards to the ground and he fell on top of me. He let go of my arm and quickly put his arm across my throat and bared down. I began to choke. I saw sparks flying through the air. Pain shot through my throat and my eyes felt like they were going to pop out of my head! After that, he didn't have to warn me not to scream, I couldn't even talk.

My arm fell, helpless. He grabbed my other arm and pulled it under me so that I laid on it. With his weight on me, both of my arms were lost to me.

He ripped my underclothes off and grabbed my crotch and squeezed until I croaked like a frog. He then grabbed my inner thighs on each side of my crotch, one then the other and squeezed, I rolled my head back and forth trying to scream but nothing came out. It felt like he was ripping the flesh off.

He put his mouth close to my ear, "I want you to remember, I was there! I like you. This won't be the last you'll see of me."

I don't know when he penetrated me. It was all one big pain and my crotch and thighs were on fire. I looked up at the morning sky and wished myself away.

Somehow, I don't remember when, I ended up in the back seat with him on top of me. He was sleeping. His snoring brought me back to reality.

I tried to move. My whole body hurt. Willing myself, I began to move out from under him. I would move a little bit at a time. Without waking him, slowly I slipped out from under him.

My body felt disjointed, like I was made of rubber. My head kept wobbling. It was like my neck wasn't strong enough to hold my head up. I tried to hurry but my body didn't listen to my commands. Holding onto the car, I started to look for my purse. Slowly I made my way around the front of the car. I wanted to go to the passenger side. When I got there, the door was open. I found my purse laying on the floorboard. I took it and leaning against the car for support, looked around to see where I was and which way was town. Fog hung low and I could see light from the city. I looked in to see if he had woken up. His head was facing the front of the car. His mouth was open and slobber ran onto the seat as he snored. I looked back at the light from the city and headed in that direction.

Wobbling, I tried to run. Too weak, I fell down. Using all my strength, I got up. Not looking back, I had the feeling he was chasing me. It was like he was going to catch me any second. Fear gripped my insides again but I held back from screaming. I came to a little knoll and started to climb up. When I got to the top I looked back, he wasn't there!

Somehow, all my strength left me. Like a rubber doll, I fell forward, face first. I couldn't move. My mouth opened and spit ran out. I could feel it and tried to close my mouth but I had no control. My mind was clear but nothing else worked. Every now and then, my body would twitch. I felt no pain. Again, I tried to move but couldn't. The life was draining out of me! I gave up and closed my eyes. Slowly my mind drifted away.

Then, from somewhere, I felt a breeze sweep over me. I began to hear birds singing in the trees. I heard a dog barking in the distance.

1944 – Age 8
Trailing along behind the wagon, Manny was feeling bad about the sheep. "I hope those dogs don't start killing the pigs or the chickens."

"You're right Manny, we have to do something about that," I said.

Ernie gave me a firm look, "You bet we will."

"You mean, we're going to kill them?" Manny asked.

"Wait and see, Manny. Let's go and get a gun and have it ready," Ernie said as we headed for the house.

Running along behind us, Manny begged, "Can I shoot, please, can I shoot?"

Trying to calm him, "Yes, Manny. You'll get your turn," I promised. As we neared the house, we could see the dark blood spots where each sheep died.

I'm not sure how long I laid there. I opened my eyes and tried to move. I could feel a little strength returning. Still weak, I began to move my arms, then my legs. When I lifted my head, it felt heavy. Using all my strength, I was able to sit up. I peeled off the grass and pine needles that stuck to my cheek and neck. I wiped the spit from my mouth.

I sat on the hill facing the car. It no longer looked shiny and beautiful. It looked black and dull, like something from Hell. The pain began to return in my thighs and crotch. My insides began to catch fire. It felt like he took a knife and carved my guts out.

I felt anger building up. Fear left me. His words came back, "I like you... this won't be the last you'll see of me... I want you to remember, I was there...."

It was on Manny's watch when he came downstairs all excited, "They're coming. I saw them. There's three dogs and they're big! Hurry, get the gun!"

Dropping everything we were doing, Ernie and I ran for the house. Ernie grabbed the gun while I went for the shells.

"Let's go upstairs, we can see where they are," Ernie said while he loaded the gun.

The upstairs window had a broken pane, giving us a place to stick the gun out to make the shot. From there, the dogs wouldn't see us and would come close enough. Seeing them in the distance, we waited with our eyes glued on their every move. There was a black dog, one with white and reddish brown large spots and the third was gray and black.

As they got close, the black one would stop, stretch his neck and smell the air, then put his nose to the ground and trot on.

Getting anxious, Manny whispered, "Ernie, shoot. What are you waiting for?"

With the barrel out the window, his cheek on the gun, his finger on the trigger and one eye closed, "I'm waiting for them to get closer. I don't want to miss."

I could see the barrel of the gun move with the dogs as they got closer. Then I saw Ernie hold his breath. Bang! The gray and black one dropped and didn't move. The shot startled the other two dogs. They stopped in their tracks and looked at the dead dog. Not moving, they looked around and sniffed the ground. Then they came closer to the house.

In the meantime, it was my turn. I took the rifle, loaded it and took my place at the window. The red and white dog had stopped and looked up at the window. I quickly took aim and pulled the trigger. One shot put it down.

Reaching for the gun, Manny said, "Now it's my turn. Give the gun to me." Taking the gun, being little, he rested the barrel on the floor while he loaded it and went to the window. Since he wasn't tall enough to see out the window we had to put down a stick of wood for him to stand on.

With the barrel of the gun out the window, he aimed and pulled the trigger. Bang! The black dog fell and started to howl. Getting up on its front legs, it went around in a circle, howling.

Then I remembered my pocketknife in my purse. *We'll see, you son-of-a-bitch. I'm going to kill you. I'll slice your damn throat with one move!* I got up and started down the hill. *Yes sir, if you scream nobody will hear you.*

"You wounded him!" Ernie shouted. "Hurry, we got to go down there and finish him off. Hurry!" When we got outside, the dog looked up at us and howled.

Ernie said, "It's your dog, you kill him."

Manny put a shell in the gun and aimed. Looking down the barrel at the dog looking back, Manny put the gun down. "Ernie, you do it, I can't."

"No, you do it!"

"I can't!" The whole time the dog is howling.

I took the gun, put it to his head and pulled the trigger.

When I got to the car and looked in, he was still laying on his stomach. *Good, I'll grab you by the hair, pull your head back and slice your damn throat! I want you to try and scream, you son-of-a-bitch!*

I sat my purse on the ground and started looking through it. I couldn't find the knife*! Damn, I know it's there, I always keep it in my purse.*

I dumped everything in the purse on the ground. It wasn't there! *Shit!* I wondered who took it. I sat on the ground, angry! *Mannn... he has to pay for this some way! But it's just him, me and the car. That's it... the car. If he doesn't pay with his life, he'll pay with his car!* I put everything back in my purse, sat it on the ground and went to the back of the car.

I took off the gas cap and began to pour sand in the tank. After several handfuls, I went to the driver's side, opened the door and pulled the latch. While there, I pulled as many wires loose as I could from under the dashboard. On my way to the front, I bent the aerial and the windshield wipers.

I opened the hood and looked for any type of hole. I took off the radiator cap and poured sand until it filled up. I took out the oil stick and poured in the sand. I used the stick to work the sand in.

It took awhile to get the caps off the battery, then I filled them with sand. I unscrewed the nut and filled the carburetor with sand.

I went around the back and put a few more handfuls of sand in the gas tank. I left the cap on the ground so he couldn't miss how well his limousine loved sand! I went to the other side and looked in. He was still sleeping.

I stood back and looked at the car. *Let me see, what else could I do so he will remember, I was there?*

I saw his slacks and jacket. I jerked them off the seat. I looked through his pockets and found $41.00. I took $40.00 and threw the dollar on the seat. I took a key ring out of his jacket pocket that had several keys on it and threw them out in the field as far as I could.

I gathered up his clothes, his slacks, jacket, belt, shirt, tie, socks and shoes. They were all neatly placed on the front seat. How and when he removed his clothes, I don't remember. The only thing he had on was a t-shirt. With my arms full, I looked in on him. Sleeping.

I turned and looked at the ground where the rape took place. The grass was flattened out, deep skid marks marred the ground. A lump grew in my throat. I tried to swallow but it hurt. I had to take a deep breath to keep from crying out.

When the sun comes up, the grass will rise and stand up. The wind and rain will pass over the dirt and smooth it out. In time, my wounds will heal but it will forever leave the scar that I will not let anyone see.

When I turned to leave, I saw a rock. I picked it up and made three passes around the car scratching the beautiful shiny black car. Still sleeping.

As I walked away, I wondered what he was dreaming about. I knew for sure I gave him something he'll never forget or, if he dares, a story to tell his children and grandchildren. But one thing he'll never know is how close he came to never being able to tell the story. He may get a new car to replace this one, but he'll have to explain why to everyone. And, every time he looks at the new one, he will remember, I was there.

When I got to the top of the little knoll I stopped and looked back. *Dear God, leave my pain there.*

The sun was just beginning to show itself as I walked along a fence line towards Spokane. One by one, I tore his clothes and threw them along the way. By the time I got to the main highway, I threw the last shoe.

I walked on the right side of the highway. As I walked and the inside of my thighs rubbed together, it was as if the skin was gone leaving the flesh that burned like fire with every step. Through my anger, only now did I really begin to feel the rawness of the pain. My shoulder, arm and wrist felt like they were out of joint.

I heard a car coming down the highway. I didn't bother looking back. A taxi cab slowly passed by me going towards the city. The driver stopped, backed up and stopped beside me. He leaned towards me and asked if he could take me where I was going. I nodded, he got out and opened the back door for me. I told him where I lived. As we drove along, he asked if I was okay. I didn't say anything.

When we got to my apartment, he refused payment. "Take it easy, Miss. You'll be alright."

"Thanks, Mister. I needed the ride."

I went into my apartment, closed the door and locked it. I threw my purse on the table, went to the bedroom, pulled back the covers and fell into bed.

I slept until late in the afternoon. When I woke up, I turned over and looked at the ceiling, *Did the nightmare really happen or was I dreaming?* The pain in my thighs and crotch soon told me the answer. My arm hurt when I tried to move it.

I got up and undressed. The little blue dress no longer looked the same. Now I knew why the taxi cab driver stopped. The back of the dress and crinoline was covered with dried mud and was ripped. It dragged on the ground as I walked.

Standing in the shower with the hot water pouring on me, I prayed the pain would wash off and go down the drain. I thought of him, of the fear that gripped me on the way out to the country wondering if I would come out of it dead or alive, of the fear when he towered over me and the pain that followed. My stomach tightened up and I fell to my knees and cried.

When the water from the shower began to get cold, I came to my senses. I dried off and got dressed. I gathered up the little blue dress and the white shoes, took them out to the dumpster, lifted the lid and threw them in.

When I got back to the apartment, I saw my purse on the table. I took the $40.00 out, reached for the old picture on the wall, took the back off and put the money in it. Then I put it back on the wall making sure I covered the light spot where it hung. *It will pay next month's rent. I will give myself that much time to put this behind me.*

Looking down, my pocketknife was on the floor. I picked it up and stared at it. Squeezing the knife in my hand, "You said, 'This won't be the last you'll see me.' Next time you son-of-a-bitch, I will have my knife with me."

To ease the pain, I made cold packs and held it to my thighs and crotch to take down the swelling. When the cold ice touched my skin, it burned like fire. Laying down with my head back and closing my eyes, I agonized and relived the rape over and over. I killed him over and over. I could see the blood come out of his throat as he fought for breath. I held his head back by the hair and watched. I held back from screaming! Then I visualized myself kneeling next to him and crying after his last breath left him.

Suddenly, I became aware of sounds and movements. I wondered where I was, then I heard the clock ticking, the refrigerator turning on and the drip of the faucet. *I'm home!*

Then I heard a car drive up and stop. I heard the doors open and I knew there was more than one person getting out of the car. Laying still, I listened. I could hear them talking but couldn't hear what they were saying. Then they walked up to my door. There was a hard knock. I laid still. The knock did not sound friendly. There was anger. Again, the knock rattled the door.

"Miss, I know you're in there. We need to talk to you. Open up!" the man scolded.

I opened my knife, got up and stood by the door. "Who are you and what do you want?!"

"My name is Mr. Jamison, I represent Mr. Garrett. You have a lot of explaining to do young lady. You have totally destroyed Mr. Garrett's car and there is a law against such an act."

"If there is such a law, then what is the law against rape?!"

"Listen Miss, you flirted with Mr. Garrett last night. You knew exactly what you were doing which led him to believe you wanted to spend the night with him."

"If that was true, then why did he have to rape me?!"

He chuckled, "Miss, that will be up to the judge. I'm sure he won't think kindly to the destruction of a new automobile, the damage to Mr. Garrett's belongings and taking his money. Now I suggest you open this door!"

"No! Go ahead and break down the door, I dare you!"

"You could lessen the charges by returning the $40.00."

Ignoring Mr. Jamison, "Bill, I want you to listen to me and listen good. At first, I left you sleeping in the car. But after thinking about what you did to me I went back to kill you. Yes! To kill you! The only thing that saved your life was I didn't have my knife. I was going to grab you by the hair, pull your head back and slit your throat while you slept! So, the loss of your car and $40.00, I think you got by pretty cheap. They can be replaced."

There was a silence, then I heard them talking quietly.

"Miss, you haven't heard the last of us." Mr. Jamison said, "We will see you in court. The judge will settle this."

"You know where I live and where I work, it won't be hard to find me. I'll be looking forward to seeing the judge. And, Mr. Jamison, when I'm standing before the judge, he will be charging me with MURDER!"

There was a long silence, then I heard them say something in a low voice. I listened while they walked to the car. I heard the doors shut and they drove off. When I knew they were gone, I felt a weakness coming on. I made my way back to the bed and the weakness began to take over. I began to lose control of my body, my arms, my legs. On its own, my body would twitch every now and then. All I could do was breathe.

So devastated, I stayed in bed the rest of the day. I pushed all the bad things out of my mind. Making it blank, I went to sleep. It was late in the night before I managed to get up. I prepared for work.

Walking to work that morning, it felt good to have the sun on my face. I began to work on my mind. *Make believe it didn't happen... it was a nightmare... I'm awake now... I don't hurt any more... it's time for work.*

Maybelle was happy to see me, "Chris, did you have a good time?"

Epilogue

Through the years, many people have asked me, "How did you make it? How did you do it?" Writing my story was like the prospector mining for gold. He scoops up the dirt with his pan then washes it away, what is left is the gold. It was quite an experience. It pulled out the deepest buried feelings of sorrow, hurt, joy, anger and love I felt for my family. As I wrote, I became a shadow of myself and watched this little girl go through life. I cried for her, I laughed with her, I felt her loneliness and the fears she lived with. And when she went through hard times, I'd say, "Hang in there, you're going to be okay," then I'd go on writing.

DADDY

After Mama was laid to rest and we said our goodbyes I remembered Daddy's words, "Tissie, it's a tough world out there. Set your goals and don't give up but remember who you are and where you came from." When I think of my daddy, it makes me smile. He was truly a man of few words but when he said something you better listen because he knew what he was talking about and he only said it once. Through the years, Daddy roamed the country. He would go to Canada and visit with friends. He would come and visit me and stay a few days. He would go to Okanogan and spend time with my half-sister, his first born.

On one of his visits, I asked him how he was doing since Mama had passed. Sitting at the table, he looked out the window, giving it some thought. "You know Tissie, after Mama died, I woke up one morning and asked, 'How long has it been since Mama died?' I was told it had been one year." He turned and looked at me. "Tissie, I was drunk for the whole year." I saw a tear in his eye. After blinking it away he said, "I put the bottle down and now a fifth lasts me a month just like old times." With those words, a smile crept at the corner of his mouth. I let out a sigh of relief. Listening to him, I didn't realize I was holding my breath. I knew now he would be alright.

Then in February 1966, almost 10 years since Mama died, I received a call from my half-sister. I was living in Richland, Washington at the time. Daddy was in the hospital in Omak. She told me to hurry, he was very, very sick. When I got there and entered his ward, I was shocked! He was skin and bones and I saw death in his eyes. He greeted me with a big smile. "Tissie, I knew you would come." Closing his eyes, he smiled, "Oh, Tissie I almost saw her last night, she's waiting for me."

I went to the side of the bed, hugged him and asked him what happened. Through labored breathing he told me that when he would receive his social security check each month and knowing he had money, Manny, Ernie, and their friends would come and take him out on the town. Anxious to spend time with them, he was happy to go. It didn't take much to drink up all the money he had. When the night was over they would take him home.

He had been sick for a couple weeks when his next check arrived and the boys were waiting. They went out partying. It was a cold night and there was a lot of snow. During the night, they went off the road and got stuck in the snow. After several attempts to get out of the snow and back on the road, they gave up and went to sleep.

Daddy woke up in the early morning and was chilled to the bone. He tried to wake up the boys but they kept on sleeping. After about a half hour, a man in a pickup stopped. It didn't take long before he had the boys awake. He handed them a shovel then hooked a chain to the car and pulled them out. They took Daddy back to Canada and left.

He laid in bed for the next two weeks with pneumonia. The doctor told me that if he had waited one more night to go to the hospital, he would have died. The day I arrived, which was on Monday, the doctor had already made plans to send Daddy to Edgecliff Sanatorium in Spokane. I asked why they would send him to a hospital for TB patients. He told me that Daddy's lung showed black on the x-ray and, to make sure, he wanted tests run on him. When I kissed Daddy goodbye at the ambulance, as they lifted him into the back, I told him I would be there on Saturday. He passed away on Friday. It broke my heart when the nurse told me he cried. He told her everybody left him. I wished I had gone with him when he was taken to the Edgecliff instead of going back to work. It haunts me to this day.

I had Daddy taken to Omak to hold his wake. He was then taken to St. Mary's Mission for the mass to be said for him. From there I had him taken to Ellisford Cemetery to be buried next to my mother. It was a beautiful day, like the day so long ago, when Mama was laid to rest. The two little puffs of clouds were back. This time they came for Daddy. I just knew Mama was up there waiting and they were now together.

ERNIE

As the years passed, "the bottle" ruled the lives of my brothers. I had to divorce myself from them. However, it took 12 years to let go. I prayed Mama would forgive me. There was nothing I could do to help them. Being an enabler had its price. It broke my heart to see what they were doing to themselves. I saw the nightmares they were living but I had to move on with the fear that one day the phone would ring.

The call came February 23, 1984. Ernie was drinking in a tavern in Omak. He was soon joined by two men. They knew a per capita payment was given out to the tribal members the day before. Happy with a few dollars in his pocket and new "friends", Ernie paid for the rounds. When the bartender called out, "Last call", the last drink was served. The three men left the tavern and headed to East Omak which, after crossing the bridge, was on the reservation. When Ernie and the two men were last seen, they were standing on the Omak side of the bridge. The next morning, Ernie was found under the bridge. His head had been crushed with a rock and his pockets were turned inside out. The two men were arrested, held for 72 hours and released. No other action was ever taken. As the saying goes, "It's just another dead Indian."

MANNY

Manny still lives with his demons. Several years ago, he spent a week with me. It was a nice visit. However, I could clearly see the toll that drinking had taken on his life. He was thin and mentally stuck back in time.

When he first started drinking, he was 15 years old. It was right after I went to the sanatorium. The guys he associated with were in their 20's and 30's. Through the years, with their passing, he became lost. I think the short time he spent with me gave him a brief insight to where he was in his life. He kept saying, "Sis, all my friends are gone," as he cried. I did my best to explain to him the reasons. Then he added, "Sis, I wish I could talk to people and live like you."

Looking at him, I knew he was lost to this world. He has worn a deep moccasin trail from one reservation to the other where he has friends that live in his world. I pray for him but again, I wait for the phone to ring.

FULL CIRCLE

After receiving my cosmetology license, Mrs. Cady wished me well and said, "Chris, you have a gift, make the best of it." At the time, I didn't know what she meant but I strived to do the best I could in everything. My home away from home became the salon. My friends became the clients and those friends were widespread. No matter what the weather was, snow, rain or a blizzard, I made my way to the salon.

Through the years, I had two marriages, two divorces, five hair salons and in 1979 I opened a beauty school. By 1995 all of my children left the nest to fly on their own. They even took the dog. It was a hard time for me.

One evening after the school closed, the students and instructors said goodnight and left. I sat at my desk and thought about things. The school felt hollow and cold. It was a constant battle to keep the business alive and now everything that I lived for, that had meaning to me and made the fight worthwhile, was gone. I had come to a crossroad. Should I take the high road by putting the school up for sale and wait or should I just pull the plug and let it go?

I drove home and when I walked in to the house it looked stale and empty. When I went to bed that night, I heard the faucet drip. The house no longer breathed. It was like a part of me had died. Staring in the dark at the dimly lit doorway, I felt small. All that seemed large was my eyes. I couldn't close them. The silence was loud. I made up my mind it was time to go home.

At the end of the month I closed the doors of the school. The Tribe foreclosed on my house and 60 acres of land that I had inherited. Yes, I had hit rock bottom! But this time, I knew how to make dreams come true. I looked up to the Heavens, closed my eyes and said, "Dear Lord, this is a tough one, at my age I can't make any mistakes. Guide me, I'm in your hands."

A goal was set, I must build me a house. I went back to work in a salon for the next 10 years. With my stuff in storage, I lived out of a suitcase and put every dime I could save in "my sock". With the help of family and friends by giving me a place to lay my weary head, the years flew by. There were 10 such beds in all. However, there were many anxious times. When I would see a moving van drive by or a Christmas tree in a window, a tear would blur my vision. I would blink it away and say, "One day… but it will have wallpaper instead of cardboard on the walls."

ABOUT THE AUTHOR

As a professional, Christine won hairstyling competitions at the local, state, national and international levels, culminating her competitive career as the Champion of the 1991 International Americas Cup.
As the owner of Christine's Institute of Hair Design, she trained students to the top in Artistic Hairstyling with multiple National Champions. Her students placed 1st, 2nd, and 3rd in the 1985 Nationals to represent the United States in the World Competition.
Retiring after 58 years as a hairstylist, her children gave her a gold watch inscribed, "Your sun has reached the mountain, now you are home."

Christine lives on the Colville Indian Reservation in the home she built in Inchelium, Washington.